DISCARDED

MID-AMERICAN
★ FRONTIER ★

This is a volume in the Arno Press collection

MID-AMERICAN ★ FRONTIER ★

Advisory Editor
Jerome O. Steffen

Editorial Board
Richard S. Brownlee
William W. Savage, Jr.

*See last pages of this volume
for a complete list of titles*

WESTERN CHARACTERS

OR

TYPES OF BORDER LIFE

IN THE

WESTERN STATES

J[ohn] L[udlum] McConnel

ARNO PRESS
A New York Times Company
New York — 1975

Editorial Supervision: ANDREA HICKS

Reprint Edition 1975 by Arno Press Inc.

Reprinted from a copy in
  The University of Illinois Library

THE MID-AMERICAN FRONTIER
ISBN for complete set: 0-405-06845-X
See last pages of this volume for titles.

Manufactured in the United States of America

Library of Congress Cataloging in Publication Data

McConnel, John Ludlum, 1826-1862.
    Western characters.

    (The Mid-American frontier)
    Reprint of the 1853 ed. published by Redfield,
New York.
    1. Frontier and pioneer life--Mississippi Valley.
2. Mississippi Valley--Social life and customs.
I. Title. II. Series.
F353.M12   1975   977'.02   75-110
ISBN 0-405-06877-8

THE PEDDLER.

WESTERN CHARACTERS

OR

TYPES OF BORDER LIFE

IN THE

WESTERN STATES

BY J. L. McCONNEL

AUTHOR OF "TALBOT AND VERNON,"—"THE GLENNS," ETC.

WITH ILLUSTRATIONS BY DARLEY

REDFIELD,
110 AND 112 NASSAU STREET, NEW YORK.
1853.

Entered, according to Act of Congress, in the year 1853,

By J. S. REDFIELD,

in the Clerk's Office of the District Court of the United States, in and for the Southern District of New York.

STEREOTYPED BY C. C. SAVAGE,
13 Chambers Street, N. Y.

PREFATORY NOTE.

ATTEMPTS to delineate local character are always liable to misconstruction; for, the more truthful the sketch, the greater is the number of persons, to whom resemblance may be discovered; and thus, while in fact only describing the characteristics of a class, authors are frequently subjected, very unjustly, to the imputation of having invaded the privacy of individuals. Particularly is this so, when the class is idealized, and an imaginary type is taken, as the representative of the species.

I deem it proper, therefore, to say in advance, that no attempt has been made in the following pages, to portray any individual; and that—although I hope I have not been so unsuccessful, as to paint pictures which have no originals—if there be a portrait in any sketch, it consists, not in the likeness of the picture to the person, but of both to the type.

As originally projected, the book would have borne this explanation upon its face; but the circumstances which have reduced its dimensions, and changed its plan, have also rendered necessary a disclaimer, which would, otherwise, have been superfluous.

One or two of the sketches might have been made more complete had I been fortunate enough to meet with certain late publications, in time to use them. Such is the elaborate work of Mr. Schoolcraft upon Indian History and Character; and such, also, is that of Mr. Shea, upon the voyages and labors of Marquette—a book whose careful accuracy, clear style, and lucid statement, might have been of much service in writing the sketch entitled "*The Voyageur.*" Unfortunately, however, I saw neither of these admirable publications, until my work had assumed its present shape—a fact which I regret as much for my reader's sake as my own.

J. L. McC.

July 15, 1853.

CONTENTS.

	PAGE.
INTRODUCTORY	7
I.	
THE INDIAN	19
II.	
THE VOYAGEUR	62
III.	
THE PIONEER	106
IV.	
THE RANGER	157
V.	
THE REGULATOR	171
VI.	
THE JUSTICE OF THE PEACE	246
VII.	
THE PEDDLER	268
VIII.	
THE SCHOOLMASTER	288
IX.	
THE SCHOOLMISTRESS	319
X.	
THE POLITICIAN	340

INTRODUCTORY.

*——" Our Mississippi, rolling proudly on,
Would sweep them from its path, or swallow up,
Like Aaron's rod, those streams of fame and song."*
            MRS. HALE.

THE valley of a river like the channel of a man's career, does not always bear proportion to the magnitude or volume of the current, which flows through it. Mountains, forests, deserts, physical barriers to the former — and the obstacles of prejudice, and accidents of birth and education, moral barriers to the latter — limit, modify, and impair the usefulness of each. A river thus confined, an intellect thus hampered, may be noisy, fretful, turbulent, but, in the contemplation, there is ever a feeling of the incongruity between the purpose and the power; and it is only when the valley is extended, the field of effort open, that we can avoid the impression of energy wasted, and strength frittered away. The great intellect, whose scope is not confined by ancient landmarks, or old prejudices, is thus typified by the broad, deep river, whose branches penetrate the Earth on every hand, and add to the current the tributaries of all climes. In this view, how noble an object is the Mississippi!

In extent, fertility, variety of scenery, and diversity of climate, its valley surpasses any other in the world. It is the great aorta of the continent, and receives a score of tributary rivers, the least of which is larger than the vaunted streams of mighty empires. It might furnish natural boundaries to all Europe, and yet leave, for every country, a river greater than the Seine. It discharges, in one year, more water than has issued from the Tiber in five centuries; it swallows up near fifty nameless rivers longer than the Thames; the addition of the waters of the Danube would not swell it half a fathom; and in a single bend, the navies of the world might safely ride at anchor, five hundred miles from sea.

It washes the shores of twelve powerful states, and between its arms lies space enough for twenty more. The rains which fall upon the Alleganies, and the snows that shroud the slopes and cap the summits of the Rocky mountains, are borne upon its bosom, to the regions of perpetual summer, and poured into the sea, more than fifteen hundred leagues from their sources. It has formed a larger tract of land, by the deposites of its inundations, than is contained in Great Britain and Ireland; and every year it roots up and bears away more trees, than there are in the Black Forest. At a speed unknown to any other great river, it rolls a volume, in whose depths the cathedral of St. Paul's might be sunk out of sight; and five hundred leagues from its mouth, it is wider than at thirty.

It annually bears away more acres than it would require to make a German principality, engulfing more than the revenues of many a petty kingdom. Beneath its turbid waters lie argosies of wealth, and floating palaces, among whose gilded halls and rich saloons are sporting slimy creatures; below your very feet, as you sail along its current, are resting in its bed, half buried in the sand, the bodies of bold men and tender maidens; and their imploring hands are raised toward Heaven, and the world which floats, unheeding, on the surface. There lies, entombed, the son whose mother knows not of his death; and there the husband, for whose footstep, even yet, the wife is listening—here, the mother with her infant still clasped fondly to her breast; and here, united in their lives, not separated in their death, lie, side by side, the bride and bridegroom of a day;—and, hiding the dread secrets from all human ken, the mighty and remorseless river passes onward, like the stream of human life, toward "the land of dreams and shadows!"

To the contemplative mind, there is, perhaps, no part of the creation, in which may not be found the seed of much reflection; but of all the grand features of the earth's surface, next to a lofty mountain, that which impresses us most deeply is a great river. Its pauseless flow, the stern momentum of its current—its remorseless coldness to all human hopes and fears—the secrets which lie buried underneath its waters, and the myriad purposes of those it bears upon its bosom—are all so clearly typical of Time. The waters will not pause, though dreadful battles may be fought upon their shores—as Time will steadily march forward, though the fate of nations hang upon the conflict. The moments fly as swiftly, while a mighty king is breathing out his life, as if he were a lowly peasant; and the current flows as coldly on, while men are struggling in the eddies, as if each drowning wretch were but a floating weed. Time gives no warning of the hidden dangers on which haughty conquerors are rushing, as the perils of the waters are revealed but in the crashing of the wreck.

But the parallel does not stop here. The sources of the Mississippi — were it even possible that they should ever be otherwise — are still unknown to man. Like the stream of history, its head-springs are in the regions of fable — in the twilight of remote latitudes; and it is only after it has approached us, and assumed a definite channel, that we are able to determine which is the authentic stream. It flows from the country of the savage, toward that of civilization; and like the gradations of improvement among men, are the thickening fields and growing cultivation, which define the periods of its course. Near its mouth, it has reached the culmination of refinement — its last ripe fruit, a crowded city; and, beyond this, there lies nothing but a brief journey, and a plunge into the gulf of Eternity!

Thus, an emblem of the stream of history, it is still more like a march along the highway of a single human life. As the sinless thoughts of smiling childhood are the little rivulets, which afterward become the mighty river; like the infant, airy, volatile, and beautiful — sparkling as the dimpled face of innocence — a faithful reflex of the lights and shadows of existence; and revealing, through the limpid wave, the golden sands which lie beneath. Anon, the errant channels are united in one current — life assumes a purpose, a direction — but the waters are yet pure, and mirror on their face the thousand forms and flashing colors of Creation's beauty — as happy boyhood, rapidly perceptive of all loveliness, gives forth, in radiant smiles, the glad impressions of unfaded youth.

Yet sorrow cometh even to the happiest. Misfortune is as stern a leveller as Death; and early youth, with all its noble aspirations, gorgeous visions, never to be realized, must often plunge, like the placid river over a foaming cataract, down the precipice of affliction — even while its current, though nearing the abyss, flow softly as "the waters of Shiloah." It may be the death of a mother, whom the bereaved half deemed immortal — some disappointment, like the falsehood of one dearly loved — some rude shock, as the discovery of a day-dream's hollowness; happy, thrice happy! if it be but one of these, and not the descent from innocence to sin!

But life rolls on, as does the river, though its wave no longer flows in placid beauty, nor reveals the hidden things beneath. The ripples are now whirling eddies, and a hundred angry currents chafe along the rocks, as thought and feeling fret against the world, and waste their strength in vain repining or impatient irritation. Tranquillity returns no more; and though the waters seem not turbid, there is a shadow in their depths — their transparency is lost.

Tributaries, great and small, flow in — accessions of experience to the man, of weight and volume to the river; and, with force augmented, each rolls on its current toward the ocean. A character, a purpose, is imparted to the life, as to the stream, and usefulness becomes an element of being. The river is a chain which links remotest latitudes, as through the social man relations are established, binding alien hearts: the spark of thought and feeling, like the fluid of the magnet, brings together distant moral zones.

On it rushes — through the rapids, where the life receives an impulse — driven forward — haply downward — among rocks and dangerous channels, by the motives of ambition, by the fierce desire of wealth, or by the goad of want! But soon the mad career abates, for the first effect of haste is agitation, and the master-spell of power is calmness. Happy are they, who learn this lesson early—for, thence, the current onward flows, a tranquil, noiseless, but resistless, tide. Manhood, steady and mature, with its resolute but quiet thoughts, its deep, unwavering purposes, and, more than all, its firm, profound affections, is passing thus, between the shores of Time—not only working for itself a channel broad and clear, but bearing on its bosom, toward Eternity, uncounted wealth of hopes.

But in the middle of its course, its character is wholly changed; a flood pours in, whose waters hold, suspended, all impurities. A struggle, brief but turbulent, ensues: the limpid wave of youth is swallowed up. Some great success has been achieved; unholy passions are evoked, and will not be allayed; thenceforward there is no relenting; and, though the world—nay! Heaven itself!—pour in, along its course, broad tributaries of reclaiming purity, the cloud upon the waters can never be dispelled. The marl and dross of Earth, impalpable, but visibly corrupting, pervade the very nature; and only when the current ceases, will its primitive transparency return.

Still it hurries onward, with velocity augmented, as it nears its term. Yet its breadth is not increased ; the earth suspended in its waters, like the turbid passions of the human soul, prevents expansion ;* for, in man's career through time, the heart grows wider only in the pure.

Along the base of cliffs and highlands — through the deep alluvions of countless ages — among stately forests and across extended plains, it flows without cessation. Beyond full manhood, character may change no more — as, below its mighty tributaries, the river is unaltered. Its full development is reached among rich plantations, waving fields, and swarming cities; while, but the journey of a day beyond, it rushes into Eternity, leaving a melancholy record, as it mingles with the waters of the great gulf, even upon the face of Oblivion.

—Within the valley of this river, time will see a population of two hundred millions ; and here will be the seat of the most colossal power Earth has yet contained. The heterogeneous character of the people is of no consequence : still less, the storms of dissension, which now and then arise, to affright the timid and faithless. The waters of all latitudes could not be blended in one element, and purified, without

---

* " Were it a clear stream, it would soon scoop itself out a channel from bluff to bluff."—*Flint's Geography,* p. 103.

the tempests and cross-currents, which lash the ocean into fury. Nor would a stagnant calmness, blind attachment to the limited horizon of a homestead, or the absence of all irritation or attrition, ever make one people of the emigrants from every clime.

And, when this nation shall have become thoroughly homogeneous — when the world shall recognise *the race*, and, above this, *the power* of the race — will there be no interest in tracing through the mists of many generations, the outlines of that foundation on which is built the mighty fabric? Even the infirmities and vices of the men who piled the first stones of great empires, are chronicled in history as facts deserving record. The portrait of an ancient hero is a treasure beyond value, even though the features be but conjectural. How much more precious would be a faithful portrait of *his character*, in which the features should be his salient traits — the expression, outline, and complexion of his nature!

To furnish a series of such portraits — embracing a few of the earlier characters, whose "mark" is traceable in the growing civilization of the West and South — is the design of the present work. The reader will observe that its logic is not the selection of actual, but of ideal, individuals, each representing a class; and that, although it is arranged chronologically, the periods are not historical, but characteristic. The design, then, is double; *first*, to select a *class*, which indicates a certain stage of social or political advancement; and, *second*, to present a picture of an imaginary individual, who combines the prominent traits, belonging to the class thus chosen.

The series halts, beyond the Rubicon of contemporaneous portraiture, for very obvious reasons; but there are still in existence abundant means of verifying, or correcting, every sketch. I have endeavored to give the consciousness of this fact its full weight — to resist the temptation (which, I must admit, was sometimes strong) to touch the borders of satire; and, in conclusion, I can only hope that these wishes, with an earnest effort at fidelity, have enabled me to present truthful pictures.

I.

THE INDIAN.

> "In the same beaten channel still have run
> The blessed streams of human sympathy;
> And, though I know this ever hath been done,
> The why and wherefore, I could never see!"
>
> PHEBE CAREY.

IN a work which professes to trace, even indistinctly, the reclamation of a country from a state of barbarism, some notice of that from which it was reclaimed is, of course, necessary; and an attempt to distinguish the successive periods, each by its representative character, determines the logic of such notice. Were we as well acquainted with the gradations of Indian advancement—for such unquestionably, there were—as we are with those of the civilized man, we should be able to distinguish eras and periods, so as to represent them, each by its separate *ideal*. But civilization and barbarism are comparative terms; and, though it is difficult, perhaps impossible, precisely to fix the point at which one ceases and the other begins, yet, within that limit, we must consider barbarism as *one* period. Of this period, in our plan, the Indian, without reference to distinction of tribe, or variation in degree of advancement, is the representative. As all triangles agree in certain properties, though widely different in others, so all Indians are alike in certain characteristics, though differing, almost radically, each from every other: But, as the points of coincidence in triangles are those which determine the class, and the differences only indicate subspecies, so the similar characteristics in the Indian, are those which distinguish the species, and the variations of character are, at most, only tribal limits. An Indian who should combine all the equivalent traits, without any of the inequalities, would, therefore, be the pure ideal of his race. And his composition should include the evil as well as the good; for a portrait of the savage, which should represent him as only generous and brave, would be as far from a complete ideal, as one which should display only his cruelty and cunning.

My object in this article is, therefore, to combine as many as possible — or as many as are necessary — of the general characteristics of the

Indian, both good and bad — so as to give a fair view of the character, according to the principle intimated above. And I may, perhaps without impropriety, here state, that this may be taken as the key to all the sketches which are to follow. It is quite probable that many examples of each class treated, might be found, who are exceptions to the rules stated, in almost every particular; and it is possible, that no *one*, of *any* class treated, combined *all* the characteristics elaborated. Excepting when historical facts are related, or well-authenticated legends worked in, my object is not to give portraits of individuals, however prominent. As was hinted above — the logic of the book points only to the ideal of each class.

And this view of the subject excludes all those discussions, which have so long puzzled philosophers, about the origin of the race — our business is with the question *What is he?* rather than with the inquiry, *Whence did he come?* The shortest argument, however — and, if the assumption be admitted, the most conclusive — is that, which assumes the literal truth of the Mosaic account of the creation of man; for from this it directly follows, that the aboriginal races are descendants of Asiatic emigrants; and the minor questions, as to the route they followed — whether across the Pacific, or by Behring's strait — are merely subjects of curious speculation, or still more curious research. And this hypothesis is quite consistent with the evidence drawn from Indian languages, customs, and physical developments. Even the arguments against the theory, drawn from differences in these particulars among the tribes, lose their force, when we come to consider that the same, if not wider differences, are found among other races, indisputably of a single stock. These things may be satisfactorily accounted for, by the same circumstances in the one case, as in the other — by political and local situation, by climate, and unequal progress. Thus, the Indian languages, says Prescott, in his "Conquest of Mexico," "present the strange anomaly of differing as widely in etymology, as they agree in organization;" but a key to the solution of the problem, is found in the latter part of the same sentence: "and, on the other hand," he continues,* "while they bear some slight affinity to the languages of the Old World, in the former particular, they have no resemblance to them whatever, in the

* Vol. III., page 394.

latter." This is as much as if he had said, that the incidents to the lives of American Indians, are totally different to those of the nations of the Old World: and these incidents are precisely the circumstances, which are likely to affect organization, more than etymology. And the difficulty growing out of their differences among themselves, in the latter, is surmounted by the fact, that there is a sufficient general resemblance among them all, to found a comparison with "the languages of the Old World." I believe, a parallel course of argument would clear away all other objections to the theory.*

But, as has been said, the scope of our work includes none of these discussions; and we shall, therefore, pass to the Indian character, abstracted from all antecedents. That this has been, and is, much misunderstood, is the first thought which occurs to one who has an oppor-

* There is, however, little necessity for any argument on the subject: For, leaving out of the question the highest and most sacred of authorities, almost all respectable writers upon ethnology, including Buffon, Volney, Humboldt, &c., agree in assigning a common origin to all nations,— though the last deduces from many particulars, the conclusion that the American Indian was "isolated in the infancy of the world, from the rest of mankind."— *Ancient Inhabitants of America*, vol. i, p. 250.

tunity personally to observe the savage. Nor is it justly a matter of surprise. The native of this continent has been the subject of curious and unsatisfactory speculation, since the discovery of the country by Columbus: by the very *want* of those things, which constitute the attraction of other nations, he became at once, and has continued, the object of a mysterious interest. The absence of dates and facts, to mark the course of his migration, remits us to conjecture, or the scarcely more reliable resource of tradition — the want of history has made him a character of romance. The mere name of Indian gives the impression of a shadowy image, looming, dim but gigantic, through a darkness which nothing else can penetrate. This mystery not only interests, but also disarms, the mind; and we are apt to see, in the character, around which it hovers, only those qualities which give depth to the attraction. The creations of poetry and romance are usually extremes; and they are, perhaps, necessarily so, when the nature of the subject furnishes no standard, by which to temper the conception.

"The efforts of a poet's imagination are, more or less, under the control of his opinions:" but opinions of men are founded upon their history; and there is, properly, *no* historical Indian character. The consequence has been, that poets and novelists have constructed their savage personages according to a hypothetical standard, of either the virtues or vices, belonging, potentially, to the savage state. The same rule, applied to portraiture of civilized men, would at once be declared false and pernicious; and the only reason why it is not equally so, in its application to the Indian, is, because the separation between him and us is so broad, that our conceptions of his character can exert little or no influence upon our intercourse with mankind.

Sympathy for what are called the Indian's misfortunes, has, also, induced the class of writers, from whom, almost exclusively, our notions of his character are derived, to represent him in his most genial phases, and even to palliate his most ferocious acts, by reference to the injustice and oppression, of which he has been the victim. If we were to receive the authority of these writers, we should conclude that the native was not a savage, at all, until the landing of the whites; and, instead of ascribing his atrocities to the state of barbarism in which he lived — thus indicating their only valid apology — we should degrade both the white and the red men, by attributing to the former all imaginable vices, and, to the latter, a peculiar aptitude in acquiring them. These mistakes are natural and excusable — as the man who kills another in self-defence is justifiable; but the Indian character is not the less misconceived, just as the man slain is not less dead, than if malice had existed in both cases. To praise one above his merits, is as fatal to his consideration, as decidedly to disparage him. In either case, however, there is a chance that a just opinion may be formed; but, when both extremes are asserted with equal confidence, the mind is confused, and can settle upon nothing. The latter is precisely the condition of the Indian; and it is with a view of correcting such impressions, that this article is written.

The American Indian, then, is the ideal of a savage — no more, no less: and I call him the ideal, because he displays *all* those qualities, which the history of the human race authorizes us to infer, as the characteristics of an unenlightened people, for many ages isolated from the rest of mankind?* He differs, in many

---

* It will be observed, that I assume the *unity* of the Indian race; and I am not sufficiently acquainted with the recent discussions on the subject, to be certain whether the question is still considered open. But the striking analogies between

particulars, from the other barbarians of the world; but the broadest distinction lies in this *completeness* of his savage character. The peculiarities of the country in which their lives assume their direction, its climate, isolation, or connection with the world — all these things contribute to modify the aspects presented by native races. In such points as are liable to modification by these causes, the American differs from every other savage; and without entering into an elaborate comparison of circumstances — for which we have neither the material, the inclination, nor the space — it may be proper briefly to consider *one* of these causes, and endeavor to trace its effects in the Indian's moral physiognomy.

The state of this continent, when the first Asiatic wanderers landed upon its shores, was, of course, that of a vast, unbroken solitude; and the contemplation of its almost boundless extent and profound loneliness, was certainly the first, and probably the most powerful agency, at work in modifying their original character. What the primary effects of this cause

the customs, physical formation, and languages of all the various divisions, (except the Esquimaux, who are excluded), I think, authorize the assumption.

were likely to be, we may observe in the white emigrants, who have sought a home among the forests and upon the plains of the west: whatever they may have been before their migration, they soon become meditative, abstracted, and taciturn. These, and especially the last, are the peculiar characteristics of the Indian; his taciturnity, indeed, amounts to austerity, sometimes impressing the observer with the idea of affectation. The dispersion, which must have been the effect of unlimited choice in lands — the mode of life pursued by those who depended upon the chase for subsistence — the gradual estrangement produced among the separate tribes, by the necessity of wide hunting-grounds — the vast expanse of territory at command — causes operating so long, as to produce a fixed and corresponding nature — are the sources, to which we may trace almost all the Indian's distinctive traits.

"Isolation," Carlyle says, "is the sum total of wretchedness to man;" and, doubtless, the idea which he means to convey is just. "But," in the words of De Quincey, "no man can be truly *great*, without at least chequering his life with solitude." Separation from his kind, of course, deprives a man of the humanizing influences, which are the consequences of association; but it may, at the same time, strengthen some of the noblest qualities of human nature. Thus, we are authorized to ascribe to this agency, a portion of the Indian's fortitude under hardships and suffering, his contempt for mere meanness, and above all, the proud elevation of his character. The standards of comparison, which were furnished by his experience, were few, and, of course, derived from the ideas of barbarians; but all such as were in any way modified by the solitude of his existence, were rendered impressive, solemn, and exalted.

In the vast solitudes of Asia, whence the Indian races migrated to this continent, so far as the loneliness of savage deserts and endless plains might exert an influence, we should expect to find the same general character. But the Asians are almost universally pastoral — the Americans never; the wildest tribes of Tartary possess numerous useful domesticated animals — the Americans, even in Mexico,* had none ; the Tartars are acquainted with the use of milk, and have been so from time immemorial — the Indian, even at this day, has adopted it only in a few localities, among the more enlightened tribes. The migration of the latter either took place at a period before even

* *Conquest of Mexico*, vol. iii., p. 416.

his Asiatic father had discovered its use, or the accidents which brought him to this continent, were such as to preclude importing domesticated animals; and the lapse of a few generations was sufficient to obliterate even the recollection of such knowledge. "And," says Prescott,* "he might well doubt, whether the wild, uncouth monsters, whom he occasionally saw bounding with such fury over the distant plains, were capable of domestication, like the meek animals which he had left grazing in the green pastures of Asia." To this leading distinction — the adoption and neglect of pastoral habits — may be referred most of the diversities among races, unquestionably of one stock.

Reasoning from the effects upon human character, produced by the face of different countries, we might expect to find, in the Indian, among other things, a strong tendency toward poetical thought, embodied, not in the mode of expression usually denominated poetry, but in the style of his addresses, the peculiarities of his theories, or the construction of his mythology, language, and laws. This expectation is totally disappointed; but when we examine the *degree* and *character* of his advancement, and

* *Conquest of Mexico,* vol. iii., p. 417.

recollect a few of the circumstances, among which the poetry looked for would be obliged to grow, our disappointment loses its element of surprise. The contemplation of Nature in her primitive, terrible, and beautiful forms — the habit of meditation, almost the necessary consequence of solitude — the strange, wild enchantment of an adventurous life — have failed to develop in the Indian, any but selfish and sensual ideas. Written poetry was, of course, not to be expected, even from the indigenous civilization of Mexico and Peru; yet we might, with some ground for hope, seek occasional traces of poetical thought and feeling. We look in vain for any such thing.

"Extremes meet," says one of the wisest of adages; and the saying was never more singularly and profoundly vindicated, than in its application to civilization and barbarism. The savage rejects all that does not directly gratify his selfish wants — the highly-civilized man is, in like manner, governed by the principle of *utility;* and, by both, the merely fanciful and imaginative is undervalued. Thus, as Mr. Macaulay[*] ingeniously says, "A great poem, in a highly-polished state of society, is the most wonderful and splendid proof of genius."

[*] *Essays*—Art. 'Milton.'

But, for the same reasons, the savage, who should display any remarkably poetical feeling or tone of thought, would be quite as great a prodigy. Poetry flourishes most luxuriantly midway between the two extremes. Its essence is the contemplation of great passions and actions — of love, revenge, ambition. Imagination is then vivified by the means of expression or articulation; and, in the half-civilized state, neither a refined public sentiment, nor the other extreme of barbarous isolation, restrains the exhibition of great (and poetical) emotions.

The best of Hazlitt's numerous definitions of poetry, determines it to be "the excess of imagination, beyond the actual or ordinary impression of any object or feeling."* But the Indian was destitute of all imagination; apparently, the composition of his nature included no such element; and, certainly, the rude exigencies of his life did not admit its action. Even the purity of his mythology, compared to that of the Greeks and Romans,† has been (by Lord Lindsay) attributed to this want — though, if such were its only effects, it might very well be supplied.

* *Lectures on English Poets,* p. 4.
† No very high compliment, but as high as it deserves. We shall see anon.

THE INDIAN. 33

The Indian has no humor, no romance — how could he possess poetical feeling? The gratification of sensual wants is the end of his life — too often, *literally* the end! "He considers everything beneath his notice, which is not necessary to his advantage or enjoyment."* To him a jest is as unmeaning as the babbling of a brook; his wife is a beast of burden; and even his courting is carried on by gifts of good things *to eat*, sent to the parents.† Heaven is merely a hunting-ground; his language has no words to express abstract qualities, virtues, vices, or sentiments.‡ His idea of the Great Spirit, and the word which expresses it, may be applied with equal propriety to a formidable (though not beneficent) *animal;* indeed, the Indian words which we translate "spirit," mean only superior power, without the qualification of good or evil. He has not even the ordinary inhabitive instinct of the human race; his attachment to any region of country depends upon its capacity to furnish game, and the fading of the former keeps pace with the disappearance of the latter. "Attachment to the graves of his fathers," is an agreeable fiction — unfortunately, only a fic-

* Warburton's *Conquest of Canada*, vol. i., p. 177.
† Bancroft's *United States*, vol. iii., p. 256.
‡ Hunter's *Memoirs*, p. 236.   *Western Annals*, p. 712.

tion.* He has always been nomadic, without the pastoral habits which the word supposes: a mere wandering savage, without purpose or motive, beyond the gratification of the temporary want, whim, or passion, and void of *everything* deserving the name of sentiment.

An extravagant, and, I am sorry to say, groundless, notion has obtained currency, among almost all writers upon the Indian character, that he is distinguished for his *eloquence*. But the same authors tell us, that his language, the vehicle of the supposed eloquence, can express only material ideas.† Now, if we knew no more of his character than this, we should be authorized to infer (what is, indeed, true), that he possesses no standard for the distinction of good and evil, and that his imagination is bounded by the lines of his sensible experience. How any degree of eloquence can be compatible with this state of things, passes comprehension. And what reflection would conclude, a little examination will confirm. The mistake has, doubtless, grown out of a misconception of the

---

* Flint's *Geography*, p. 108.
† "All ideas are expressed by figures addressed to the senses." *Warburton*, vol. i., p. 175. Bancroft, ut supra.

nature of eloquence itself.* If eloquence were all *figure* — even if it were, in any considerable degree, *mere* figure — then the tawdriest rhetorician would be the greatest orator. But it is not so. On the contrary, the use of many words (or figures) to express an idea, denotes not command of language, but the absence of that power — just as the employment of numerous tools, to effect a physical object, indicates, not skill in the branch of physics, to which the object belongs, but rather awkwardness. Of course, much must be placed, in both cases, to the account of clumsy instruments; but the instrument of speech differs from others in this: it is fashioned *by*, as well as *for*, its use; and a rude, unpolished language is, therefore, an index, in two ways, of the want of eloquence among the people who employ it.

In this view, the figurative elocution of the Indian, so far from affording evidence of oratorical power, if it proves anything, proves the opposite. It is the barrenness of his language, and not the luxuriance of his imagination, which enforces that mode of speech.† Imagi-

---

* See Bancroft, Hunter, Catlin, Flint, Jefferson, &c.—passim —all supporters of Indian eloquence, but all informing us, that "combinations of material objects were his *only* means of expressing abstract ideas."

† Vide Bancroft's *United States*, vol. iii., pp. 257, 266, etc.

nation is the first element of oratory, simplicity its first condition. We have seen that the Indian is wholly destitute of the former; and the stilted, meretricious, and ornate style, of even his ordinary communications, entirely excludes the latter from our conception of his character.*

For example: take the expressions "bury the hatchet," for "make peace," and "a cloudless sky," for "prosperity"—the latter being the nearest approximation to an abstract idea observed in Indian oratory. Upon examining these, and kindred forms of speech, we shall at once perceive that they are not the result of imagination, but are suggested by *material* analogies. Peace, to the savage, is, at best, but a negative idea; and the *state* of peacefulness, abstracted from the absence of war, finds no corresponding word in his language. Even friendship only means that relation, in which friends may be of *use* to each other. As his dialects are all synthetic,† his ideas are all con-

---

* *E. G.* "They style themselves the 'beloved of the Great Spirit.'"—*Warburton*, vol. i., p. 186. "In the Iroquois language, the Indians gave themselves the appellation of 'Angouconoue, or 'Men of Always.'"—*Chateaubriand's Travels in America*, vol. ii., p. 92. Note, also, their exaggerated boastfulness, even in their best speeches: "Logan never knew fear," &c.

† "The absence of all reflective consciousness, and of all

crete. To say, "*I love*," without expressing *what* or *whom* I love, would be, so to speak, very bad Indian grammar. He can not even say "two" correctly, without applying the numeral to some object. The notion of absolute being, number, emotion, feeling, posture, or relation, is utterly foreign to his mode of thought and speech.

So, also, of the " cloudless sky," used to express a state of prosperity. He does not mean, by the phrase, the serenity of mind which prosperity produces, nor any other abstract inflexion or suggestion of the figure. He is constantly exposed to the storms of heaven, in the chase, and on the war path; and, even in his best "lodge," he finds but little shelter from their fury. Clear weather is, therefore, grateful to him — bright sunshine associates itself, in his mind, with comfort, or (that supremest of Indian pleasures) undisturbed indolence. And the transition, though, as we have said, an approach to an abstract conception, is easy, even to the mind of a savage. His employment of such illustrations is rather an evidence of rudeness, than of eloquence — of barrenness, than of luxuriance of idea.*

logical analysis of ideas, is the great peculiarity of American speech."—*Bancroft,* vol. iii., p. 257.

* Warburton's *Conquest of Canada,* vol. i., p. 180.

From these considerations, it results, that even the very best specimens of Indian oratory, deserve the name of *picturesque*, rather than of *eloquent* — two characteristics which bear no greater affinity to each other, than do the picture-writing of the Aztec and the alphabetical system of the Greek. The speech of Logan — the most celebrated of Indian harangues — even if genuine,* is but a feeble support to the theory of savage eloquence. It is a mixture of the lament and the song of triumph, which may be found in equal perfection among all barbarous people; but, so far as we are aware, was never elsewhere dignified with that sounding name. The slander of a brave and honorable man,† which it contains, might

---

* I have seen it hinted, though I have forgotten where, that Jefferson, and not Logan, was the author of this speech; but the extravagant manner in which Jefferson himself praises it, seems to exclude the suspicion. "I may challenge the whole orations of Demosthenes and Cicero," he says, "and of any other more eminent orator, if Europe has furnished more eminent, to produce a single passage superior to the speech of Logan!" Praise certainly quite high enough, for a mixture of lamentation and boastfulness.

† The evidence in this matter has long ago been thoroughly sifted; and it is now certain that, so far from being present aiding at the massacre of Logan's family, Colonel Cresap earnestly endeavored to dissuade the party from its purpose. And yet the falsehood is perpetuated even in the common school-books of

be the result of a mistake easily made; the wrongs of which this chief was the victim, might render even a savage eloquent; and the mixture of bloody vaunting with profound grief, is scarcely to be expected in any *but* a savage. "Logan never knew fear," he says; "he would not turn on his heel to save his life." This species of boasting is perfectly in keeping with the Indian character; but the pathetic reason for this carelessness, which follows — "There is no one to mourn for Logan" — is one not likely to have occurred to an Indian, even in his circumstances. And, granting that the expression *was* used by the orator, and not (as it seems probable it was) added by Jefferson, it is, I believe, the only example on record of poetical feeling in any Indian speech.

The *religion* of the Indian has given as much troublesome material to the builders of systems, as has been furnished by all his other characteristics combined. The first explorers of America supposed that they had found a people, quite destitute of any religious belief. But faith in a higher power than that of man,

the country, while its object has been mouldering in his grave for a quarter of a century.— *Western Annals,* p. 147. *Ameri can Pioneer,* vol. i., p. 7, *et seq.*

is a necessity of the human mind; and its organization, more or less enlightened, is as natural, even to the most degraded savage, as the formation of his language. Both depend upon general laws, common to the intellect of all races of men; both are affected by the external circumstances of climate, situation, and mode of life; and the state of one may always be determined by that of the other. "No savage horde has been caught with its language in a state of chaos, or as if just emerging from the rudeness of undistinguishable sounds. Each appears, not as a slow formation by painful processes of invention, but as a perfect whole, springing directly from the powers of man."* And though this rigor of expression is not equally applicable to the Indian's religion, the fact is attributable solely to the difference in nature of the subjects. As the "primary sounds of a language are essentially the same everywhere," the impulses and instincts of piety are common to all minds. But, as the written language of the Indian was but the pictorial representation of visible objects, having no metaphysical signification, so the symbols of his religion, the objects of his adoration, were drawn from

* Bancroft, vol. iii., p. 254.

THE INDIAN. 41

external nature.* Even his faith in the Great Spirit is a graft upon his system, derived from the first missionaries;† and, eagerly as he adopted it, it is probable that its meaning, to him, is little more exalted, than that of the "Great Beaver," which he believes to be the first progenitor, if not the actual creator, of that useful animal.

We often see the fact, that the Indian believes in his *manitou*, cited as an evidence, that he has the conception of a spiritual divinity. But the word never conveyed such a meaning; it is applicable more properly to material objects, and answers, with, if possible, a more intense and superstitious significance, to the term *amulet*. The Indian's *manitou* might be, indeed always was, some wild animal, or some part of a beast or bird — such as a bear's claw, a buffalo's hoof, or a dog's tooth.‡ And, though he ascribed exalted powers to this primitive guardian, it must be remembered that

---

* Bancroft, vol. iii., p. 285.—" The God of the savage was what the metaphysician endeavors to express by the word *substance*." But the Indian's idea of substance was altogether *concrete*.

† The best authority upon this subject is found in the *Jesuit* "*Relaciones*:" but it is at least probable, that the preconceptions of the good Fathers colored, and, perhaps, shaped, many of the religious wonders there related.

‡ "Lettres Edifiantes," vol. vi., p. 200, *et seq.* Warburton, vol. i., p. 187.

these powers were only physical — such, for example, as would enable it to protect its devotee from the knife of his enemy, or give him success in hunting.

Materialism, then, reigns in the religion, as in the language, of the Indian; and its effects are what might be expected. His whole system is a degraded and degrading superstition; and, though it has been praised for its superior purity, over that of the ancients, it seems to have been forgotten, that this purity is only the absence of *one kind* of *im*purity : and that its cruel and corrupting influences, of another sort, are ten-fold greater than those of the Greek mythology. The faith of the Greek embodied itself in forms, ceremonies, and observances — regularly appointed religious rites kept his piety alive; the erection of grand temples, in honor of his deity, whatever might be his conception of that deity's character, attested his genuine devotion, and held constantly before his mind the abstract idea of a higher power. The Indian, before the coming of the white man, erected no temples* in honor of his divinities; for he

---

* The extravagant stories told of the Natchez Indians (among whom there was said to be a remarkable temple for worship) are quite incredible, even if they had not been disproved.

venerated them only so long as they conferred physical benefits* upon him; and his idea of beneficence was wholly concrete. He had no established form of worship; the ceremonies, which partook of a religious character, were grotesque in their conception, variable in their conduct, and inhuman in their details. Such, for example, are the torturing of prisoners, and the ceremonies observed on the occasion of a young Indian's placing himself under his guardian power.

The dogmas of the Indian religion, until varied by the teaching of missionaries, were few and simple — being circumscribed, like everything else belonging to him, by the material world. He believed in a good spirit, and an evil spirit; but his conception was limited by the ideas of benefit or injury, *to himself;* indeed, it may safely be doubted, whether the word "spirit," in its legitimate sense, is at all applicable to his belief. "Power in a state of exertion," is the more accurate description of

* When the *manitou* of the Indian has failed to give him success in the chase, or protection from danger, "he upbraids it with bitterness and contempt, and threatens to seek a more effectual protector. If the *manitou* continues useless, this threat is fulfilled." Warb. *ut supra.* *Vide,* also, Catlin's "American Indians," vol. i., p. 36, *et seq.*

his imperfect notion: abstract existence he never conceived; the verb "*to be*," except as relating to time, place, and action, had no meaning in his language.* He believed, also, in subordinate powers of good and evil; but, since his life was occupied more in averting danger and calamity, than in seeking safety or happiness, he paid far more respect to the latter than to the former — he prayed oftener and more fervently to the devils, than to the angels. His clearest notion of divinity, was that of a being able to injure him; and, in this sense, his devotion might be given to man, bird, or beast.

There seems to be no doubt, that he believed in a sort of immortality, even before the missionaries visited his country. But it was not so much a new state of existence, as a continuation of present life.† He killed horses upon the grave of the departed warrior, that he might be mounted for his long journey; and buffalo meat and roasted maize were buried with him,

---

* Bancroft, vol. iii., p. 253.

† "He calls it [the soul] the shadow or image of his body, but its acts and enjoyments are all the same as those of its earthly existence. He only pictures to himself a continuation of present pleasures." Warb. vol. i., p. 190. *Vide*, also, Catlin's "*American Indians*," vol. i., p. 158, *et seq.*

that he might not suffer from hunger.* On arriving in the land of the blest, he believed, that the dead pursued the game of that country, as he had done in this; and the highest felicity of which he conceived, was the liberty to hunt unmolested by the war-parties of his enemies. Heaven was, therefore, in his conception, only a more genial earth, and its inheritors but keener sportsmen.

That this idea of immortality involved that of accountability, in some form, seems to admit of no doubt; but this doctrine, like almost all others belonging to the primitive savage, has been moulded to its present definite shape, by the long-continued labors of Christian missionaries.† He believed, indeed, that the bad Indians never reached the happy hunting-grounds, but the distinction between the good and the bad, in his mind, was not at all clear; and, since the idea of the passage across the gulf of

* The Indian never believed in the resurrection of the body; but even corn and venison were supposed to possess a spirit, which the spirit of the dead warrior might eat.—*Jesuit " Relacion,"* 1633, p. 54.

† "The idea of retribution," says Bancroft, vol. iii., p. 299, "as far as it has found its way among them, was derived from Europeans." And the same remark may be made, of most of the other wonders, in which enthusiastic travellers have discovered coincidences with Christianity.

death most prevalent among all tribes, is that of a narrow bridge, over which only steady nerves and sure feet may carry the wanderer, it seems probable that the line was drawn between the brave warrior and the successful hunter, on the one hand, and the coward and the unskilful, on the other. If these views be correct, the inferences to be drawn from the Indian's belief in immortality and accountability, are of but slender significance.

Corrupt manners and degrading customs never exist, in conjunction with a pure religious system. The outlines of social institutions are metaphysically coincident with the limits of piety; and the refinement of morals depends upon the purity of faith. We may thus determine the prevailing spirit of a national religion, by observation of domestic manners and habits; and, among all the relations of life, that of parent and child is the best index to degree of advancement. Filial piety is but the secondary manifestation of a devotional heart; and attachment and obedience to a father on earth, are only imperfect demonstrations of love to our Father in heaven. What, then — to apply the principle — is the state of this sentiment in the Indian? By the answer to that question, we shall be able to estimate the value of his religious notions, and to determine the amount of hope, for his conversion, justified by their possession. The answer may be given in a few words: There is no such sentiment in the Indian character. Children leave their infirm parents to die alone, and be eaten by the wolves;* or treat them with violent indignity,† when the necessity of migration gives no occasion for this barbarous desertion. Young savages have been known to beat their parents, and even to kill them; but the display of attachment or reverence for them, is quite unknown. Like the beast of the forest, they are no sooner old enough to care for themselves, than they cease even to remember, by whose care they have become so; and the slightest provocation will produce a quarrel with a father, as readily as with a stranger. The unwritten law of the Indian, about which so many writers have dreamed, enacts no higher penalty for parricide, than for any other homicide; and a command to honor his father and mother because they *are* his father and mother, would strike the mind of an Indian as simply absurd.

* James's "*Expedition*," vol. i., p. 237.—Catlin's "*American Indians*," vol. i., pp. 216–'18. The latter is a zealous apologist for Indian cruelties and barbarisms.

† "*Conquest of Canada,*" vol. i., pp. 194–'5.

If the possession of a religion, whose fruits are no better than these, can, of itself, give ground for hope to the Christian philanthropist, let him cherish it fondly. But it is much to be feared, that the existence of such a system indefinitely postpones, if it does not entirely preclude, the Indian's conversion. Even a bird which has never known the forest, will eventually escape to the wilds which God has made its home; and the young Indian, who has been reared in the city, will fly to the woods and prairies, and return to the faith of his fathers, because these, and only these, will satisfy his nature.*

A theme of praise, in itself more just, has been the Indian's courage; but the same circumstances of poetical interest, which have magnified men's views of his other qualities,

* The following may serve to indicate the sort of impression of Christianity which even the most earnest and enlightened preaching has been able to make upon the Indian mind: "Here I saw a most singular union; one of the [Indian] graves was surmounted by a cross, while close to it a trunk of a tree was raised, covered with hieroglyphics, recording the number of enemies slain by the tenant of the tomb. Here presenting a hint to those who are fond of system-making on the religion of these people," &c.—*Beltrami's Pilgrimage, &c.*, vol. ii., p. 307. Bancroft's *United States*, vol. iii., pp. 303-'4. Flint's *Geography*, pp. 109, 126.

have contributed to exaggerate this also. If calm steadiness of nerve, in the moment of action, be an element in true courage, that of the primitive savage was scarcely genuine. In all his battles, there were but two possible aspects — the furious onset, and the panic retreat: the firmness which plants itself in line or square, and stubbornly contends for victory, was no part of his character. A check, to him, always resulted in a defeat; and, though this might, in some measure, be the consequence of that want of discipline, which is incident to the savage state, the remark applies with equal justice, whether he fought singly or in a body. He was easily panic-struck, because the impulse of the forward movement was necessary to keep him strung to effort; and the retrograde immediately became a rout, because daring, without constancy, collapses with the first reaction.

Notwithstanding the enervating influences attributed to refinement and luxury, genuine, steady courage is one of the fruits borne by a high civilization. It is the result of combination, thought, and the divinity which attaches to the cultivated man. And, though it may seem rather unfair to judge a savage by the rules of civilization, it has long been received as a canon, that true valor bears an inverse ratio to ferocious cruelty. Of all people yet discovered upon earth, the Indian is the most ferocious. We must, therefore, either vary the meaning of the word, when applied to different people, or deny the savage the possession of any higher bravery, than that which lives only through the onset.

Cunning supplied the place of the nobler quality; the object of his warfare was to overcome by wily stratagem, rather than by open combat. "Skill consisted in surprising the enemy. They followed his trail, to kill him when he slept; or they lay in ambush near a village, and watched for an opportunity of suddenly surprising an individual, or, it might be, a woman and her children; and, with three strokes to each, the scalps of the victims being suddenly taken off, the brave flew back with his companions, to hang the trophies in his cabin."* If they succeeded in taking prisoners, it was only that they might be reserved for the most infernal torments, and the gratification of a brutal ferocity, not the trial and admiration of the victim's courage, was the purpose of their infliction.†

* Bancroft, vol. iii., p. 281.

† "To inflict blows that can not be returned," says this his-

The fortitude of the Indian under suffering, has often been referred to, in evidence of moral courage. And it is certainly true, that the display so frequently made of triumph in the hour of death by torture, indicates,* in part, an elevation of character, seldom found among more civilized men. It is, however, the elevation of a barbarian; and its manifestations are as much the fruit of impotent rage, as of a noble fortitude. The prisoner at the stake knows that there is no escape; and his intense hatred of his enemies takes the form of a wish, to deprive them of a triumph. While his flesh is crisping and crackling in the flames, therefore, he sings of the scalps he has taken, and heaps opprobrious epithets upon the heads of his tormentors. But his song is as much a cry of agony, as of exultation — his pain only adopts this mode of expression. It is quite certain, also, that he does not suffer so deeply, as would a white man in the same circumstances. By long exposure, and the endurance of hard-

torian (Bancroft, vol. iii., p. 282), "is a proof of full success, and the entire humiliation of the enemy. It is, moreover, an experiment of courage and patience." But we think such things as much mere brutality, as triumph.

* The frequent change of tense in this article, refers to those circumstances in which the *present* differs from the *past* character of the Indian.

ships incident to his savage life, his body acquires an insensibility akin to that of wild animals.* His nerves do not shrink or betray a tendency to spasm, even when a limb is amputated. Transmitted from one generation to another, this physical nature has become a peculiarity of the race. And when assisted by the fierce hatred above referred to, it is not at all strange that it should enable him to bear with fortitude, tortures which would conquer the firmness of the most resolute white man.†

The Indian's dignified stoicism has been as much exaggerated, as his courage and fortitude. It is not quite true that he never expresses surprise, or becomes loquacious. But he has a certain stern impassibility of feature — a coldness of manner — which have been mistaken for dignity. His immobility of countenance, however, may be the effect of sluggish sensibilities, or even of dull perceptions;‡ and

* It is to be doubted, whether some part of this vaunted stoicism be not the result of a more than ordinary degree of physical insensibility."—*Flint's Geography*, vol. i., p. 114.

† Many white men, however, have endured the utmost extremities of Indian cruelty. See cases of Brebeuf, and Lallemand, in *Bancroft*, vol. iii., p. 140.

‡ "It is intellectual culture which contributes most to diversify the features."—*Humboldt's Personal Narrative*, vol. iii., p. 228.

the same savage vanity, which leads him to make a display of strength or agility before friend or enemy, prevents his acknowledging ignorance, by betraying surprise.* We have been in company with Indians from the Far West, while they saw a railroad for the first time. When they thought themselves unnoticed, they were as curious about the singular machinery of the locomotive, and as much excited by the decorations and appointments of the cars, as the most ignorant white man. But the moment they discovered that their movements were observed, they resumed their dignified composure; and, if you had judged of the Indian country by their subsequent deportment, you might have believed that the vast prairies of the Missouri were everywhere intersected by railroads — that the Indian had, in fact, never known any other mode of travelling. "On first seeing a steamboat, however," says Flint, who well understands his character, "he never represses his customary ' *Ugh!*'"

Generally, among white men, he who is fondest of inflicting pain, is least able to endure it.

* "They have probably as much curiosity [as the white], but a more stern perseverance in repressing it."—*Flint's Geography*, vol. i., p. 124.

But the Indian reverses almost all the principles, which apply to civilized life; and, accordingly, we find that, with all his so-called fortitude, he is the most intensely cruel of all living men. Before possession of the continent was taken by Europeans, war was more constantly the occupation of his life, than it has been since; but even now his only object in taking his enemies alive, is to subject them to the most inhuman tortures.* And in these brutal orgies, the women are most active, even taking the lead, in applying the cord and the brand.† Nor is this cruelty confined to enemies, as the practice of leaving the aged and infirm to die of starvation sufficiently proves.

And his treachery is equal to his cruelty. No treaty can bind him longer than superior force compels him to observe it. The discovery that his enemy is unprepared for an attack, is sufficient reason to him for making it; his only object in concluding peace, is to secure an ad-

---

* "The enemy is assailed with treachery, and, if conquered, treated with revolting cruelty." * * "A fiendish ferocity assumes full sway."—*Conquest of Canada,* vol. i., p. 206.

† It is perhaps not very remarkable, however, that the women are most cruel to the aged and infirm — the young and vigorous being sometimes adopted by them, to console them for the loss of those who have fallen.—*Idem,* p. 210.

THE INDIAN. 55

vantage in war; and before the prospect of a bloody inroad, his faith melts away, like snow before the sun. The claims of gratitude he seldom acknowledges; he cherishes the memory of a benefit, only until he finds an opportunity of repaying it with an injury ; and forbearance to avenge the latter, only encourages its repetition.* The numerous pretty stories published of Indian gratitude, are either exceptional cases, or unmixed romances.

There have been some tribes of Indians in a measure reclaimed from their state of barbarism; the Cherokees, I believe, (and perhaps one or two other nations,) have even increased in numbers, under the influence of civilization. But this is the result of numerous favorable causes combined, and proves nothing, from which to infer the Indian's docility. Other savages, on coming in contact with civilized men, have discovered a disposition to acquire some of the useful arts — their comforts have been increased, their sufferings diminished, and their condition ameliorated, by the grafting of new ideas upon

* "We consider them a treacherous people, easily swayed from their purpose, paying their court to the divinity of good fortune, and always ready to side with the strongest. We should not rely upon their feelings of to-day, as any pledge for what they will be to-morrow."—*Flint's Geography*, vol. i., p. 120.

the old. But, between the red man and the white, contiguity has brought about little more than an exchange of vices.

Almost the only things coveted by the "redskin" from the "paleface," were his arms, his trinkets, and his "firewater." He could appreciate whatsoever gave him superiority in war, gratified his childish vanity, or ministered to his brutal appetite. But the greater comfort of the white man's house — the higher excellence of his boat — his improved agricultural implements or extended learning — none of these things appealed to the Indian's passions or desires. The arts of peace were nothing to him — refinement was worse than nothing. He would spend hours in *decorating* his person, but not a moment in *cleansing* it: I believe no tradition exists of an Indian ever having used soap or bought a fine-tooth comb! He is, indeed, a "pattern of filthiness;" but even in civilized life, we find that this is not at all incompatible with an extravagant love of ornament; and, in this respect, the savage is not behind his more enlightened brethren and sisters. Beads, ribands, and scarlet cloth — with powder and lead, guns, tomahawks, and knives — are the acquisitions which he prizes most highly.

Pre-eminent, however, above all these in his estimation, is the greatest curse which has yet reached him — the liquid fire called whiskey! He is, by nature, a drunkard, and the fury of his intoxication equals the ferocity of his warfare. "All words would be thrown away," says Mr. Flint,* "in attempting to portray, in just colors, the effects of whiskey upon such a race." Fire should be kept away from combustibles — whiskey from the Indian, and for the same reason. With drunkenness, he possesses, also, its inseparable companion, the vice of gambling.† He is the most inveterate gamester: Before the demon of avarice everything gives way. He even forgets his taciturnity, in the excitement of the game, and becomes loquacious and eager. He will stake all his most valuable possessions, and, losing these, will even risk his own liberty, or life, on the turn of a card. We were once witness to a game in San Antonio (in Western Texas), among a party of Lipans,‡ a race of fine-looking men, who range the table-lands north of the

* "*Geography of the Mississippi Valley,*" vol. i., p. 121.

† "The Indians are immoderately fond of play."— *Warburton*, vol. i., p. 218.

‡ These used cards; but they have, among themselves, numerous games of chance, older than the discovery of the continent.

sources of the Nueces. Two of them, one the handsomest warrior among them, lost, first, the money, which they had just received as the price of skins, brought to the city for sale. They then staked, successively, their horses, their arms, their mocassins, and their blankets. The "luck" was against them — everything was lost; and we supposed the game was over. But — as a last resource, like drawing blood from their beating hearts — each produced *a little leathern bottle*, containing whiskey! And, as if these possessed a higher value than all the articles yet lost, the game went on with increased interest! Even the potent "spirit" thus evoked, could not prevail upon Fortune to change her face: the whiskey was lost with the rest! Each rose to his feet, with the usual guttural exclamation, and, afoot, and unarmed as he was, silently took his way to the prairies; while the winners collected in a group, and with much glee, proceeded to consume the liquid poison so cheaply obtained.

We come, finally to the question of the Indian's fate: What is to become of the race? The answer presents no difficulties, save such as grow out of men's unwillingness to look unpleasant truths in the face. There has been, of late years, much lamentation, among our own people, over the gradual extinction of these interesting savages; and in Europe we have been made the subject of indignant eloquence, for (what those, who know nothing about it, are pleased to call) "our oppression of the Indian." But, in the first place, the decay of the American races is neither so rapid nor so universal, as is generally supposed;* and, in the second place, if the fact were otherwise, we could, at the worst, be charged only with accelerating a depopulation already begun. "The ten thousand mounds in the Mississippi Valley, the rude memorials of an immensely numerous former population, but, to our view, no more civilized than the present races, are proofs that the country *was depopulated*, when the white man first became acquainted with it. If we can infer nothing else from these mounds, we can clearly infer, that this country once had its millions."† What

* "The Cherokee and Mobilian families of nations are more numerous now than ever."—*Bancroft*, vol. iii., p. 253. In speaking of this declamation about the extinction of the race, Mr. Flint very pertinently remarks: "One would think it had been discovered, that the population, the improvements, and the social happiness of our great political edifice, ought never to have been erected in the place of these habitations of cruelty.'—*Geography*, vol. i., p. 107.

† Idem.

had become of this immense population? The successive invasions of new hordes of barbarians from the north, intestine wars, and the law, that men shall advance toward civilization, or decay from the earth — these are the only causes to which we may ascribe their disappearance.

The extinction of the Indian race is decreed, by a law of Providence which we can not gainsay. Barbarism *must* give way to civilization. It is not only inevitable, but *right*, that it should be so. The tide of empire, which has been flowing since the earliest times, has set steadily toward the West. The Indian emigrated in the wrong direction: and now, after the lapse of many centuries, the descendants of the first Asians, having girdled the globe, meet on the banks of the Mississippi! On the one side, are enlightenment, civilization, Christianity: on the other, darkness, degradation, barbarism: and the question arises, which shall give way? The Indian recedes: at the rate of seventeen miles a year,* the flood rolls on! Already it has reached the shores of the Pacific: One century will reduce the whole continent to the possession of the white man; and,

---

* This is De Tocqueville's estimate.—*Democracy in America,* vol. ii., chap. 10.

THE INDIAN. 61

then, the lesson which all history teaches, will be again taught — that two distinct races cannot exist in the same country on equal terms. The weaker must be incorporated with the stronger — or exterminated.*

* "We may as well endeavor to make the setting sun stand still on the summit of the Rocky Mountains, as attempt to arrest the final extermination of the Indian race!"— *Merivale on Colonization—Lecture* 19.

The principle stated in the text will apply with equal force to the negro-race; and those who will look the facts firmly in the face, can not avoid seeing, that the ultimate solution of the problem of American Slavery, can be nothing but *the sword.*

II.

THE VOYAGEUR.

> " Spread out earth's holiest records here,
> Of days and deeds to reverence dear:
> A zeal like this, what pious legends tell?"

THE shapeless knight-errantry of the thirteenth and fourteenth centuries, rich as it was in romance and adventure, is not to be compared, in any valuable characteristic, to the noiseless self-devotion of the men who first explored the Western country. The courage of the knight was a part of his savage nature; his confidence was in the strength of his own right arm; and if his ruggedness was ever softened down by gentler thoughts, it was only when he asked forgiveness for his crimes, or melted in sensual idolatry of female beauty.

It would be a curious and instructive inquiry, could we institute it with success, how much of the contempt of danger manifested by the wandering knight was referable to genuine valor, and what proportion to the strength of a Milan coat, and the temper of a Toledo or Ferrara blade. And it would be still more curious, although perhaps not so instructive, to estimate the purity and fidelity of the heroines of chivalry; to ascertain the amount of true devotion given them by their admirers, "without hope of reward."

But without abating its interest by invidious and ungrateful inquiries, we can see quite enough — in its turbulence, its cruelty, arrogance, and oppression — to make us thank Heaven that "the days of chivalry are gone." And from that chaotic scene of rapine, raid, and murder, we can turn with pleasure to contemplate the truer, nobler chivalry — the chivalry of love and peace, whose weapons were the kindness of their hearts, the purity of their motives, and the self-denial of their lives.

The term "*voyageur*"* literally signifies "traveller;" and by this modest name are indicated some of the bravest adventurers the world has ever seen. But it is not in its usual, common-place signification that I employ the

* In common use, this word was restricted so as to indicate only the boatmen, the carriers of that time; but I am writing of a period anterior, by many years, to the existence of the Trade which made their occupation.

word, nor yet in that which is given it by most writers on the subject of early French settlements and explorations. Men are often affected by the names given them, either of opprobrium or commendation; but words are quite as frequently changed, restricted, or enlarged in meaning, by their application to men. For example: you apply the word soldier to a class of men; and if robbery be one of the characteristics of that class, "soldier" will soon come to mean "robber" too. And thus, though the parallel is only logical, has it been with the term "*voyageur*." The class of men to whom it is applied were travellers—*voyageurs;* but they were *more;* and as the habits and qualities of men came in time to be better understood than the meaning of French words, the term, used in reference to Western history, took much of its significance from the history and character of the men it assumed to describe. Thus, *un voyageur* means not only a traveller, but a traveller with a purpose; an adventurer among the Western wilds; a chivalrous missionary, either in the cause of science or religion. It includes high courage, burning zeal for church and country, and the most generous self-devotion. It describes such men as Marquette, La Salle, Joliet, Gravier, and hundreds of others equally illustrious, who lived and died among the dangers and privations of the wilderness; who opened the way for civilization and Christianity among the savages, and won, many of them, crowns of martyrdom.

They were almost all Frenchmen. The Spaniards who came to this continent were mere gold-seekers, thirsting only for wealth; and if they sought to propagate Christianity, or rather the Christian *name*, it was only a sanguinary bigotry that prompted them. On the other hand, the English emigrants came to take possession of the country for themselves. The conversion of the natives, or territorial acquisition for the mother-country, were to them objects of barely secondary importance. They believed themselves persecuted — some of them *were* persecuted — and they fled: it was only safety for themselves, and the rich lands of the Indian, that they sought. Providence reserved for the French chevaliers and missionaries the glory of leaving their homes without compulsion, real or imaginary, to penetrate an inhospitable wilderness; to undergo fatigues; to encounter dangers, and endure privations of a thousand kinds; enticed by no golden glitter, covetous of no riches, save such as are "laid up in heaven!" They came not as conquerors, but as ministers of peace, demanding only hospitality. They never attacked the savages with sword or fagot; but extending hands not stained by blood, they justified their profession by relief and love and kindly offices. Sometimes, indeed, they received little tracts of land; not seized by the hand of power, nor grasped by superior cunning, but possessed as the free gift of simple gratitude; and upon these they lived in peace, surrounded by savages, but protected by the respect inspired by blameless and beneficent lives. Many of those whose vows permitted it, intermarried among the converted natives, and left the seeds of many meliorations in a stony soil; and many of them, when they died, were as sincerely mourned by the simple children of the forest, as if they had been chiefs and braves.

Such were the men of peace who penetrated the wilderness through the French settlements in Canada, and preached the gospel to the heathen, where no white man had ever before been seen; and it is particularly to this class that I apply the word at the head of this article. But the same gentle spirit pervaded other orders of adventurers—men of the sword and buckler, as well as of the stole and surplice.

These came to establish the dominion of *La Belle France;* but it was not to oppress the simple native, or to drive him from his lands. Kindness marked even the conduct of the rough soldier; and such men as La Salle, and Iberville, who were stern enough in war, and rigid enough in discipline, manifested always an anxious solicitude for the *rights*, as well as for the spiritual welfare of the Indian. They gave a generous confidence where they were conscious of no wish to injure; they treated frankly and on equal terms, with those whom their religion and their native kindness alike taught them to consider brethren and friends. Take, for example, that significant anecdote of La Salle, related by the faithful chronicler* of his unfortunate expeditions. He was building the fort of *Crevecœur*, near the spot where now stands the city of Peoria, on the Illinois river; and even the name of his little fortress (*Crevecœur*, Broken Heart) was a mournful record of his shattered fortunes. The means of carrying out his noble enterprise (the colonizing of the Mississippi valley) were lost; the labor of years had been rendered in-

---

* Joutel, who was one of La Salle's party, and afterward wrote an account of the enterprise, entitled *Journal Historique*, published in Paris, 1713. Its fidelity is as evident upon its face, as is the simplicity of the historian.

effectual by one shipwreck; his men were discontented, even mutinous, "attempting," says Hennepin, "first to poison, and then desert him;" his mind was distracted, his heart almost broken, by accumulated disasters. Surrounded thus by circumstances which might well have rendered him careless of the feelings of the savages around him, he observed that they had become cold and distant — that in effect they no longer viewed him as their friend. The Iroquois,* drifting from the shores of Lake Ontario, where they had always been the bitterest foes of the French, had instilled fear and hatred into their minds; it was even said that some of his own men had encouraged the growing discontent. In this juncture, what measures does he take? Strengthen his fortifications, and prepare for war, as the men of other nations had done? Far from it. Soldier and adventurer as he was, he had no wish to shed innocent blood; though with his force he might have defied all the nations about him. He went as a friend, frankly and generously,

---

* This was in the winter of 1679–'80; and the Five Nations, included in the general term Iroquois, had not then made the conquest upon which the English afterward founded their claim to the country. They were, however, generally regarded as enemies by all the Illinois tribes.

among them, and demanded the reasons of their discontent. He touched their hearts by his confidence, convinced them of his friendship, and attached them to himself more devotedly than ever. A whole history in one brief passage!

But it is more especially to the *voyageurs* of the church — the men of faith and love — that I wish to direct my readers' attention: To such men as Le Caron, a Franciscan, with all the zeal and courage and self-abnegation of his order, who wandered and preached among the bloody Iroquois, and upon the waters of Huron, as early as 1616: to Mesnard, a devoted missionary of the same order, who, in 1660, founded a mission at the Sault de Ste. Marie, and then went into the forest to induce the savages to listen to the glad tidings he had brought, and never came back: to Father Allouez, who rebuilt the mission five years afterward (the first of these houses of God which was not destroyed or abandoned), who subsequently crossed the lakes, and preached to the Indians on Fox river, where, in one of the villages of the Miamis and Mascoutens, Marquette found a cross still standing, after the lapse of years, where Allouez had raised it, covered with the offerings of the simple natives to an unknown God.

He is the same, too, who founded Kaskaskia, probably the earliest settlement in the great valley, and whose history ends (significant fact!) with the record of his usefulness. To Father Pinet, who founded Cahokia, and was so successful in the conversion of the natives, that his little chapel could not contain the numbers who resorted to his ministrations: to Father Marest, the first preacher against intemperance; and, finally, to Marquette, the best and bravest of them all, the most single-hearted and unpretending!

Enthusiasm is a characteristic of the French nation; a trait in some individuals elevated to a sublime self-devotion, and in others degraded to mere excitability. The vivacity, gesticulation, and grimace, which characterize most of them, are the external signs of this nature; the calm heroism of the seventeenth century, and the insane devotion of the nineteenth, were alike its fruits. The *voyageur* possessed it, in common with all his countrymen. But in him it was not noisy, turbulent, or egotistical; military glory had "neither part nor lot" in his schemes; the conquests he desired to make were the conquests of faith; the dominion he wished to establish was the dominion of Jesus.

In the pursuit of these objects, or rather of this single object, I have said he manifested the enthusiasm of his race; but it was the noblest form of that characteristic. The fire that burned in his bosom was fed by no selfish purpose. To have thought of himself, or of his own comforts, or glory, to the detriment of any Christian enterprise, however dangerous or unpromising, would, in his eyes, have been a deadly sin.

At Sault de Ste. Marie, Father Marquette heard of many savages (whom he calls "God's children") living in barbarism, far to the west. With five boatmen and one companion, he at once set out for an unexplored, even unvisited wilderness. He had what they had not—the gospel; and his heart yearned toward them, as the heart of a mother toward an afflicted child. He went to them, and bound them to him "in the bond of peace." If they received him kindly—as they usually did, for even a savage recognises and respects genuine devotion—he preached to them, mediated among them, softened their hearts, and gathered them into the fold of God. If they met him with arms in their hands—as they sometimes did, for savages, like civilized men, do not always know their friends—he resolutely offered peace; and, in his own simple and pious language, "God touched their hearts," and they cast aside their weapons and received him kindly.

But the *voyageur* had higher qualities than enthusiasm. He was capable of being so absorbed in a cause as to lose sight of his own identity; to forget that he was more than an instrument in the hands of God, to do God's work: and the distinction between these traits is broad indeed! Enthusiasm is noisy, obtrusive—self-abnegation is silent, retiring; enthusiasm is officious, troublesome, careless of time and place—self-abnegation is prudent, gentle, considerate. The one is active and fragmentary—the other passive, but constant.

Thus, when the untaught and simple native was to be converted, the missionary took note of the spiritual capacity as well as of the spiritual wants; he did not force him to receive, at once, the whole creed of the church, as a mere enthusiast would have done; for *that* wisdom would feed an infant with strong meats, even before it had drawn its mother's milk. Neither did he preach the gospel with the sword, like the Spaniard, nor with fire and fagot, like the puritan. He was wise as the serpent, but gentle as the dove. He took the wondering

Indian by the hand; received him as a brother; won him over to listen patiently; and then taught him first that which he could most easily comprehend : he led him to address the throne of grace, or, in the language of the time, " to embrace the prayer;" because even the savage believed in Deity. As his understanding was expanded, and his heart purified — as every heart must be which truly lifts itself to God — he gradually taught him the more abstruse and wonderful doctrines of the Church of Christ. Gently and imperceptibly he led him on, until the whole tremendous work was done. The untutored savage, if he knew nothing else, yet knew the name of his Redeemer. The bloody warfare, the feuds and jealousies of his tribe, if not completely overcome, at least were softened and ameliorated. When he could not convert, he endeavored to humanize; and among the tribes of the Illinois,* though they were never thoroughly Christianized, the influence of the good fathers soon prevailed to abolish the barbarous practice of torturing captives.† For though they might not embrace

* A collective name, including a number, variously stated, of different tribes confederated.

† *Annals of the West*, by J. H. Perkins and J. M. Peck, p. 679. St. Louis. 1850.

the religion, the savages venerated its teachers, and loved them for their gentleness.

And this gentleness was not want of courage; for never in the history of the world has truer valor been exhibited than that shown by the early missionary and his compeers, the first military adventurers! Read Joutel's account of the melancholy life and death of La Salle; read the simple, unpretending "Journal" of Marquette;* and compare their constancy and heroism with that displayed at any time in any cause! But the *voyageur* possessed higher qualities than courage, also; and here again we recur to his perfect abnegation of himself; his renunciation of all personal considerations.

Courage takes note of danger, but defies it: the *voyageur* was careless of danger, because he counted it as nothing; he gave it no thought, because it only affected *himself;* and he valued not his own safety and comfort, so long as he could serve the cause by forgetting them. Mere courage is combative, even pugnacious; but the *voyageur* fought only "the good fight;" he had no pride of conquest, save in the victories of Faith, and rather would suffer, himself, than

* The substance of the Journal may be found, republished by Dr. Sparks, in the second edition of *Butler's Kentucky*, p. 493, *et seq.*, and in vol. x. of his *American Biography*.

inflict suffering upon others. Mere courage is restless, impatient, purposeless: but the *voyageur* was content to remain wherever he could do good, tentative only in the cause of Christ, and distracted by no objects from his mission. His religion was his inspiration; his conscience his reward. His system may have been perverted, his zeal mistaken, his church a sham; we are not arguing that question. But the purity of his intentions, the sincerity of his heart, can not be doubted; and the most intolerant protestant against "the corruptions of Rome" will, at least, admit that even catholicism was better than the paganism of the savage.

"There is not," says Macaulay,* "and there never was on this earth, a work of human policy so well deserving of examination as the Roman Catholic Church." And certainly all other systems combined have never produced one tithe of the astounding results brought about by this alone. Whether she has taught truth or falsehood; whether, on the whole, it had been better or worse for the cause of Christianity, had no such organization ever existed; whether her claims be groundless or well-founded, are questions foreign to our purpose.

* *Miscellanies*, "Review of Ranke's History of the Popes."

But that her polity is the most powerful — the best adapted to the ends she has in view — of all that man has hitherto invented, there can be no doubt. Her missionaries have been more numerous and more successful, ay, and more devoted, than those of any other church. They have gone where even the sword of the conqueror could not cleave his way. They have built churches in the wilderness, which were time-worn and crumbling when the first emigrant penetrated the forests. They have preached to youthful savages who never saw the face of another white man, though they lived to three-score years and ten. They have prayed upon the shores of lonely lakes and rivers, which were not mapped by geographers for centuries after their deaths. They have travelled on foot, unarmed and alone, where an army could not march. And everywhere their zeal and usefulness have ended only with their lives; and always with their latest breath they have mingled prayers for the salvation of their flocks, with aspirations for the welfare of their church. For though countless miles of sea and land were between her and them, their loyalty and affection to the great spiritual Mother were never forgotten. "In spite of oceans and deserts; of hunger and pestilence;

of spies and penal laws; of dungeons and racks, of gibbets and quartering-blocks," they have been found in every country, at all times, ever active and zealous. And everywhere, in palace, or hovel, or wilderness, they have been true sons of the church, loyal and obedient.

An organization capable of producing such results is certainly well worth examination. For the influence she has wielded in ages past gives promise of her future power; and it becomes those who think her permanence pernicious to the world, to avoid her errors and yet imitate her wisdom. If the system be a falsehood and a sham, it is a most gigantic and successful one, and it is of strange longevity. It has lived now more than fifteen hundred years, and one hundred and fifty millions of people yet believe it. If it be a counterfeit, it is high time the cheat were detected and exposed. Let those who have the truth give forth its light, that the falsehood may wither and die. Unless they do so, the life which has already extended over so many centuries may gain fresh vigor, and renew its youth. Even yet the vision of the essayist may be realized: "She may still exist in undiminished vigor, when some traveller from New Zealand shall, in the midst of a vast solitude, take his stand on a broken arch of London Bridge to sketch the ruins of St. Paul's!"

It was to this church that the early *voyageurs* belonged. And I do not use that word "belonged" as it is employed in modern times among protestants: I mean *more* than that convenient, loosely-fitting profession, which, like a garment, is thrown on and off, as the exigencies of hypocrisy or cupidity may require. These men actually *did belong* to the church. They were hers, soul and body; hers, in life and in death; hers to go whithersoever she might direct, to do whatsoever she might appoint. They believed the doctrines they taught with an abiding, *active* faith; and they were willing to be spent in preaching them to the heathen.

It has always been a leading principle in the policy of the Roman church, to preserve her unity, and she has been enabled to do so, principally by the ramified and elastic polity for which she has been distinguished, to which she owes much of her extent and power, as well as no small part of the reproach so liberally bestowed upon her in the pages of history. There are many "arms" in her service: a man must be impracticable indeed, when she can find no place in which to make him useful, or to prevent his being mischievous. She never drives one from the pale of the church who can benefit it as a communicant, or injure it as a dissenter. If he became troublesome at home, she has, in all ages, had enterprises on foot in which she might clothe him with authority, and send him to the uttermost parts of the earth; thus ridding herself of a dangerous member, and, by the same act, enlarging the sphere of her own dominion. Does an enthusiast become noisy, or troublesome upon unimportant points, the creed is flexible, and the mother will not quarrel with her child, for his earnestness may convince and lead astray more valuable sons and daughters. She will establish a new order, of which the stubborn fanatic shall be founder; the new order is built into the old church organization, and its founder becomes a dignitary of the ecclesiastical establishment. Instead of becoming a dangerous heretic and schismatic, he is attached to orthodoxy by cords stronger than steel; henceforth all his earnest enthusiasm shall be directed to the advancement of his order, and consequently of his church. Does one exhibit inflexibility in some matter of conscience upon which the church insists, there are many of God's children in the wilderness starving in spirit for the bread of life; and to these, with that bread, shall the refractory son be sent. He receives the commission; departs upon his journey, glad to forget a difference with his spiritual superiors; preaches to the heathen; remembers only that the church is his mother; wins a crown of martyrdom, and is canonized for the encouragement of others!

Thus she finds a place for all, and work enough for each; and thus are thrown off the elements of schism and rebellion. Those who had most courage in the cause of right; all who were likely to be guided in matters of conscience by their own convictions; the most sincere and single-hearted, the firmest and purest and bravest, were, in matters of controversy, the most dangerous champions, should they range themselves against the teaching of the church. They were consequently, at the period of which I am writing, the men whom it was most desirable to send away; and they were eminently well fitted for the arduous and wasting duties of the missionary.

To this class belonged the large majority of the *voyageur* priests: men who might be inconvenient and obtrusive monitors, or formidable adversaries in controversy, if they remained at home; but who could only be useful — who of all men could be *most* useful — in gathering the heathen into the fold of the church. There were, doubtless, a few of another class; the restless, intriguing, and disobedient, who, though not formidable, were troublesome. But even when these joined the missionary expeditions, they did but little to forward the work, and are entitled to none of the honor so abundantly due to their more sincere brethren. To this class, for example, belonged the false and egotistical Hennepin, who only signalized himself by endeavoring to appropriate the reputation so hardly won by the brave and unfortunate La Salle.*

It does not appear upon the record that any of these men — of either the restless and ambitious, or of the better class — were literally *sent away*. But such has been the politic practice of this church for many ages; and we may safely believe, that when she was engaged in an unscrupulous and desperate contest for the recovery, by fair means or foul, of her immense losses, there might be many in the ranks of her pious priesthood whom it would be inconvenient to retain at home. And during that conflict

* In a book which he published at Utrecht, in 1697, entitled *A New Discovery of a Vast Country*, he claims to have gone down the Mississippi to its mouth before La Salle. The whole book is a mere plagiarism. See Sparks's *Life of La Salle*, where the vain father is summarily and justly disposed of.

especially, with the most formidable enemies she ever had, she could not afford to be encumbered.

But whatever may have been the motives of their spiritual superiors, the missionaries themselves were moved only by the considerations of which we have spoken — the truest piety and the most burning zeal. Of these influences they were conscious; but we shall perhaps not do the character injustice if we add another spur to action, of which they were *not* conscious. There is a vein of romance in the French composition; a love of adventure for the sake of the adventure itself, which, when not tamed or directed, makes a Frenchman fitful, erratic, and unreliable. When it is toned by personal ambition, it becomes a sort of Paladin contempt for danger; sometimes a crazy furor. When accompanied by powerful intellect, and strengthened by concentration on a purpose, it makes a great commander — great for the quickness of his comprehension, the suddenness of his resolutions, the rapidity of their execution. When humanized by love, and quickened by religious zeal, it is purified of every selfish thought, and produces the chivalrous missionary, whom neither fire nor flood, neither desert nor pathless wilderness, shall deter from obeying the command of Him who sent his gospel "unto every creature." And thus are even those traits, which so often curse the world with insane ambition and sanguinary war, turned by the power of a true benevolence to be blessings of incalculable value.

Such were the purposes, such the motives, of this band of noble men; and whatever may have been their errors, we must at least accord them the virtues of *sincerity, courage, and self-denial*. But let us look a little more closely at the means by which they accomplished undertakings which, to any other race of men, would have been not only impracticable, but utterly desperate. Take again, as the representative of his class, the case of Father Marquette, than whom, obscure as his name is in the wastes of history, no man ever lived a more instructive and exemplary life.

From the year 1668 to 1671,* Marquette had been preaching at the Sault de Sainte Marie, a little below the foot of Lake Superior. He was associated with others in that mission; but the largest type, though it thrust itself no higher than the smallest, will make the broadest impress on the page of history; and even in the

* Most of these dates may be found in Bancroft's *United States*, vol iii.

meager record of that time, we may trace the influence of his gentle but firm spirit—those by whom he was accompanied evidently took their tone from him. But he was one of the Church's pioneers; that class whose eager, single-hearted zeal is always pushing forward to new conquests of the faith; and when he had put aside the weapons that opposed their way, to let his followers in, his thoughts at once went on to more remote and suffering regions. During his residence at the Sault, rumors and legends were continually floating in of the unknown country lying to the west—"the Land of the Great River," the Indians called it—until the mind of the good father became fully possessed with the idea of going to convert the nations who dwelt upon its shores. In the year 1671, he took the first step in that direction, moving on to Point St. Ignatius, on the main land, north of the island of Mackinac. Here, surrounded by his little flock of wondering listeners, he preached until the spring of 1673; but all the time his wish to carry the gospel where its sound had never been heard was growing stronger. He felt in his heart the impulse of his calling, to lead the way and open a path for the advance of light. At the period mentioned, he received an order from the wise intendant in New France, M. Talon, to explore the pathless wilderness to the westward.

Then was seen the true spirit of the man, and of his order. He gathered together no armament; asked the protection of no soldiers; no part of the cargo of his little boat consisted of gunpowder, or of swords or guns; his only arms were the spirit of love and peace; his trust was in God for protection. Five boatmen, and one companion, the Sieur Joliet, composed his party. Two light bark canoes were his only means of travelling; and in these he carried a small quantity of Indian corn and some jerked meat, his only means of subsistence.

Thus equipped, he set out through Green Bay and up Fox river, in search of a country never yet visited by any European. The Indians endeavored to dissuade him, wondering at his hardihood, and still more at the motives which could induce him thus to brave so many dangers. They told him of the savage Indians, to whom it would be only pastime to torture and murder him; of the terrible monsters which would swallow him and his companions, "canoes and all;" of the great bird called the *Piasau*,* which devoured men, after car-

* The legend of the Piasau is well known. Within the recollection of men now living, rude paintings of the monster

rying them in its horrible talons to inaccessible cliffs and mountains; and of the scorching heat, which would wither him like a dry leaf. "I thanked them kindly," says the resolute but gentle father, "for their good counsel; but I told them that I could not profit by it, since the salvation of souls was at stake, for which object I would be overjoyed to give my life." Shaking them by the hand, one by one, as they approached to bid him farewell, as they thought, for the last time, he turned his back upon safety and peace, and departed upon his self-denying pilgrimage.

Let him who sits at ease in his cushioned pew at home — let him who lounges on his velvet-covered sofa in the pulpit, while his well-taught choir are singing; who rises as the strains are dying, and kneels upon a cushioned stool to pray; who treads upon soft carpets while he preaches, in a white cravat, to congregations clad in broadcloth, silk, and satin — let him pause and ponder on the difference between his works, his trials, his zeal — ay, and his glory, both of earth and heaven! — and those of Father James Marquette!

were visible on the cliffs above Alton, Illinois. To these images, when passing in their canoes, the Indians were accustomed to make offerings of maize, tobacco, and gunpowder. They are now quite obliterated.

The little party went upon their way; the persuasions of their simple-hearted friends could not prevail, for the path of duty was before them, and the eye of God above. Having passed through Green Bay, and painfully dragged their canoes over the rapids of Fox river, they reached a considerable village, inhabited by the united tribes of Kickapoos, Miamis, and Mascoutimes. Here they halted for a time, as the mariner, about to prove the dangers of a long voyage, lingers for a day in the last port he is likely to enter for many months. Beyond this point no white man had ever gone; and here, if anywhere, the impulses of a natural fear should have made themselves felt. But we hear of no hesitation, no shrinking from the perilous task; and we know from the unpretending "Journal" of the good father, that a retreat, nay, even a halt—longer than was necessary to recruit exhausted strength, and renew the memory of former lessons among the natives—was never thought of. "My companion," said Marquette, referring to Joliet, "is an envoy from the king of France, and I am an humble minister of God. I have no fear, *because I shall consider it the highest happiness to die in the service of my master!*" There was no bravado in this, for, unlike many from whom you may, any day, hear the same declaration, he set forth immediately to encounter the perils of his embassy.

The Indians, unable to prevail with him to abandon the enterprise, made all their simple provision for his comfort; and, furnishing him with guides and carriers across the portage to the Wisconsin river, parted with him as one bound for eternity. Having brought them safely to the river, the guides left them "alone in that unknown country, in the hand of God;" and, trusting to the protection of that hand, they set out upon their journey down the stream.* Seven days after, "with inexpressible joy," they emerged upon the bosom of the great river. During all this time they had seen no human being, though, probably, many a wandering savage had watched them from the covert of the bank, as they floated silently between the forests. It was an unbroken solitude, where the ripple of their paddles sounded loudly on the ear, and their voices, subdued by the stillness, were sent back in lonely echoes from the shore.

They were the first white men who ever floated on the bosom of that mighty river[†]—

* June 10, 1673.

† I mean, of course, the upper Mississippi; for De Soto had

"the envoy from the king of France, and the embassador of the King of kings." What were their thoughts we know not, but from Marquette's simple "Journal;" for, in returning to Quebec, Joliet's boat was wrecked in sight of the city, and all his papers lost.* Of the Sieur himself, we know nothing, save as the companion of Marquette on this voyage; but from this alone his fame is imperishable.

They sailed slowly down the river, keeping a constant outlook upon the banks for signs of those for whose spiritual welfare the good father had undertaken his perilous journey. But for more than sixty leagues not a human form or habitation could be seen. They had leisure, more than they desired, to admire the grand and beautiful scenery of that picturesque region. In some places the cliffs rose perpendicularly for hundreds of feet from the water's edge; and nodding over their brows, and towering against the sky, were stately pines and cedars of the growth of centuries. Here,

reached it lower down one hundred and thirty-two years before.

* It was announced, some months since, that our minister at Rome, Mr. Cass, had made discoveries in that city which threw more light upon this expedition. But how this can be, consistently with the fact stated in the text (about which there is no doubt), I am at a loss to divine.

there lay between the river and the cliffs, a level prairie, waving in all the luxuriance of "the leafy month of June;" while beyond, the bluffs, enclosing the natural garden, softened by the distance, and clothed in evergreen, seemed but an extension of the primitive savanna. Here, a dense, primeval forest grew quite down to the margin of the water; and, hanging from the topmost branches of the giant oaks, festoons of gray and graceful moss lay floating on the rippled surface, or dipped within the tide. Here, the large, smooth roots of trees half undermined, presented seats and footholds, where the pleasant shade invited them to rest, and shelter from the sultry summer sun. Anon, an open prairie, with no cliff or bluff beyond, extended undulating from the river, until the eye, in straining to measure its extent, was wearied by the effort, and the plain became a waving sea of rainbow colors; of green and yellow, gold and purple. Again, they passed a gravelly beach, on which the yellow sand was studded with a thousand sets of brilliant shells, and little rivulets flowed in from level prairies, or stealthily crept out from under roots of trees or tangled vines, and hastened to be hidden in the bosom of the great father of waters.

They floated on, through the dewy morning hours, when the leaves were shining in the sunlight, and the birds were singing joyously; before the summer heat had dried the moisture, or had forced the feathered songsters to the shade. At noon, when the silence made the solitude oppressive; when the leaves hung wilting down, nor fluttered in the fainting wind: when the prairies were no longer waving like the sea, but trembling like the atmosphere around a heated furnace: when the *mirage* hung upon the plain: tall trees were seen growing in the air, and among them stalked the deer, and elk, and buffalo: while between them and the ground, the brazen sky was glowing with the sun of June: when nothing living could be seen, save when the *voyageur's* approach would startle some wild beast slaking his thirst in the cool river, or a flock of waterfowl were driven from their covert, where the willow branches, drooping, dipped their leaves of silvery gray within the water. They floated on till evening, when the sun approached the prairie, and his broad, round disc, now shorn of its dazzling beams, defined itself against the sky and grew florid in the gathering haze: when the birds began to reappear, and flitted noiselessly among the trees, in busy preparation for the night: when beasts of prey crept out from lurking-places, where they had dozed and panted through the hours of noon: when the wilderness grew vocal with the mingled sounds of lowing buffalo, and screaming panther, and howling wolf; until the shadows rose from earth, and travelled from the east; until the dew began to fall, the stars came out, and night brought rest and dreams of home!

Thus they floated on, "from morn till dewy eve," and still no sign of human life, neither habitation nor footprint, until one day — it was the twenty-fifth of June, more than two weeks since they had entered the wilderness — in gliding past a sandy beach, they recognised the impress of a naked foot! Following it for some distance, it grew into a trail, and then a path, once more a place where human beings habitually walked.

Whose feet had trodden down the grass, what strange people lived on the prairies, they knew not, what dangers might await them, they cared not. These were the people whom the good father had come so far to convert and save! And now, again, one might expect some natural hesitation; some doubt in venturing among those who were certainly barbarians, and who might, for aught they knew, be brutal cannibals. We could forgive a little wavering, indeed, especially when we think of the frightful stories told them by the Northern Indians of this very people. But fear was not a part of these men's nature; or if it existed, it lay so deep, buried beneath religious zeal and pious trust, that its voice never reached the upper air. Leaving the boatmen with the canoes, near the mouth of the river now called Des Moines, Marquette and Joliet set out alone, to follow up the trail, and seek the people who had made it. It led them to an open prairie, one of the most beautiful in the present state of Iowa, and crossing this, a distance of six miles, they at last found themselves in the vicinity of three Indian villages. The very spot* where the chief of these stood might now be easily found, so clear, though brief, is the description of the simple priest. It stood at the foot of a long slope, on the bank of the river Moingona (or Des Moines), about six miles due west of the Mississippi; and at the top of the rise, at the distance of half a league, were built

* The place of Marquette's landing — which should be classic ground — from his description of the country, and the distance he specifies, could not have been far from the spot where the city of Keokuk now stands, a short distance above the mouth of the Des Moines. The locality should, if possible, be determined.

the two others. "We commended ourselves unto God," writes the gentle father; for they knew not at what moment they might need his intervention; and crying out with a loud voice, to announce their approach, they calmly advanced toward the group of lodges. At a short distance from the entrance to the village, they were met by a deputation of four old men, who, to their great joy, they perceived bore a richly-ornamented pipe of peace, the emblem of friendship and hospitality. Tendering the mysterious calumet, they informed the Frenchmen that they belonged to one of the tribes called "Illinois" (or "Men"), and invited them to enter their lodges in peace: an invitation which the weary *vogageurs* were but too glad to accept.

A great council was held, with all the rude but imposing ceremonies of the grave and dignified Indian; and before the assembled chiefs and braves, Marquette published his mission from his heavenly Master. Passing, then, from spiritual to temporal things — for we do not hear of any address from Joliet, who probably was no orator — he spoke of his earthly king, and of his viceroy in New France; of his victories over the Iroquois, the dreaded enemies of the peaceful Western tribes; and then made many inquiries about the Mississippi, its tributaries, and the nations who dwelt upon their banks. His advances were kindly received, his questions frankly answered, and the council broke up with mutual assurances of good-will. Then ensued the customary festival. Homminy, fish, buffalo, and *dog-meat*, were successively served up, like the courses of a more modern table; but of *the last* " we declined to partake," writes the good father, no doubt much to the astonishment and somewhat to the chagrin of their hospitable friends; for even yet, among the western Indians, dog-meat is a dish of honor.

Six days of friendly intercourse passed pleasantly away, diversified by many efforts on the part of Marquette to instruct and convert the docile savages. Nor were these entirely without result; they excited, at least, the wish to hear more; and on his departure they crowded round him, and urgently requested him to come again among them. He promised to do so, a pledge which he afterward redeemed. But now he could not tarry; he was bent upon his hazardous voyage down the Great River, and he knew that he was only on the threshold of his grand discoveries. Six hundred warriors, commanded by their most distinguished chief, accompanied him back to his boats; and, after hanging around his neck the great calumet, to protect him among the hostile nations of the south, they parted with him, praying that the Great Spirit, of whom he had told them, might give him a prosperous voyage, and a speedy and safe return.

These were the first of the nations of the Mississippi Valley visited by the French, and it is from them that the state of Illinois takes its name. They were a singularly gentle people; and a nature originally peaceful had been rendered almost timid by the cruel inroads of the murderous Iroquois.* These, by their traffic with the Dutch and English of New-York, and by their long warfare with the French of Canada, had acquired the use of fire-arms, and, of course, possessed an immense advantage over those who were armed only with the primitive bow and arrow. The restless and ambitious spirit of the singular confederacy, usually called the Five Nations, and known among their neighbors by the collective name of Iroquois, had carried their incursions even as far as the hunting-grounds of the Shawanese, about

* It was by virtue of a treaty of purchase — signed at Fort Stanwix on the 5th of November, 1768 — with the Six Nations, who claimed the country as their conquest, that the British asserted a title to the country west of the Alleghanies, Western Virginia, Kentucky, etc.

the mouth of the Ohio; and their successes had made them a terror to all the western tribes. The Illinois, therefore, knowing the French to be at war with these formidable enemies, were the more anxious to form an alliance with them; and the native gentleness of their manners was, perhaps, increased by the hope of assistance and protection. But, whatever motives may have influenced them, besides their natural character, their forethought was of vital service to the wanderers in the countries of the south, whither they proceeded.

The little party of seven resumed their voyage on the last day of June, and floating with the rapid current, a few days afterward passed the rocks, above the site of Alton, where was painted the image of the ravenous *Piasau*, of which they had been told by the Northern Indians, and on the same day reached the mouth of the Pekitanoni, the Indian name for the rapid and turbulent Missouri. Inwardly resolving, at some future time, to ascend its muddy current, to cross the ridge beyond, and, descending some river which falls into the Great South sea (as the Pacific was then called), to publish the gospel to all the people of the continent, the zealous father passed onward toward the south. Coasting slowly along the wasting shore, lingering in the mouths of rivers, or exploring dense forests in the hope of meeting the natives, they continued on their course until they reached the mouth of a river which they called the *Ouabache*, or Wabash, none other than the beautiful Ohio.* Here they found the advanced settlement of Shawanese, who had been pushed toward the southwest by the incessant attacks of the Iroquois. But by this time, fired with the hope of ascertaining the outlet of the Mississippi, they postponed their visit to these people until their return, and floated on.

It is amusing, as well as instructive, to observe how little importance the travellers gave to the river Ohio, in their geographical assumptions. In the map published by Marquette with his " Journal," the " *Ouabisquigou*," as he denominates it, in euphonious French-Indian, compared to the Illinois or even to the Wisconsin, is but an inconsiderable rivulet! The lonely

* The geographical mistakes of the early French explorers have led to some singular discussions about Western history — have even been used by diplomatists to support or weaken territorial claims. Such, for example, is the question concerning the antiquity of Vincennes, a controversy founded on the mistake noticed in the text. Vide *Western Annals*. 2d Ed. Revised by J. M. Peck.

wanderers were much farther from the English settlements than they supposed; a mistake into which they must have been led, by hearing of the incursions of the Iroquois; for even at that early day they could not but know that the head-waters of the Ohio were not distant from the hunting-grounds of that warlike confederacy. Even this explanation, however, scarcely lessens our wonder that they should have known so little of courses and distances; for had this river been as short as it is here delineated, they would have been within four hundred miles of Montreal.

After leaving the Ohio, they suffered much from the climate and its incidents; for they were now approaching, in the middle of July, a region of perpetual summer. Mosquitoes and other venomous insects (in that region we might even call them *ravenous* insects) became intolerably annoying; and the *voyageurs* began to think they had reached the country of the terrible heats, which, as they had been warned in the north, " would wither them up like a dry leaf." But the prospect of death by torture and savage cruelty had not daunted them, and they were not now disposed to be turned back by any excess of climate. Arranging their sails in the form of awnings to protect them from the sun by day and the dews by night, they resolutely pursued their way.

Following the course of the river, they soon entered the region of cane-brakes, so thick that no animal larger than a cat could penetrate them; and of cotton-wood forests of immense size and of unparalleled density. They were far beyond the limits of every Indian dialect with which they had become acquainted — were, in fact, approaching the region visited by De Soto, on his famous expedition in search of Juan Ponce de Leon's fountain of youth.* The country was possessed by the Sioux and Chickasaws, to whom the *voyageurs* were total strangers; but they went on without fear. In the neighborhood of the southern boundary of the present state of Arkansas, they were met in hostile array by great numbers of the natives, who approached them in large canoes made from the trunks of hollow trees. But Marquette held aloft the symbol of peace, the ornamented calumet, and the hearts of the savages were melted, as the pious father believed, by the touch of God. They threw aside their

* In 1541, De Soto crossed the Mississippi about the thirty-fifth parallel of latitude, or near the northern boundary of the state of that name. It is not certain how far below this Marquette went, though we are safe in saying that he did not turn back north of that limit.

weapons, and received the strangers with rude but hearty hospitality. They escorted them, with many demonstrations of welcome, to the village of Michigamia; and, on the following day, having feasted their strange guests plentifully, though not with the unsavory meats of the Illinois, they marched in triumphal procession to the metropolis of Akansea, about ten leagues distant, down the river.

This was the limit of their voyage. Here they ascertained, beyond a doubt, that the Mississippi flowed into the gulf of Mexico, and not, as had been conjectured, into the great South sea. Here they found the natives armed with axes of steel, a proof of their traffic with the Spaniards; and thus was the circle of discovery complete, connecting the explorations of the French with those of the Spanish, and entirely enclosing the possessions of the English. No voyage so important has since been undertaken—no results so great have ever been produced by so feeble an expedition. The discoveries of Marquette, followed by the enterprises of La Salle and his successors, have influenced the destinies of nations; and passing over all political speculations, this exploration first threw open a valley of greater extent, fertility, and commercial advantages, than any other in the world. Had either the French or the Spanish possessed the stubborn qualities which *hold*, as they had the useful which *discover*, the aspect of this continent would, at this day, have been far different.

On the seventeenth of July, having preached to the Indians the glory of God and the Catholic faith, and proclaimed the power of the *Grand Monarque*—for still we hear nothing of speech-making or delivering credentials on the part of Joliet—he set out on his return. After severe and wasting toil for many days, they reached a point, as Marquette supposed, some leagues below the mouth of the Moingona, or Des Moines. Here they left the Mississippi, and crossed the country between that river and the Illinois, probably passing through the very country which now bears the good father's name, entering the latter stream at a point not far from the present town of Peoria. Proceeding slowly up that calm river, preaching to the tribes along its banks, and partaking of their hospitality, he was at last conducted to Lake Michigan, at Chicago, and by the end of September was safe again in Green Bay, having travelled, since the tenth of June, more than three thousand miles.

It might have been expected that one who had made so magnificent a discovery — who had braved so much and endured so much — would wish to announce in person, to the authorities in Canada, or in France, the results of his expedition. Nay, it would not have been unpardonable had he desired to enjoy, after his labors, something of the consideration to which their success entitled him. And, certainly, no man could ever have approached his rulers with a better claim upon their notice than could the unpretending *voyageur*. But vain-glory was no more a part of his nature, than was fear. The unaspiring priest remained at Green Bay, to continue, or rather to resume, as a task laid aside only for a time, his ministrations to the savages. Joliet hastened on to Quebec to report the expedition, and Marquette returned to Chicago, for the purpose of preaching the gospel to the Miami confederacy; several allied tribes who occupied the country between Lake Michigan and the Des Moines river. Here again he visited the Illinois, speaking to them of God, and of the religion of Jesus; thus redeeming a promise which he had made them, when on his expedition to the South.

But his useful, unambitious life was drawing

to a close. Let us describe its last scene in the words of our accomplished historian:—

"Two years afterward, sailing from Chicago to Mackinac, he entered a little river in Michigan. Erecting an altar, he said mass, after the rites of the Catholic church; then, begging the men who conducted his canoe to leave him alone for a half hour,

> ——'In the darkling wood,
> Amid the cool and silence, he knelt down,
> And offered to the mightiest solemn thanks
> And supplication.'

At the end of the half hour they went to seek him, *and he was no more*. The good missionary, discoverer of a world, had fallen asleep on the margin of the stream that bears his name. Near its mouth, the canoe-men dug his grave in the sand. Ever after, the forest rangers, in their danger on Lake Michigan, would invoke his name. The people of the West will build his monument."*

The monument is not yet built; though the name of new counties in several of our western states testifies that the noble missionary is not altogether forgotten, in the land where he spent so many self-denying years.

* Bancroft's *History of the United States*, vol. iii., p. 161, *et seq.*, where the reader may look for most of these dates.

Such was the *voyageur* priest; the first, in chronological order, of the succession of singular men who have explored and peopled the great West. And though many who have followed him have been his equals in courage and endurance, none have ever possessed the same combination of heroic and unselfish qualities. It ought not to be true that this brief and cursory sketch is the first distinct tribute yet paid to his virtues; for no worthier subject ever employed the pen of the poet or historian.

Note.—Struck with the fact that the history of this class of men, and of their enterprises and sufferings, has never been written, except by themselves in their simple "Journals" and "Relations" — for the *résumé* given of these by Sparks, Bancroft, and others, is of necessity a mere unsatisfactory abstract — the writer has for some time been engaged in collecting and arranging materials, with the intention of supplying the want. The authorities are numerous and widely scattered; and such a work ought to be thoroughly and carefully written, so that much time and labor lies between the author and his day of publication. Should he be spared, however, to finish the work, he hopes to present a picture of a class of men, displaying as much of true devotion, genuine courage, and self-denial, in the humble walk of the missionary, as the pages of history show in any other department of human enterprise.

III.

THE PIONEER.

"I hear the tread of pioneers,
  Of nations yet to be —
The first low wash of waves where soon
  Shall roll a human sea."

WHITTIER.

The axe rang sharply 'mid those forest shades
Which, from creation, toward the sky had towered
In unshorn beauty."

SIGOURNEY.

Next, in chronological order, after the missionary, came the military adventurer — of which class La Salle was the best representative. But the expeditions led by these men, were, for the most part, wild and visionary enterprises, in pursuit of unattainable ends. They were, moreover, unskilfully managed and unfortunately terminated — generally ending in the defeat, disappointment, and death of those who had set them on foot. They left no permanent impress upon the country; the most

THE PIONEER.

acute moral or political vision can not now detect a trace of their influence, in the aspect of the lands they penetrated; and, so far from hastening the settlement of the Great Valley, it is more probable that their disastrous failures rather retarded it — by deterring others from the undertaking. Their history reads like a romance; and their characters would better grace the pages of fiction, than the annals of civilization. Further than this brief reference, therefore, I find no place for them, in a work which aims only to notice those who either aided to produce, or indicated, the characteristics of the society in which they lived.

Soon after them, came the Indian-traders — to whose generosity so many of the captives, taken by the natives in those early times, were indebted for their ransom. But — notwithstanding occasional acts of charity — their unscrupulous rapacity, and, particularly, their introduction of spirituous liquors among the savages, furnish good reason to doubt, whether, on the whole, they did anything to advance the civilization of the lands and people they visited. And, as we shall have occasion to refer again, though briefly, to the character in a subsequent article, we will pass over it for the present, and hasten on to the *Pioneer*.

Of this class, there are two sub-divisions: the floating, transitory, and erratic frontierman — including the hunter, the trapper, the scout and Indian-fighter: men who can not be considered *citizens* of any country, but keep always a little in advance of permanent emigration. With this division of the class, we have little to do: first, because they are already well understood, by most readers in this country, through the earlier novels of Cooper, their great delineator; and, second, because, as we have intimated, our business is chiefly with those, whose footprints have been stamped upon the country, and whose influence is traceable in its civilization. We, therefore, now desire to direct attention to the other sub-division — the genuine "settler;" the firm, unflinching, permanent emigrant, who entered the country to till the land and to possess it, for himself and his descendants.

And, in the first place, let us inquire what motives could induce men to leave regions, where the axe had been at work for many years — where the land was reduced to cultivation, and the forest reclaimed from the wild beast and the wilder savage — where civilization had begun to exert its power, and society had assumed a legal and determined shape — to depart from all these things, seeking a new home in an inhospitable wilderness, where they could only gain a footing by severe labor, constant strife, and sleepless vigilance? To be capable of doing all this, from *any* motive, a man must be a strange compound of qualities; but that compound, strange as it is, has done, and is doing, more to reclaim the west, and change the wilderness into a garden, than all other causes combined.

A prominent trait in the character of the genuine American, is the desire "to better his condition"—a peculiarity which sometimes embodies itself in the disposition to forget the good old maxim, "Let well-enough alone," and not unfrequently leads to disaster and suffering. A thorough Yankee — using that word as the English do, to indicate national, not sectional, character — is never satisfied with doing well; he always underrates his gains and his successes; and, though to others he may be boastful enough, and may, even truly, rate the profits of his enterprise by long strings of "naught," he is always whispering to himself, "I ought to do better." If he sees any one accumulating property faster than himself, he becomes emulous and discontented — he is apt to think, unless he goes more rapidly than any one else, that he is not moving at all. If he can find no one of his neighbors advancing toward fortune, with longer strides than he, he will imagine some successful "speculator," to whom he will compare himself, and chafe at his inferiority to a figment of his own fancy. If he possessed " a million a minute," he would cast about for some profitable employment, in which he might engage, " to pay expenses." He will abandon a silver-mine, of slow, but certain gains, for the gambling chances of a gold "placer;" and if any one within his knowledge dig out more wealth than he, he will leave the " diggings," though his success be quite encouraging, and go quixoting among the islands of the sea, in search of pearls and diamonds. With the prospect of improvement in his fortunes — whether that prospect be founded upon reason, be a naked fancy, or the offspring of mere discontent — he regards no danger, cares for no hardship, counts no suffering. Everything must bend before the ruling passion, "to better his condition."

His spirit is eminently encroaching. Rather than give up any of his own "rights," he will take a part of what belongs to others. Whatever he thinks necessary to his welfare, to that he believes himself entitled. To whatever point he desires to reach, he takes the straightest course, even though the way lie across the corner of his neighbor's field. Yet he is intensely jealous of his own possessions, and warns off all trespassers with an imperial menace of "the utmost penalty of the law." He has, of course, an excellent opinion of himself — and justly: for when not blinded by cupidity or vexed by opposition, no man can hold the scales of justice with a more even hand.

He is seldom conscious of having done a wrong: for he rarely moves until he has ascertained "both the propriety and expediency of the motion." He has, therefore, an instinctive aversion to all retractions and apologies. He has such a proclivity to the forward movement, that its opposite, even when truth and justice demand it, is stigmatized, in his vocabulary, by odious and ridiculous comparisons. He is very stubborn, and, it is feared, sometimes mistakes his obstinacy for firmness. He thinks a safe retreat worse than a defeat with slaughter. Yet he never rests under a reverse, and, though manifestly prostrate, will never acknowledge that he is beaten. A check enrages him more than a decided failure: for so long as his end is not accomplished, nor defeated, he can see no reason why he should not succeed. If his forces are driven back, shattered and destroyed, he is not cast down, but angry — he forthwith swears vengeance and another trial. He is quite insatiable — as a failure does not dampen him, success can never satisfy him. His plans are always on a great scale; and, if they sometimes exceed his means of execution, at least, "he who aims at the sun," though he may lose his arrow, "will not strike the ground." He is a great projector — but he is eminently practical, as well as theoretical; and if *he* cannot realize his visions, no other man need try.

He is restless and migratory. He is fond of change, for the sake of the change; and he will have it, though it bring him only new labors and new hardships. He is, withal, a little selfish — as might be supposed. He begins to lose his attachment to the advantages of his home, so soon as they are shared by others. He does not like near neighbors — has no affection for the soil; he will leave a place on which he has expended much time and labor, as soon as the region grows to be a "settlement." Even in a town, he is dissatisfied if his next neighbor lives so near that the women can gossip across the division-fence. He likes to be at least one day's journey from the nearest plantation.

I once heard an old pioneer assign as a reason why he must emigrate from western Illinois, the fact that "people were settling right under his nose"—and the farm of his nearest neighbor was twelve miles distant, by the section lines! He moved on to Missouri, but there the same "impertinence" of emigrants soon followed him; and, abandoning his half-finished "clearing," he packed his family and household goods in a little wagon, and retreated, across the plains to Oregon. He is—or was, two years ago—living in the valley of the Willamette, where, doubtless, he is now chafing under the affliction of having neighbors in the same region, and nothing but an ocean beyond.

His character seems to be hard-featured.

But he is neither unsocial, nor morose. He welcomes the stranger as heartily as the most hospitable patriarch. He receives the sojourner at his fireside without question. He regales him with the best the house affords: is always anxious to have him "stay another day." He cares for his horse, renews his harness, laughs at his stories, and exchanges romances with him. He hunts with him; fishes, rides, walks, talks, eats, and drinks with him. His wife washes and mends the stranger's shirts, and lends him a needle and thread to sew a button on his only pair of pantaloons. The children sit on his knee, the dog lies at his feet, and accompanies him into the woods. The whole family are his friends, and only grow cold and distant when they learn that he is looking for land, and thinks of "settling" within a few leagues. If nothing of the sort occurs — and this only "leaks out" by accident, for the pioneer never pries inquisitively into the business of his guest, he keeps him as long as he can; and when he can stay no longer, fills his saddle-bags with flitches of bacon and "pones" of corn-bread, shakes him heartily by the hand, exacts a promise to stop again on his return, and bids him "God-speed" on his journey.

Such is American character, in the manifestations which have most affected the settlement and development of the West; a compound of many noble qualities, with a few — and no nation is without such — that are not quite so respectable. All these, both good and bad, were possessed by the early pioneer in an eminent, sometimes in an extravagant degree; and the circumstances, by which he found himself surrounded after his emigration to the West, tended forcibly to their exaggeration.

But the qualities — positive and negative — above enumerated, were, many of them, at least, peculiarities belonging to the early emigrant, as much before as after his removal. And there were others, quite as distinctly marked, called into activity, if not actually created by his life in the wilderness. Such, for example, was his self-reliance — his confidence in his own strength, sagacity, and courage. It was but little assistance that he ever required from his neighbors, though no man was ever more willing to render it to others, in the hour of need. He was the swift avenger of his own wrongs, and he never appealed to another to ascertain his rights. Legal tribunals were an abomination to him. Government functionaries he hated, almost as the Irish hate excisemen. Assessments and taxes he could not endure, for, since he was his own protector, he had no interest in sustaining the civil authorities.

Military organizations he despised, for subordination was no part of his nature. He stood up in the native dignity of manhood, and called no mortal his superior. When he joined his neighbors, to avenge a foray of the savages, he joined on the most equal terms — each man was, for the time, his own captain; and when the leader was chosen — for the pioneers, with all their personal independence, were far too rational to underrate the advantages of a head in the hour of danger — each voice was counted in the choice, and the election might fall on any one. But, even after such organization, every man was fully at liberty to abandon the expedition, whenever he became dissatisfied, or thought proper to return home. And if this want of discipline sometimes impaired the strength, and rendered unavailing the efforts, of communities, it at least fostered the manly spirit of personal independence; and, to keep that alive in the breasts of a people, it is worth while to pay a yearly tribute, even though that tribute be rendered unto the King of Terrors!

This self-reliance was not an arrogant and vulgar egotism, as it has been so often represented in western stories, and the tours of superficial travellers. It was a calm, just estimate of his own capabilities — a well-grounded confidence in his own talents — a clear, manly understanding of his own individual rights, dignity, and relations. Such is the western definition of independence; and if there be anything of it in the western character at the present day, it is due to the stubborn and intense individuality of the first pioneer. He it was who laid the foundation of our social fabric, and it is his spirit which yet pervades our people.

The quality which next appears, in analyzing this character, is his *courage*.

It was not mere physical courage, nor was it stolid carelessness of danger. The pioneer knew, perfectly well, the full extent of the peril that surrounded him; indeed, he could not be ignorant of it; for almost every day brought some new memento, either of his savage foe, or of the prowling beast of prey. He ploughed, and sowed, and reaped, and gathered, with the rifle slung over his shoulders; and, at every turn, he halted, listening, with his ear turned toward his home; for well he knew that, any moment, the scream of his wife, or the wail of his children, might tell of the uplifted tomahawk, or the murderous scalping-knife.

His courage, then, was not ignorance of danger—not that of the child, which thrusts its hand within the lion's jaws, and knows naught of the penalty it braves. His ear was ever listening, his eye was always watching, his nerves were ever strung, for battle. He was stout of heart, and strong of hand—he was calm, sagacious, unterrified. He was never disconcerted — excitement seldom moved him — his mind was always at its own command. His heart never lost its firmness — no suffering could overcome him — he was as stoical as the savage, whose greatest glory is to triumph amidst the most cruel tortures. His pride sustained him when his flesh was pierced with burning brands — when his muscles crisped and crackled in the flames. To the force of character, belonging to the white, he added the savage virtues of the red man; and many a captive has been rescued from the flames, through his stern contempt for torture, and his sneering triumph over his tormentors. The highest virtue of the savage was his fortitude; and he respected and admired even a "pale face," who emulated his endurance.

But fortitude is only passive courage — and the bravery of the pioneer was eminently active. His vengeance was as rapid as it was sometimes cruel. No odds against him could deter him, no time was ever wasted in deliberation. If a depredation was committed in the night, the dawn of morning found the sufferer on the trail of the marauder. He would follow it for days, and even weeks, with the sagacity of the blood-hound, with the patience of the savage: and, perhaps, in the very midst of the

Indian country, in some moment of security, the blow descended, and the injury was fearfully avenged! The debt was never suffered to accumulate, when it could be discharged by prompt payment — and it was never forgotten! If the account could not be balanced now, the obligation was treasured up for a time to come — and, when least expected, the debtor came, and paid with usury!

It has been said, perhaps truly, that a fierce, bloody spirit ruled the settlers in those early days. And it is unquestionable, that much of that contempt for the slow vengeance of a legal proceeding, which now distinguishes the people of the frontier west, originated then. It was, doubtless, an unforgiving — eminently an unchristian — spirit: but vengeance, sure and swift, was the only thing which could impress the hostile savage. And, if example, in a matter of this sort, could be availing, for their severity to the Indians, they had the highest!

The eastern colonists — good men and true — "willing to exterminate the savages," says Bancroft,[*] who is certainly not their enemy, offered a bounty for every Indian scalp — as

[*] *History of the United States*, vol. iii., p. 336. Enacted in Massachusetts.

we, in the west, do for the scalps of wolves! "To regular forces under pay, the grant was *ten* pounds — to volunteers, in actual service, *twice that sum;* but if men would, of themselves, without pay, make up parties and patrol the forests in search of Indians, *as of old the woods were scoured for wild beasts*, the chase was invigorated by the promised "encouragement of *fifty* pounds per scalp!'" The "fruitless cruelties" of the Indian allies of the French in Canada, says the historian, gave birth to these humane and nicely-graduated enactments! Nor is our admiration of their Christian spirit in the least diminished, when we reflect that nothing is recorded in history of "bounties on scalps" or "encouragement" to murder, offered by Frontenac, or any other French-Canadian governor, as a revenge for the horrible massacre at Montreal, or the many "fruitless cruelties" of the bloody Iroquois!*

The descendants of the men who gave these "bounties" and "encouragements," have, in our own day, caressed, and wept and lamented over the tawny murderer, Black-Hawk, and his "wrongs" and "misfortunes;" but the theatre

* A detailed and somewhat tedious account of these savage inroads, may be found in Warburton's *Conquest of Canada*, published by Harpers. New-York. 1850.

of Indian warfare was then removed a little farther west; and the atrocities of Haverhill and Deerfield were perpetrated on the western prairies, and not amid the forests of the east! Yet I do not mean, by referring to this passage of history — or to the rivers of wasted sentiment poured out a few years ago — so much to condemn our forefathers, or to draw invidious comparisons between them and others, as to show, that the war of extermination, sometimes waged by western rangers, was not without example — that the cruelty and hatred of the pioneer to the barbarous Indian, might originate in exasperation, which even moved the puritans; and that the lamentations, over the fictitious "wrongs" of a turbulent and bloody savage, might have run in a channel nearer home.

Hatred of the Indian, among the pioneers, was hereditary; there was scarcely a man on the frontier, who had not lost a father, a mother, or a brother, by the tomahawk; and not a few of them had suffered in their own persons. The child, who learned the rudiments of his scanty education at his mother's knee, must decipher the strange characters by the straggling light which penetrated the crevices between the logs; for, while the father was absent, in the field or on the war-path, the mother was obliged to bar the doors and barricade the windows against the savages. Thus, if he did not literally imbibe it with his mother's milk, one of the first things the pioneer learned, was dread, and consequently hatred, of the Indian. That feeling grew with his growth, strengthened with his strength — for a life upon the western border left but few days free from sights of blood or mementoes of the savage. The pioneer might go to the field in the morning, unsuspecting; and, at noon, returning, find his wife murdered and scalped, and the brains of his little ones dashed out against his own doorpost! And if a deadly hatred of the Indian took possession of his heart, who shall blame him? It may be said, the pioneer was an intruder, seeking to take forcible possession of the Indian's lands — and that it was natural that the Indian should resent the wrong after the manner of his race. Granted: and it was quite as natural that the pioneer should return the enmity, after the manner of *his* race!

But the pioneer was *not* an intruder.

For all the purposes, for which reason and the order of Providence authorize us to say, God made the earth, this continent was vacant — uninhabited. And — granting that the savage was in possession — for this is his only ground of title, as, indeed, it is the foundation of all primary title — there were at the period of the first landing of white men on the continent, between Lake Superior and the Gulf of Mexico, east of the Mississippi, about one hundred and eighty thousand Indians.* That region now supports at least twenty millions of civilized people, and is capable of containing quite ten times that number, without crowding! Now, if God made the earth for any purpose, it certainly was *not* that it should be monopolized by a horde of nomad savages!

But an argument on this subject, would not be worth ink and paper; and I am, moreover, aware, that this reasoning may be abused. *Any* attempt to construe the purposes of Deity must be liable to the same misapplication. And, besides, it is not my design to go so far back; I seek not so much to excuse as to account for — less to justify than to analyze — the characteristics of the class before me. I wish to establish that the pioneer hatred of the Indian was not an unprovoked or groundless hatred, that the severity of his warfare was not

---

* This is the estimate of Bancroft — and, I think, at least, thirty thousand too liberal. If the number were doubled, however, it would not weaken the position in the text.

a mere gratuitous and bloody-minded cruelty. There are a thousand actions, of which we are hearing every day, that are indefensible in morals: and yet we are conscious while we condemn the actors, that, in like circumstances, we could not have acted differently. So is it with the fierce and violent reprisals, sometimes made by frontier rangers. Their best defence lies in the statement that they were men, and that their manhood prompted them to vengeance. When they deemed themselves injured, they demanded reparation, in such sort as that demand could then be made — at the muzzle of a rifle or the point of a knife. They were equal to the times in which they lived.— Had they not been so, how many steamboats would now be floating on the Mississippi?

There was no romance in the composition of the pioneer — whatever there may have been in his environment. His life was altogether too serious a matter for poetry, and the only music he took pleasure in, was the sound of a violin, sending forth notes remarkable only for their liveliness. Even this, he could enjoy but at rare periods, when his cares were forcibly dismissed. He was, in truth, a very matter-of-fact sort of person. It was principally with facts that he had to deal — and most of them were very "stubborn facts." Indeed, it may be doubted — notwithstanding much good poetry has been written (in cities chiefly), on solitude and the wilderness — whether a life in the woods is, after all, very suggestive of poetical thoughts. The perils of the frontier must borrow most of their "enchantment" from the "distance;" and its sufferings and hardships are certainly more likely to evoke pleasant fancies to him who sits beside a good coal fire, than to one whose lot it is to bear them. Even the (so-called) "varied imagery" of the Indian's eloquence — about which so much nonsense has been written — is, in a far greater measure, the result of the poverty and crude materialism of his language, than of any poetical bias, temperament, or tone of thought. An Indian, as we have said before, has no humor — he never understands a jest — his wife is a beast of burthen — heaven is a hunting-ground — his language has no words to express abstract qualities, virtues, or sentiments. And yet he lives in the wilderness all the days of his life! The only trait he has, in common with the poetical character, is his laziness.

But the pioneer was not indolent, in any sense. He had no dreaminess — meditation was no part of his mental habit — a poetical fancy would, in him, have been an indication of insanity. If he reclined at the foot of a tree, on a still summer day, it was to sleep: if he gazed out over the waving prairie, it was to search for the column of smoke which told of his enemy's approach: if he turned his eyes toward the blue heaven, it was to prognosticate to-morrow's storm or sunshine: if he bent his gaze upon the green earth, it was to look for "Indian sign" or buffalo trail. His wife was only a help-mate — he never thought of making a divinity of her — she cooked his dinner, made and washed his clothes, bore his children, and took care of his household. His children were never "little cherubs," — "angels sent from heaven" — but generally "tow-headed" and very earthly responsibilities. He looked forward anxiously, to the day when the boys should be able to assist him in the field, or fight the Indian, and the girls to help their mother make and mend. When one of the latter took it into her head to be married — as they usually did quite early in life; for beaux were plenty and belles were "scarce" — he only made one condition, that the man of her choice should be brave and healthy. He never made a "parade" about anything — marriage, least of all.

He usually gave the bride — not the "blushing" bride — a bed, a lean horse, and some good advice: and, having thus discharged his duty in the premises, returned to his work, and the business was done.

The marriage ceremony, in those days, was a very unceremonious affair. The parade and drill which now attend it, would then have been as ridiculous as a Chinese dance; and the finery and ornament, at present understood to be indispensable on such occasions, then bore no sway in fashion. Bridal wreaths and dresses were not known; and white kid gloves and satin slippers never heard of. Orange blossoms — natural and artificial — were as pretty then as now; but the people were more occupied with substance, than with emblem.

The ancients decked *their* victims for the sacrifice with gaudy colors, flags, and streamers; the moderns do the same, and the offerings are sometimes made to quite as barbarous deities.

But the bride of the pioneer was clothed in linsey-wolsey, with hose of woollen yarn; and moccasins of deer-skin — or as an extra piece of finery, high-quartered shoes of calf-skin — preceded satin slippers. The bridegroom came in copperas-colored jeans — domestic manufacture — as a holiday suit; or, perhaps, a hunting-shirt of buckskin, all fringed around the skirt and cape, and a "coon-skin" cap, with moccasins. Instead of a dainty walking-stick, with an opera-dancer's leg, in ivory, for head, he always brought his rifle, with a solid maple stock; and never, during the whole ceremony, did he divest himself of powder-horn and bullet-pouch.

Protestant ministers of the gospel were few in those days; and the words of form were usually spoken by a Jesuit missionary. Or, if the Pioneer had objections to Catholicism — as many had — his place was supplied by some justice of the peace, of doubtful powers and mythical appointment. If neither of these could be procured, the father of the bride, himself, sometimes assumed the functions, *pro hâc vice*, or *pro tempore*, of minister or justice. It was always understood, however, that such left-handed marriages were to be confirmed by the first minister who wandered to the frontier: and, even when the opportunity did not offer for many months, no scandal ever arose — the marriage vow was never broken. The pioneers were simple people — the refinements of high cultivation had not yet penetrated the forests or crossed the prairies — and good faith and virtue were as common as courage and sagacity.

When the brief, but all-sufficient ceremony was over, the bridegroom resumed his rifle, helped the bride into the saddle — or more frequently to the pillion behind him — and they calmly rode away together.

On some pleasant spot — surrounded by a shady grove, or point of timber — a new log-cabin has been built: its rough logs notched across each other at the corners, a roof of oaken clapboards, held firmly down by long poles along each course, its floor of heavy "puncheons," its broad, cheerful fireplace, large as a modern bed-room — all are in the highest style of frontier architecture. Within — excepting some anomalies, such as putting the skillet and tea-kettle in the little cupboard, along with the blue-edged plates and yellow-figured tea-cups — for the whole has been arranged by the hands of the bridegroom himself — everything is neatly and properly disposed. The oaken bedstead, with low square posts, stands in one corner, and the bed is covered by a pure white counterpane, with fringe — an heirloom in the family of the bride. At the foot of this is seen a large, heavy chest — like a camp-chest — to serve for bureau, safe, and dressing-case.

In the middle of the floor — directly above a trap-door which leads to a "potato-hole" beneath — stands a ponderous walnut table, and on it sits a nest of wooden trays; while, flanking these, on one side, is a nicely-folded table-cloth, and, on the other, a wooden-handled butcher-knife and a well-worn Bible. Around the room are ranged a few "split-bottomed" chairs, exclusively for use, not ornament. In the chimney-corners, or under the table, are several three-legged stools, made for the children, who — as the bridegroom laughingly insinuates while he points to the uncouth specimens of his handiwork — "will be coming in due time." The wife laughs in her turn — replies, "no doubt"— and, taking one of the graceful tripods in her hand, carries it forth to sit upon while she milks the cow — for she understands what she is expected to do, and does it without delay. In one corner — near the fireplace — the aforesaid cupboard is erected — being a few oaken shelves neatly pinned to the logs with hickory forks — and in this are arranged the plates and cups; — not as the honest pride of the housewife would arrange them, to display them to the best advantage — but piled away, one within another, without reference to show. As yet there is no sign of female taste or presence.

But now the house receives its mistress. The "happy couple" ride up to the low rail-fence in front — the bride springs off without assistance, affectation, or delay. The husband leads away the horse or horses, and the wife enters the dominion, where, thenceforward, she is queen. There is no coyness, no blushing, no pretence of fright or nervousness — if you will, no romance — for which the husband has reason to be thankful! The wife knows what her duties are and resolutely goes about performing them. She never dreamed, nor twaddled, about "love in a cottage," or "the sweet communion of congenial souls" (who never eat anything): and she is, therefore, not disappointed on discovering that life is actually a serious thing. She never whines about " making her husband happy"— but sets firmly and sensibly about making him *comfortable*. She cooks his dinner, nurses his children, shares his hardships, and encourages his industry. She never complains of having too much work to do, she does not desert her home to make endless visits — she borrows no misfortunes, has no imaginary ailings. Milliners and mantua-makers she ignores —"shopping" she never heard of — scandal she never invents or listens to. She never wishes for fine carriages, professes no inability to walk five hundred yards, and does not think it a "vulgar accomplishment," to know how to make butter. She has no groundless anxieties, she is not nervous about her children taking cold: a doctor is a visionary potentate to her — a drug-shop is a depot of abominations. She never forgets whose wife she is,— there is no "sweet confidante" without whom she "can not live"—she never writes endless letters about nothing. She is, in short, a faithful, honest wife: and, "in due time," the husband must make *more* "three-legged stools"— for the "tow-heads" have now covered them all!

Such is the wife and mother of the pioneer, and, with such influences about him, how could he be otherwise than honest, straightforward, and manly?

But, though a life in the woods was an enemy to every sort of sentimentalism — though a more unromantic being than the pioneer can hardly be imagined — yet his character unquestionably took its hue, from the primitive scenes and events of his solitary existence. He was, in many things, as simple as a child: as credulous, as unsophisticated. Yet the utmost cunning of the wily savage — all the strategy of Indian warfare — was not sufficient to deceive or overreach him! Though one might have expected that his life of ceaseless watchfulness would make him skeptical and suspicious, his confidence was given heartily, without reservation, and often most imprudently. If he gave his trust at all, you might ply him, by the hour, with the most improbable and outrageous fictions, without fear of contradiction or of unbelief. He never questioned the superior knowledge or pretensions of any one who claimed acquaintance with subjects of which *he* was ignorant.

The character of his intellect, like that of the Indian, was thoroughly synthetical: he had nothing of the faculty which enables us to detect falsehood, even in matters of which we know nothing by comparison and analogy. He never analyzed any story told him, he took it as a unit; and, unless it violated some known principle of his experience, or conflicted with some fact of his own observation, never doubted its truth. At this moment, there are men in every western settlement who have only vague, crude notions of what a city is—who would feel nervous if they stepped upon the deck of a steamboat—and are utterly at a loss to conjecture the nature of a railroad. Upon either of these mystical subjects they will swallow, without straining, the most absurd and impossible fictions. And this is not because of their ignorance alone, for many of them are, for their sphere in life, educated, intelligent, and, what is better, sensible men. Nor is it by any means a national trait: for a genuine Yankee will scarcely believe the truth; and, though he may sometimes trust in very wild things, his faith is usually an active " craze," and not mere passive credulity. The pioneer, then, has not derived it from his eastern fathers: it is the growth of the woods and prairies—an embellishment to a character which might otherwise appear naked and severe.

Another characteristic, traceable to the same source, the stern reality of his life, is the pioneer's gravity.

The agricultural population of this country are, at the best, not a cheerful race. Though they sometimes join in festivities, it is but seldom; and the wildness of their dissipation is too often in proportion to its infrequency. There is none of the serene contentment — none of that smiling enjoyment — which, according to travellers like Howitt, distinguishes the tillers of the ground in other lands. *Sedateness* is a national characteristic, but the gravity of the pioneer is quite another thing ; it includes pride and personal dignity, and indicates a stern, unyielding temper. There is, however, nothing morose in it: it is its aspect alone, which forbids approach ; and that only makes more conspicuous the heartiness of your reception, when once the shell is broken. Acquainted with the character, you do not expect him to *smile* much ; but now and then he *laughs:* and that laugh is round, free, and hearty. You know at once that he enjoys it, you are convinced that he is a firm friend and " a good hater."

It is not surprising, with a character such as I have described, that the pioneer is not gregarious, that he is, indeed, rather solitary. Accordingly, we never find a genuine specimen of the class, among the emigrants, who come in shoals and flocks, and pitch their tents in " colonies ;" who lay out towns and cities, projected upon paper, and call them New Boston, New Albany, or New Hartford, before one log is placed upon another; nor are there many of the unadulterated stock among that other class, who come from regions further south, and christen their towns, classically, Carthage, Rome, or Athens: or, patriotically, in commemoration of some Virginian worthy, some Maryland sharpshooter, or "Jersey blue."

The real pioneer never emigrates gregariously; he does not wish to be within "halloo" of his nearest neighbor; he is no city-builder; and, if he does project a town, he christens it by some such name as Boonville or Clarksville, in memory of a noted pioneer: or Jacksonville or Waynesville, to commemorate some "old hero" who was celebrated for good fighting.* And the reason why the outlandish and *outré* so much predominate in the names of western towns and cities, must be sought in the fact referred

---

* On the subject of naming towns, much might have been said in the preceding article in favor of French taste, and especially that just and unpretending taste, which led them almost alway to retain the Indian names. While the American has pretentiously imported from the Old World such names as Venice, Carthage, Rome, Athens, and even London and Paris, or has transferred from the eastern states, Boston, Philadelphia, Baltimore, and New York, the Frenchman, with a better judgment, has retained such Indian names as Chicago, Peoria, Kaskaskia, Cahokia, Illinois, Wisconsin, Missouri, Wabash, and Mississippi.

to above, that the western man is not essentially a town-projector, and that, consequently, comparatively few of the towns were "laid out" by the legitimate pioneer. We shall have more to say of town-building under another head; and, in the meantime, having said that the pioneer is not gregarious, let us look at the *manner* of his emigration.

Many a time, in the western highways, have I met with the sturdy "mover," as he is called, in the places where people are stationary — a family, sometimes by no means small, wandering toward the setting sun, in search of pleasant places on the lands of "Uncle Sam." Many a time, in the forest or on the prairie — generally upon some point of timber which puts a mile or two within the plain — have I passed the "clearing," or "pre-emption," where, with nervous arm and sturdy heart, the "squatter"* cleaves out, and renders habitable, a home for himself and a heritage for his children.

Upon the road, you first meet the pioneer him-

* This word is a pregnant memento of the manner in which the vain words of flippant orators fall, innocuous, to the ground, when they attempt to stigmatize, with contemptuous terms, the truly noble. "Squatter" is now, in the west, only another name for "Pioneer," and that word describes all that is admirable in courage, truth, and manhood!

self, for he almost always walks a few hundred yards ahead. He is usually above the medium height, and rather spare. He stoops a little, too; for he has done a deal of hard work, and expects to do more; but you see at once, that unless his lungs are weak, his strength is by no means broken, and you are quite sure that many a stately tree is destined to be humbled by his sinewy arm. He is attired in frontier fashion: he wears a loose coat, called a hunting-shirt, of jeans or linsey, and its color is that indescribable hue compounded of copperas and madder; pantaloons, exceedingly loose, and not very accurately cut in any part, of like color and material, defend his lower limbs. His feet are cased in low, fox-colored shoes, for of boots, he is, yet, quite innocent. Around his throat and wrists, even in midsummer, you see the collar and wristbands of a heavy, deep-red, flannel-shirt. Examine him very closely, and you will probably find no other garment on his person.

His hair is dark, and not very evenly trimmed — for his wife or daughter has performed the tonsure with a pair of rusty shears; and the longer locks seem changed in hue, as if his dingy wool hat did not sufficiently protect them against the wind and rain. Over his shoulder he carries a heavy rifle, heavier than a "Harper's ferry musket," running about " fifty to the pound." Around his neck are swung the powder-horn and bullet-pouch, the former protected by a square of deer-skin, and the latter ornamented with a squirrel's tail.

You take note of all these things, and then recur to his melancholy-looking face, with its mild blue eyes and sharpened features. You think he looks thin, and conjecture that his chest may be weak, or his lungs affected, by the stoop in his shoulders; but when he lifts his eyes, and asks the way to Thompson's ferry, or how far it is to water, you are satisfied: for the glance of his eye is calm and firm, and the tone of his voice is round and healthy. You answer his question, he nods quietly by way of thanks, and marches on; and, though you draw your rein, and seem inclined to further converse, he takes no notice, and pursues his way.

A few minutes afterward, you meet the family. A small, light wagon, easily dragged through sloughs and heavy roads, is covered with a white cotton cloth, and drawn, by either two yokes of oxen, or a pair of lean horses. A "patch-work" quilt is sometimes stretched across the flimsy covering, as a guard against the sun and rain. Within this vehicle are stowed all the emigrant's household goods, and still, it is not overloaded.

There is usually a large chest, containing the wardrobe of the family, with such small articles as are liable to loss, and the little store of money. This is always in silver, for the pioneer is no judge of gold, and, on the frontier, paper has but little exchangeable value. There are then two light bedsteads — one "a trundle-bed" — a few plain chairs, most of them tied on behind and at the sides; three or four stools, domestic manufacture; a set of tent-poles and a few pots and pans. On these are piled the "beds and bedding," tied in large bundles, and stowed in such manner as to make convenient room for the children who are too young to walk. In the front end of the wagon, sits the mother of the family : and, peering over her head and shoulders, leaning out at her side, or gazing under the edge of the cotton-covering, are numerous flaxen heads, which you find it difficult to count while you ride past.

There are altogether too many of them, you think, for a man no older than the one you met, a while ago; and you, perhaps, conjecture that the youthful-looking woman has adopted some of her dead sister's children, or, perchance, some of her brothers and sisters themselves. But you are mistaken, they are all her offspring, and the father of every one of them is the stoop-shouldered man you saw ahead. If you look closely, you will observe that the mother, who is driving, holds the reins with one hand, while, on the other arm, she supports an infant not *more* than six months old. It was for the advent of this little stranger, that they delayed their emigration: and they set out while it was very young, for fear of the approach of its successor. If they waited for their youngest child to attain a year of age, they would never "move," until they would be too old to make another "clearing."

You pass on — perhaps ejaculating thanks that your lot has been differently cast, and thinking you have seen the last of them. But a few hundred yards further, and you hear the tinkling of a bell; two or three lean cows — with calves about the age of the baby — come straggling by. You look for the driver, and see a tall girl with a very young face — the eldest of the family, though not exceeding twelve or thirteen years in age. You feel quite sure, that, besides her sun-bonnet and well-worn shoes, she wears but one article of apparel — and that a loose dress of linsey, rather narrow in the skirt, of a dirty brown color, with a tinge of red. It hangs straight down about her limbs, as if it were wet, and with every step — for she walks stoutly — it flaps and flies about her ankles, as if shotted in the lower hem. She presents, altogether, rather a slatternly figure, and her face is freckled and sunburnt.

But you must not judge her too rashly; for her eye is keen and expressive, and her mouth is quite pretty — especially when she smiles. A few years hence — if you have the *entrée* — you may meet her in the best and highest circles of the country. Perhaps, while you are dancing attendance upon some new administration, asking for a "place," and asking, probably, in vain, she may come to Washington, a beautiful and accomplished woman — the wife of some member of Congress, whose constituency is numbered by the hundred thousand!

You may pass on, now, and forget her; but, if you stop to talk five minutes, she will not forget *you* — at least, if you say anything striking or sensible. And when you meet her again, perhaps in a gilded saloon, among the brightest and highest in the land — if you seek an introduction, as you probably will — she will remind you of the meeting, and to your astonishment, will laughingly describe the scene, to some of her obsequious friends who stand around. And then she will perhaps introduce you, as an old friend, to one of those flax-haired boys, who peeped out of the wagon over his mother's shoulder, as you passed them in the wilderness: and you recognise one of the members from California, or from Oregon, whose influence in the house, though he is as yet a very young man, is already quite considerable. If you are successful in your application for a "place," it may be that the casual meeting in the forest or on the prairie was the seed which, germinating through long years of obscurity, finally sprung up *thus*, and bore a crop of high official honors!

The next time you meet a family of emigrants on the frontier, you will probably observe them a little more closely.

Not a few of those who bear a prominent part in the government of our country — more than one of the first men of the nation — men whose names are now heard in connection with the highest office of the people — twenty years ago, occupied a place as humble in the scale of influence, as that flaxen-haired son of the stoop-shouldered emigrant. Such are the elements of our civilization — such the spirit of our institutions!

We have hitherto been speaking only of the American pioneer, and we have devoted more space to him, than we shall give to his contemporaries, because he has exerted more influence, both in the settlement of the country, and in the formation of sectional character and social peculiarities, than all the rest combined.

The French emigrant was quite a different being. Even at this day, there are no two classes — not the eastern and western, or the northern and southern — between whom the distinction is more marked, than it has always been between the Saxon and the Frank. The advent of the latter was much earlier than that of the former; and to him, therefore, must be ascribed the credit of the first settlement of the country. But, for all purposes of lasting impression, he must yield to his successor. It was, in fact, the American who penetrated and cleared the forest — who subdued and drove out the Indian — who, in a word, reclaimed the country.

In nothing was the distinction between the two races broader, than in the feelings with which they approached the savage. We have seen that the hatred, borne by the American toward his red enemy, was to be traced to a

THE PIONEER.

long series of mutual hostilities and wrongs. But the Frenchman had no such injuries to avenge, no hereditary feud to prosecute. The first of his nation who had entered the country were non-combatants — they came to convert the savage, not to conquer him, or deprive him of his lands. Even as early as sixteen hundred and eight, the Jesuits had established friendly relations with the Indians of Canada — and before the stern crew of the May Flower had landed on Plymouth Rock, they had preached the gospel on the shores of Lake Huron. Their piety and wisdom had acquired an influence over the untutored Indian, long before the commencement of the hostilities, which afterward cost so much blood and suffering. They had, thus, smoothed the way for their countrymen, and opened a safe path through the wilderness, to the shore of the great western waters. And the people who followed and accompanied them, were peculiarly adapted to improve the advantages thus given them.

They were a gentle, peaceful, unambitious people. They came as the friend, not the hereditary enemy, of the savage. They tendered the calumet — a symbol well understood by every Indian — and were received as allies and brethren. They had no national prejudices to overcome: the copper color of the Indian was not an insuperable objection to intermarriage, and children of the mixed blood were not, for that reason, objects of scorn. An Indian maiden was as much a woman to a Frenchman, as if she had been a *blonde ;* and, if her form was graceful and her features comely, he would woo her with as much ardor as if she had been one of his own race.

Nor was this peculiarity attributable only to the native gallantry of the French character, as it has sometimes been asserted: the total want of prejudice, which grows up in contemplating an inferior race, held in limited subjection, and a certain easiness of temper and tone of thought, had far more influence.

The Frenchman has quite enough vanity, but very little pride. Whatever, therefore, is sanctioned by those who surrounded him, is, in his eyes, no degradation. He married the Indian woman — first, because there were but few females among the emigrants, and he could not live without "the sex;" and, second, because there was nothing in his prejudices, or in public sentiment, to deter him. The descendants of these marriages — except where, as in some cases, they are upheld by the possession of great wealth — have no consideration, and are seldom seen in the society of the whites. But this is only because French manners and feelings have long since faded out of our social organization. The Saxon, with his unconquerable prejudices of race, with his pride and jealousy, has taken possession of the country; and, as he rules its political destinies, in most places, likewise, gives tones to its manners. Had Frenchmen continued to possess the land — had French dominion not given place to English — mixture of blood would have had but little influence on one's position; and there would now have been, in St. Louis or Chicago, as many shades of color in a social assembly, as may be seen at a ball in Mexico.

The French are a more cheerful people, than the Americans. Social intercourse — the interchange of hospitalities — the enjoyment of amusements in crowds — are far more important to them than to any other race. Solitude and misery are — or ought to be — synonyms in French; and enjoyment is like glory — it must have witnesses, or it will lose its attraction. Accordingly, we find the French emigrant seeking companionship, even in the trials and enterprises of the wilderness. The American, after the manner of his race, sought places where he could possess, for himself, enough for his wants, and be "monarch of all he surveyed."

But the Frenchman had no such pride. He resorted to a town, where the amusements of dancing, *fêtes*, and social converse, were to be found — where the narrow streets were scarcely more than a division fence, "across which the women could carry on their voluble conversations, without leaving their homes."* This must have been a great advantage, and probably contributed, in no slight degree, to the singular peace of their villages — since the proximity afforded no temptation to going abroad, and the distance was yet too great to allow such whisperings and scandal, as usually break up the harmony of small circles. Whether the fact is to be attributed to this, or to some other cause, certain it is that these little communities were eminently peaceful. From the first settlement of Kaskaskia, for example, down to the transfer of the western country to the British — almost a century — I find no record, even in the voluminous epistolary chronicles, of any personal rencontre, or serious quarrel, among the inhabitants. The same praise can not be given to any American town ever yet built.

* Perkins's Western Annals.

A species of communism seems to be a portion of the French character; for we discover, that, even at that early day, *paysans*, or *habitans*, collected together in villages, had their *common fields*, where the separate portion of each family was still a part of the common stock — and their tract of pasture-land, where there was no division, or separate property. One enclosure covered all the fields of the community, and all submitted to regulations made by the free voice of the people.

If one was sick, or employed in the service of the colony, or absent on business of his own at planting or harvest time, his portion was not therefore neglected: his ground was planted, or his crop was gathered, by the associated labor of his neighbors, as thoroughly and carefully as if he had been at home. His family had nothing to fear; because in the social code of the simple villagers, each was as much bound to maintain the children of his friend as his own. This state of things might have its inconveniences and vices — of which, perhaps, the worst was its tendency to merge the family into the community, and thus — by obliterating the lines of individuality and personal independence — benumbing enterprise and checking improvements: but it was certainly productive of some good results, also. It tended to make people careful each of the other's rights, kind to the afflicted, and brotherly in their social intercourse. The attractive simplicity of manners observable, even at this day, in some of the old French villages, is traceable to this peculiar form of their early organization.

It would be well if that primitive simplicity of life and manners, could be combined with rapid, or even moderate improvement. But, in the present state of the world, this can scarcely be; and, accordingly, we find the Frenchman of the passing year, differing but little from his ancestor of sixteen hundred and fifty — still living in the old patriarchal style, still cultivating his share of the common field, and still using the antiquated processes of the seventeenth century.

But, though not so active as their neighbors, the Americans, they were ever much happier. They had no ambition beyond enough for the passing hour: with that they were perfectly contented. They were very patient of the deprivation, when they had it not; and seasons of scarcity saw no cessation of music and dancing, no abridgment of the jest and song. If the earth yielded enough in one year to sustain them till the next, the amount of labor expended for that object was never increased — superfluity they cared nothing for: and commerce, save such limited trade as was necessary to provide their few luxuries, was beyond both their capacity and desires. The prolific soil was suffered to retain its juices; it was reserved for another people to discover and improve its infinite productiveness.

They were indolent, careless, and improvident. Great enterprises were above or below them. Political interests, and the questions concerning national dominion, were too exciting to charm their gentle natures. Their intelligence was, of course, not of the highest order: but they had no use for learning — literature was out of place in the wilderness — the pursuit of letters could have found no sympathy, and for solitary enjoyment, the Frenchman cultivates nothing. Life was almost altogether sensuous: and, though their morals were in keeping with their simplicity, existence to them was chiefly a physical matter. The fertility of the soil, producing all the necessaries of life with a small amount of labor, and the amenity of the climate, rendering defences against winter but too easy, encouraged their indolence, and soothed their scanty energy.

"They made no attempt," said one* who knew them well, "to acquire land from the Indians, to organize a social system, to introduce municipal regulations, or to establish military defences; but cheerfully obeyed the priests and the king's officers, and enjoyed the present without troubling their heads about the future. They seem to have been even careless as to the acquisition of property, and its transmission to their heirs. Finding themselves in a fruitful country, abounding in game — where the necessaries of life could be procured with little labor — where no restraints were imposed by government, and neither tribute nor personal service was exacted, they were content to live in unambitious peace and comfortable poverty. They took possession of so much of the vacant land around them, as they were disposed to till, and no more. Their agriculture was rude: and even to this day, some of the implements of husbandry and modes of cultivation, brought from France a century ago, remain unchanged by the march of mind or the hand of innovation. Their houses were comfortable, and they reared fruits and flowers, evincing, in this respect, an attention to comfort and luxury, which has not

* "Sketches of the West," by Judge Hall, for many years a resident of Illinois.

been practised by the English and American first settlers. But in the accumulation of property, and in all the essentials of industry, they were indolent and improvident, rearing only the bare necessaries of life, and living from generation to generation without change or improvement."

"They reared fruits and flowers," he says; and this simple fact denotes a marked distinction between them and the Americans, not only in regard to the things themselves, as would seem to be the view of the author quoted, but in mental constitution, modes of thought, and motives to action. Their tastes were elegant, ornate, and refined. They found pleasure in pursuits which the American deems trivial, frivolous, and unworthy of exertion.

If any trees sheltered the house of the American, they were those planted by the winds; if there were any flowers at his door, they were only those with which prodigal nature has carpeted the prairies; and you may see now in the west, many a cabin which has stood for thirty years, with not a tree, of shade or fruit, within a mile of its door! Everything is as bare and as cheerless about the door-yard, as it was the first winter of its enclosure. But, stretching away from it, in every direction, sometimes for miles, you will see extensive and productive fields of grain, in the highest state of cultivation. It is not personal comfort, or an elegant residence, for which the American cares, but the enduring and solid results of unwearied labor.

A Frenchman's residence is surrounded by flower-beds and orchards; his windows are covered by creeping-vines and trellis-work; flower-pots and bird-cages occupy the sills and surround the corridors; everything presents the aspect of elegant taste, comfort, and indolence. The extent of his fields, the amount of his produce, the intelligence and industry of his cultivation, bear an immense disproportion to those of his less ornamental, though more energetic, neighbor.

The distinction between the two races is as clear in their personal appearance and bearing, as in the aspect of their plantations. The Frenchman is generally a spruce, dapper little gentleman, brisk, obsequious, and insinuating in manner, and usually betraying minute attention to externals. The American is always plain in dress — evincing no more taste in costume than in horticulture — steady, calm, and never lively in manner: blunt, straightforward, and independent in discourse. The one is amiable and submissive, the other choleric and rebellious. The Frenchman always recognises and bows before superior rank: the American acknowledges no superior, and bows to no man save in courtesy. The former is docile and easily governed: the latter is intractable, beyond control. The Frenchman accommodates himself to circumstances: the American forces circumstances to yield to him.

The consequence has been, that while the American has stamped his character upon the whole country, there are not ten places in the valley of the Mississippi, where you would infer, from anything you see, that a Frenchman had ever placed his foot upon the soil. The few localities in which the French character yet lingers, are fast losing the distinction; and a score or two of years will witness a total disappearance of the gentle people and their primitive abodes. Even now — excepting in a few parishes in Louisiana — the relics of the race bear a faded, antiquated look: as if they belonged to a past century, as, indeed, they do, and only lingered now, to witness, for a brief space, the glaring innovations of the nineteenth, and then, lamenting the follies of modern civilization, to take their departure for ever!

Let them depart in peace! For they were a

gentle and pacific race, and in their day did many kindly things!

"The goodness of the heart is shown in deeds
Of peacefulness and kindness."

Their best monument is an affectionate recollection of their simplicity: their highest wish

——"To sleep in humble life,
Beneath the storm ambition blows."

THE RANGER.

IV.

THE RANGER.

> "When purposed vengeance I forego,
> Term me a wretch, nor deem me foe;
> And when an insult I forgive,
> Then brand me as a slave, and live."
>
> SCOTT.

In elaborating the character of the pioneer, we have unavoidably anticipated, in some measure, that of the Ranger — for the latter was, in fact, only one of the capacities in which the former sometimes acted. But — since, in the preceding article, we have have endeavored to confine the inquiry, so as to use the term *Pioneer* as almost synonymous with *Immigrant* — we have, of course, ignored, to some extent, the subordinate characters, in which he frequently figured. We therefore propose, now, briefly to review one or two of them in their natural succession.

The progress of our country may be traced and measured, by the representative characters which marked each period. The missionary-priest came first, when the land was an unbroken wilderness. The military adventurer, seeking to establish new empires, and acquire great fortunes, entered by the path thus opened. Next came the hunter, roaming the woods in search of wild beasts upon which he preyed. Making himself familiar with the pathless forest and the rolling prairie, he qualified himself to guide, even while he fled from, the stream of immigration. At last came the pioneer, to drive away the savage, to clear out the forests, and reclaim the land.

At first, he was *only* a pioneer. He had few neighbors, he belonged to no community — his household was his country, his family were his only associates or companions. In the course of time others followed him — he could occasionally meet a white man on the prairies; if he wandered a few miles from home, he could see the smoke of another chimney in the distance. It he did not at once abandon his "clearing" and go further west, he became, in some sort, a member of society — was the fellow-citizen of his neighbors. The Indians became alarmed for their-hunting grounds, or the nations went to war and drew them into the contest: the frontier became unsafe: the presence of danger drew the pioneers together: they adopted a system of defence, and the ranger was the offspring and representative of a new order of things.

Rough and almost savage as he sometimes was, he was still the index to a great improvement. Rude as the system was, it gave shape and order to what had before been mere chaos.

The ranger marks a new era, then; his existence is another chapter in the history of the west. Previous to his time, each pioneer depended only on himself for defence — his sole protection, against the wild beast and the savage, was his rifle — self-dependence was his peculiar characteristic. The idea of a fighting establishment — the germ of standing armies — had never occurred to him: even the rudest form of civil government was strange to him — taxes, salaries, assessments, were all "unknown quantities."

But, gradually, all this changed; and with his circumstances, his character was also modified. He lost a little of his sturdy independence, his jealousy of neighborhood was softened — his solitary habits became more social — he acknowledged the necessity for concert of action — he merged a part of his individuality into the community, and — became a ranger.

In this capacity, his character was but little

different to what it had been before the change; and, though that change was a great improvement, considered with reference to society, it may safely be doubted whether it made the individual more respectable. He was a better *citizen*, because he now contributed to the common defence: but he was not a better *man*, because new associations brought novel temptations, and mingling with other men wore away the simplicity, which was the foundation of his manliness. Before assuming his new character, moreover, he never wielded a weapon except in his own defence — or, at most, in avenging his own wrongs. The idea of justice — claiming reparation for an injury, which he alone could estimate, because by him alone it was sustained — protected his moral sense. But, when he assumed the vindication of his neighbor's rights, and the reparation of his wrongs — however kind it may have been to do so — he was sustained only by the spirit of hatred to the savage, could feel no such justification as the consciousness of injury.

Here was the first introduction of the mercenary character, which actuates the hireling soldier; and, though civilization was not then far enough advanced, to make it very conspicuous, there were other elements mingled, which could not but depreciate the simple nobility of the pioneer's nature. Many of the qualities which, in him, had been merely passive, in the ranger became fierce and active. We have alluded, for example, to his hatred of the Indian; and this, habit soon strengthened and exaggerated. Nothing marks that change so plainly as his adoption of the barbarous practice of scalping enemies.

For this there might be some little palliation in the fact, that the savage never considered a warrior overcome, though he were killed, unless he lost his scalp; and so long as he could bring off the dead bodies of his comrades, not mutilated by the process, he was but partially intimidated. Defeat was, in that case, converted to a sort of triumph; and having gone within one step of victory — for so this half-success was estimated — was the strongest incentive to a renewal of the effort. It might be, therefore, that the ranger's adoption of the custom was a measure of self-defence. But it is to be feared that this consideration — weak as it is, when stated as an excuse for cruelty so barbarous — had but little influence in determining the ranger. Adopting the code of the savage, the practice soon became a part of his warfare; and the taking of the scalp was a ceremony necessary to the completion of his victory. It was a bloody and inhuman triumph — a custom which tended, more forcibly than any other, to degrade true courage to mere cruelty; and which, while it only mortified the savage, at the same time, by rendering his hatred of the white men more implacable, aggravated the horrors of Indian warfare. But the only measure of justice in those days, was the *lex talionis* — "An eye for an eye," a scalp for a scalp; and, even now, you may hear frontiermen justify, though they do not practise it, by quoting the venerable maxim, "Fight the devil with fire."

But, though the warfare of the ranger was sometimes distinguished by cruelty, it was also ennobled by features upon which it is far more pleasant to dwell.

No paladin, or knight, of the olden times, ever exhibited more wild, romantic daring, than that which formed a part of the ranger's daily action. Danger, in a thousand forms, beset him at every step — he defied mutilation, death by fire and lingering torture. The number of his enemies, he never counted, until after he had conquered them — the power of the tribe, or the prowess of the warrior, was no element in his calculations. Where he could strike first and most effectually, was his only inquiry. Securing an avenue for retreat was no part of his strategy — for he had never an intention or thought of returning, except as a victor. "Keeping open his communications," either with the rear or the flanks, had no place in his system; "combined movements" he seldom attempted, for he depended for victory, upon the force he chanced to have directly at hand. The distance from his "base of operations" be never measured; for he carried all his supplies about his person, and he never looked for reinforcements. Bridges and wagon-roads he did not require, for he could swim all the rivers, and he never lost his way in the forest. He carried his artillery upon his shoulder, his tactics were the maxims of Indian warfare, and his only drill was the "ball-practice" of the woods. He was his own commissary, for he carried his "rations" on his back, and replenished his havresack with his rifle. He needed no quartermaster; for he furnished his own "transportation," and selected his own encampment — his bed was the bosom of mother-earth, and his tent was the foliage of an oak or the canopy of heaven. In most cases — especially in battle — he was his own commander, too; for he was impatient of restraint, and in savage warfare knew his duty as well as any man could instruct him. Obedience was no part of his nature — subordination was irksome and oppressive. In a word, he was an excellent soldier, without drill, discipline or organization.

He was as active as he was brave — as untiring as he was fearless.

A corps of rangers moved so rapidly, as apparently to double its numbers — dispersing on the Illinois or Missouri, and reassembling on the Mississippi, on the following day — traversing the Okan timber to-day, and fording the Ohio to-morrow. One of them, noted among the Indians for desperate fighting, and personally known for many a bloody meeting, would appear so nearly simultaneously in different places, as to acquire the title of a " Great Medicine ;" and instances have been known, where as many as three distinct war-parties have told of obstinate encounters with the same men in one day! Their apparent ubiquity awed the Indians more than their prowess.

General Benjamin Howard, who, in eighteen hundred and thirteen resigned the office of governor of Missouri, and accepted the appointment of brigadier-general, in command of the militia and rangers of Missouri and Illinois, at no time, except for a few weeks in eighteen hundred and fourteen, had more than one thousand men under his orders: And yet, with this inconsiderable force, he protected a frontier extending from the waters of the Wabash, westward to the advanced settlements of Missouri — driving the savages northward beyond Peoria, and intimidating them by the promptitude and rapidity of his movements.

Our government contributed nothing to the defence of its frontiers, except an act of Congress, which authorized them to defend themselves! The Indians, amounting to at least twenty tribes, had been stirred up to hostility by the British, and, before the establishment of rangers, were murdering and plundering almost with impunity. But soon after the organization of these companies, the tide began to turn. The ranger was at least a match for the savage in his own mode of warfare; and he had, moreover, the advantages of civilized weapons, and a steadiness and constancy, unknown to the disorderly war-parties of the red men.

He was persevering beyond all example, and exhibited endurance which astonished even the stoical savage. Three or four hours' rest, after weeks of hardship and exposure, prepared him for another expedition. If the severity of his vengeance, or the success of a daring enterprise, intimidated the Indian for a time, and gave him a few days' leisure, he grew impatient of inactivity, and was straightway planning some new exploit. The moment one suggested itself, he set about accomplishing it — and its hardihood and peril caused no hesitation. He would march, on foot, hundreds of miles, through an unbroken wilderness, until he reached the point where the blow was to be struck; and then, awaiting the darkness, in the middle of the night, he would fall upon his unsuspecting enemies and carry all before him.

During the war of independence, the rangers had not yet assumed that name, nor were they as thoroughly organized, as they became in the subsequent contest of eighteen hundred and twelve. But the same material was there — the same elements of character, actuated by the same spirit. Let the following instance show what that spirit was.

In the year seventeen hundred and seventy-seven, there lived at Cahokia — on the east side of the Mississippi below Saint Louis — a Pennsylvanian by the name of Brady — a restless, daring man, just made for a leader of rangers. In an interval of inactivity, he conceived the idea of capturing one of the British posts in Michigan, the nearest point of which was at least three hundred miles distant! He forthwith set about raising a company — and, at the end of three days, found himself invested with the command of *sixteen men!* With these, on the first of October, he started on a journey of more than one hundred leagues, through the vast solitudes of the prairies and the thousand perils of the forest, to take a military station, occupied by a detachment of British soldiers! After a long and toilsome march, they reached the banks of the St. Joseph's river, on which the object of their expedition stood. Awaiting the security of midnight, they suddenly broke from their cover in the neighborhood, and by a *coup de main*, captured the fort without the loss of a man! Thus far all went well — for besides the success and safety of the party, they found a large amount of stores, belonging to traders, in the station, and were richly paid for their enterprise — but having been detained by the footsore, on their homeward march, and probably delayed by their plunder, they had only reached the Calumet, on the borders of Indiana, when they were overtaken by three hundred British and Indians! They were forced to surrender, though not without a fight, for men of that stamp were not to be intimidated by numbers. They lost in the skirmish one fourth of their number: the survivors were carried away to Canada, whence Brady, the leader, escaped, and returned to Cahokia the same winter. The twelve remained prisoners until seventeen hundred and seventy-nine.

Against most men this reverse would have given the little fort security — at least, until the memory of the disaster had been obscured by time. But the pioneers of that period were not to be judged by ordinary rules. The very next spring (1778), another company was raised for the same object, and to wipe out what they considered the stain of a failure. It was led by a man named Maize, over the same ground, to the same place, and was completely successful. The fort was retaken, the trading-station plundered, the wounded men of Brady's party released, and, loaded with spoil, the little party marched back in triumph!

There is an episode in the history of their homeward march, which illustrates another characteristic of the ranger — his ruthlessness.

The same spirit which led him to disregard physical obstacles, prevented his shrinking from even direful necessities. One of the prisoners whom they had liberated, became exhausted and unable to proceed. They could not carry him, and would not have him to die of starvation in the wilderness. They could not halt with him, lest the same fate should overtake them, which had defeated the enterprise of Brady. But one alternative remained, and though, to us, it appears cruel and inhuman, it was self-preservation to them, and mercy, in a strange guise, to the unhappy victim — *he was despatched by the hand of the leader*, and buried upon the prairie! His grave is somewhere near the head-waters of the Wabash, and has probably been visited by no man from that day to this!

Mournful reflections cluster round such a narrative as this, and we are impelled to use the word "atrocious" when we speak of it. It was certainly a bloody deed, but the men of those days were not nurtured in drawing-rooms, and never slept upon down-beds. A state of war, moreover, begets many evils, and none of them are more to be deplored than the occasional occurrence of such terrible necessities.

The ranger-character, like the pioneer-nature of which it was a phase, was compounded of various and widely-differing elements. No one of his evil qualities was more prominent than several of the good; and, I am sorry to say, none of the good was more prominent than several of the bad. No class of men did more efficient service in defending the western settlements from the inroads of the Indians; and though it seems hard that the war should sometimes have been carried into the country of the untutored savage by civilized men, with a severity exceeding his own, we should remember that we can not justly estimate the motives and feelings of the ranger, without first having been exasperated by his sufferings and tried by his temptations.

V.

THE REGULATOR.

"Thieves for their robbery have authority,
When judges steal themselves."—
MEASURE FOR MEASURE.

AT the conclusion of peace between England and America, in eighteen hundred and fifteen, the Indians, who had been instigated and supported in their hostility by the British, suddenly found themselves deprived of their allies. If they now made war upon the Americans, they must do so upon their own responsibility, and, excepting the encouragement of a few traders and commanders of outposts, whose enmity survived the general pacification, without assistance from abroad. They, however, refused to lay down their arms, and hostilities were continued, though languidly, for some years longer. But the rangers, now disciplined by the experience of protracted warfare, and vastly increased in numbers, had grown to be more than a match for them, so that not many years elapsed before the conclusion of a peace, which has lasted, with but occasional interruptions, to the present day.

When danger no longer threatened the settlements, there was no further call for these irregular troops. The companies were disbanded, and those who had families, as a large proportion of them had, returned to their plantations, and resumed the pursuits of industry and peace. Those who had neither farms nor families, and were unfitted by their stirring life for regular effort, emigrated further west. Peace settled upon our borders, never, we hope, to be seriously broken.

But as soon as the pressure of outward danger was withdrawn, and our communities began to expand, the seeds of new evils were developed — seeds which had germinated unobserved, while all eyes were averted, and which now began to shoot up into a stately growth of vices and crimes. The pioneers soon learned that there was among them a class of unprincipled and abandoned men, whose only motive in emigrating was to avoid the restraints, or escape the penalties, of law, and to whom the freedom of the wilderness was a license to commit every sort of depredation. The arm of the law was not yet strong enough to punish them.

The territorial governments were too busy in completing their own organization, to give much attention to details: where states had been formed, the statute-book was yet a blank: few officers had been appointed, and even these were strangers to their duties and charge of responsibility. Between the military rule of the rangers—for they were for internal police as well as external defence—and the establishment of regular civil government, there was a sort of interregnum, during which there was neither law nor power to enforce it. The bands of villains who infested the country were the only organizations known; and, in not a few instances, these bands included the very magistrates whose duty it was to see that the laws were faithfully executed. Even when this was not the case, it was a fruitless effort to arrest a malefactor; indeed, it was very often worse than fruitless, for his confederates were always ready to testify in his favor: and the usual consequence of an attempt to punish, was the drawing down upon the head of the complainant or prosecutor, the enmity of a whole confederacy. Legal proceedings, had provision been made for such, were worse than useless, for conviction was impossible : and the effort exasperated, while the failure encouraged, the outlaw spirit.

An *alibi* was the usual defence, and to those times may be referred the general prejudice entertained among our people, even at the present day, against that species of testimony. A jury of western men will hardly credit an *alibi*, though established by unexceptionable witnesses; and the announcement that the accused depends upon that for his defence, will create a strong prejudice against him in advance. Injustice may sometimes be done in this way, but it is a feeling of which our people came honestly in possession. They established a habit, in early days, of never believing an *alibi*, because, at that time, nine *alibis* in ten were false, and habits of thought, like legal customs, cling to men long after their reason has ceased. It is right, too, that it should be so, on the principle that we should not suspend the use of the remedy until the disease be thoroughly conquered.

In a state of things, such as we have described, but one of two things could be done: the citizens must either abandon all effort to assert the supremacy of order, and give the country over to thieves and robbers, or they must invent some new and irregular way of forcing men to live honestly. They wisely chose the latter alternative. They consulted together, and the institution of *Regulators* was the result of their deliberations.

These were small bodies of men, chosen by the people, or voluntarily assuming the duty — men upon whom the citizens could depend for both discretion and resolution. Their duties may be explained in a few words: to ferret out and punish criminals, to drive out "suspicious characters," and exercise a general supervision over the interests and police of the settlements, from which they were chosen. Their statute-book was the "code of Judge Lynch"—their order of trial was similar to that of a "drum-head court-martial"—the principles of their punishment was certainty, rapidity, and severity. They were judges, juries, witnesses, and executioners.

They bound themselves by a regular compact (usually verbal, but sometimes in writing*), to the people and to each other, to rid the community of all thieves, robbers, plunderers, and villains of every description. They scoured the

* See note at the close of this article.

country in all directions and in all seasons, and by the swiftness of their movements, and the certainty of their vengeance, rivalled their predecessors, the rangers. When a depredation had been committed, it was marvellous with what rapidity every regulator knew it; even the telegraph of modern days performs no greater wonders: and it frequently happened, that the first the quiet citizens heard of a theft, or a robbery, was the news of its punishment! Their acts may sometimes have been highhanded and unjustifiable, but on the whole — and it is only in such a view that social institutions are to be estimated — they were the preservers of the communities for whom they acted. In time, it is true, they degenerated, and sometimes the corps fell into the hands of the very men they were organized to punish.

Every social organization is liable to misdirection, and this, among others, has been perverted to the furtherance of selfish and unprincipled purposes; for, like prejudices and habits of thought, organized institutions frequently survive the necessities which call them into existence. Abuses grow up under all systems; and, perhaps, the worst abuse of all, is a measure or expedient, good though temporary, retained after the passing away of the time for which it was adopted.

But having, in the article "Pioneer," sufficiently elaborated the *character* — for the regulator was of course a pioneer also — we can best illustrate the mode of his action by a narrative of facts. From the hundreds of well-authenticated stories which might be collected, I have chosen the two following, because they distinguish the successive stages or periods of the system. The first relates to the time when a band of regulators was the only reliable legal power, and when, consequently, the vigilance of the citizens kept it comparatively pure. The second indicates a later period, when the people no longer felt insecure, and there was in fact no necessity for the system; and when, not having been disused, it could not but be abused. We derive both from an old citizen of the country, who was an actor in each. One of them, the first, has already been in print, but owing to circumstances to which it is needless to advert, it was thought better to confine the narrative to facts already generally known. These circumstances are no longer operative, and I am now at liberty to publish entire the story of "The First Grave."

THE FIRST GRAVE.

At the commencement of the war of eighteen hundred and twelve, between Great Britain and the United States, there lived, in the western part of Virginia, three families, named, respectively, Stone, Cutler, and Roberts. They were all respectable people, of more than ordinary wealth; having succeeded, by an early emigration and judicious selection of lands, in rebuilding fortunes which had been somewhat impaired east of the Blue Ridge. Between the first and second there was a relationship, cemented by several matrimonial alliances, and the standing of both had been elevated by this union of fortunes. In each of these two, there were six or seven children — the most of them boys — but Captain Roberts, the head of the third, had but one child, a daughter, who, in the year named, was approaching womanhood.

She is said to have been beautiful: and, from the extravagant admiration of those who saw her only when time and suffering must have obscured her attractions, there can be little doubt that she was so. What her character was, we can only conjecture from the tenor of our story: though we have reason to suspect that she was passionate, impulsive, and somewhat vain of her personal appearance.

At the opening of hostilities between the two countries, she was wooed by two suitors, young Stone, the eldest of the sons of that family, and Abram Cutler, who was two or three years his senior. Both had recently returned home, after a protracted absence of several years, beyond the mountains, whither they had been sent by their ambitious parents, " to attend college and see the world." Stone was a quiet, modest, unassuming young man, rather handsome, but too pale and thin to be decidedly so. Having made the most of his opportunities at " William and Mary," he had come home well-educated (for that day and country) and polished by intercourse with good society.

His cousin, Abram Cutler, was his opposite in almost everything. He had been wild, reckless, and violent, at college, almost entirely giving up his studies, after the first term, and always found in evil company. His manners were as much vitiated as his morals, for he was exceedingly rough, boisterous, and unpolished: so much so, indeed, as to approach that limit beyond which wealth will not make society tolerant. But his freedom of manner bore, to most observers, the appearance of generous heartiness, and he soon gained the good will of the neighborhood by the careless prodigality of his life. He was tall, elegantly formed, and quite well-looking; and though he is said to have borne, a few years later, a sinister and dishonest look, it is probable that most of this was attributable to the preconceived notions of those who thus judged him.

Both these young men were, as we have said, suitors for the hand of Margaret Roberts, and it is possible that the vain satisfaction of having at her feet the two most attractive young men in the country, led her to coquet with them both, but decidedly to prefer neither. It is almost certain, that at the period indicated, she was sufficiently well-pleased with either to have become his wife, had the other been away. If she *loved* either, however, it was Stone, for she was a little timid, and Cutler sometimes frightened her with his violence : but the preference, if it existed at all, was not sufficiently strong to induce a choice.

About this time, the elder Cutler died, and it became necessary for Abram, as executor of a large estate, to cross the mountains into the Old Dominion, and arrange its complicated affairs. It was not without misgiving that he went away, but his duties were imperative, and his necessities, produced by his spendthrift habits, were pressing. He trusted to a more than usually favorable interview with Margaret, and full of sanguine hopes, departed on his journey.

Whether Stone entertained the idea of taking an unfair advantage of his rival's absence, we can not say, but he straightway became more assiduous in his attentions to Margaret. He was also decidedly favored by Captain Roberts and his wife, both of whom had been alarmed by the violent character of Cutler. Time soon began to obscure the recollection of the absent suitor, and Stone's delicate and considerate gallantry rapidly gained ground in Margaret's affections. It was just one month after Cutler's departure that his triumph was complete; she consented to be his wife so soon as the minister who travelled on that circuit should enter the neighborhood. But the good man had set out on his circuit only the day before the consent was given, and it would probably be at least a month before his return. In the meantime, Cutler might recross the mountains, and Stone had seen quite enough of Margaret's capriciousness to tremble for the safety of his conquest, should that event occur before it was thoroughly secured.

This was embarrassing: but when a man is in earnest, expedients are never wanting.

There was an old gentleman living a few miles from the valley, who had once held the commission of a justice of the peace, and though he had not exercised his functions, or even claimed his dignity, for several years, Stone was advised that he retained his official power "until his successor was appointed and qualified," and that, consequently, any official act of his would be legal and valid. He was advised, moreover, and truly, that even if the person performing the ceremony were not a magistrate, a marriage would be lawful and binding upon the simple "consent" of the parties, properly published and declared.

Full-freighted with the happy news, he posted away to Captain Roberts, and without difficulty obtained his sanction. He then went to Margaret, and, with the assistance of her mother, who stood in much dread of Cutler's violence, succeeded in persuading her to consent. Without delay, the *cidevant* magistrate was called in, the ceremony was performed, and Margaret was Stone's wife!

The very day after this event, Cutler returned! What were his thoughts no one knew, for he spoke to none upon the subject. He went, however, to see "the bride," and, in the presence of others, bantered her pleasantly upon her new estate, upon his own pretensions, and upon the haste with which the ceremony had been performed. He started away with the rest of the company present; but, on reaching the door—it was afterward remembered—pretended to have forgotten something, and ran back into the room where they had left Margaret alone. Here he remained full ten minutes, and when he came out walked thoughtfully apart and disappeared. What he said to Margaret no one knew; but, that evening, when they were alone, she asked anxiously of her husband, "whether he was quite sure that their marriage had been legal?" Stone reassured her, and nothing more was said upon the subject.

Cutler had brought with him, over the mountains, the proclamation of the governor of Virginia, announcing the declaration of war, and calling upon the state for its quota of troops to repel invasion. He manifested a warm interest in the enrolling and equipment of vo'unteers, and, in order to attest his sincerity, placed his own name first upon the roll. A day or two afterward, on meeting Stone, in the presence of several others who had enrolled themselves, he laughingly observed, that the new bridegroom " was probably too comfortable at home, to desire any experience in campaigning:" and, turning away, he left the company laughing at Stone's expense.

This touched the young man's pride — probably the more closely, because he was conscious that the insinuation was not wholly void of truth — and, without a moment's hesitation, he called Cutler back, took the paper, and enrolled his name. Cutler laughed again, said *he* would not have done so, had he been in Stone's circumstances, and, after some further conversation, walked away in the direction of Stone's residence. Whether he actually entered the house is not known; but when the young husband returned home, a few hours afterward, his wife's first words indicated that she knew of his enrolment.

"Is it possible," said she, with some asperity, "that you already care so little for me as to enrol yourself for an absence of six months?"

Stone would much have preferred to break the news to her himself, for he had some foreboding as to the view she might take of his conduct. He had scarcely been married a week, and he was conscious that a severe construction of the act of enrolment, when there was notoriously not the least necessity for it, might lead to inferences, than which, nothing could be more false. If he had said, at once, that he had been taunted by his old rival, and written his name under the influence of pride, all would have been well, for his wife would then have understood, though she might not have approved his action. But this confession he was ashamed to make, and, by withholding it, laid the foundation for his own and his wife's destruction. He at once acknowledged the fact, disclaiming, however, the indifference to her, which she inferred, and placing the act upon higher ground : —

"The danger of the country," he said, " was very imminent, and it became every good citizen to do all he could for its defence. He had no idea that the militia would be called far from home, or detained for a very long time ; but, in any event, he felt that men were bound, in such circumstances, to cast aside personal considerations, and contribute, each his share, to the common defence."

His wife gazed incredulously at him while he talked this high patriotism : and well she might, for he did not speak as one moved by such feelings. The consciousness of deceit, of concealment, and of childish rashness, rendered his manner hesitating and embarrassed. Margaret observed all this, for her jealousy was aroused and her suspicions sharpened; she made no reply, however, but turned away, with a toss of the head, and busied herself, quite fiercely, with her household cares. From that moment, until the day of his departure, she stubbornly avoided the subject, listening, but refusing to reply, when her husband attempted to introduce it. When Cutler came — rather unnecessarily, as Stone thought — to consult him about the organization of a spy-company, to which both were attached, she paid no attention to their conversation, but walked away down a road over which she knew Cutler must pass on his return homeward. Whether this was by appointment with him is not known: probably, however, it was her own motion.

We need not stay to detail all that took place between her and her former suitor, when, as she had expected, they met in a wood some hundreds of yards from her home; its result will sufficiently appear in the sequel. One circumstance, however, we must not omit. She recurred to a conversation which had passed sometime before, in relation to the legality of her marriage; and though Cutler gave no positive opinion, his parting advice was nearly in the following words: —

"If you think, from your three weeks' experience, that Stone cares enough for you to make it prudent, I would advise you to have the marriage ceremony performed by Parson Bowen, immediately upon his return; and if you care enough for him to wish to retain him, you had better have it performed *before he goes away*."

With these words, and without awaiting an answer, he passed on, leaving her alone in the road. When she returned home, she did not mention the subject; and though Parson Bowen returned to the neighborhood quite a week before Stone went away, she never suggested a repetition of the ceremony. When Stone manifested some anxiety on the subject, she turned suddenly upon him and demanded —

"You do not think our marriage legal, then?"

He assured her that he only made the suggestion for her satisfaction, entertaining no doubt, himself, that they were regularly and lawfully married.

"I am content to remain as I am," she said, curtly, and the parson was not summoned.

Five days afterward the troops took up the line of march for the frontier. Hull had not yet surrendered Michigan; but Proctor had so stirred up the Indians (who, until then, had been quiet since the battle of Tippecanoe), as to cut off all communication with the advanced settlements, and even to threaten the latter with fire and slaughter. Ohio, Indiana, and Illinois, were then overrun by British and Indians; for Hopkins had not yet commenced his march from Kentucky, and Congress was still debating measures for protection. Hull's surrender took place on the sixteenth of August, eighteen hundred and twelve, and in the following month, General Harrison, having been appointed to the chief command in the northwest, proceeded to adopt vigorous measures for the defence of the country. It was to one of the regiments organized by him, that our friends from Virginia found themselves attached. They had raised a company of spies, and in this both Stone and Cutler held commissions.

They marched with the regiment, or rather in advance of it, for several weeks. By that time, they had penetrated many miles beyond the settlements, and Harrison began to feel anxious to ascertain the position of General Hopkins, and open communications with him. For this service Cutler volunteered, and was immediately selected by the general. On the following morning, he set out with five men to seek the Kentuckians. He found them without difficulty and delivered his despatches; but from that day he was not seen, either in the camp of Hopkins or in that of Harrison! It was supposed that he had started on his return, and been taken or killed by the Indians, parties of whom were prowling about between the lines of the two columns.

Stone remained with his company two or three months longer, when, the enterprise of Hopkins having failed, and operations being suspended for the time, it was thought inexpedient to retain them for the brief period which remained of their term of enlistment, and they were discharged. Stone returned home, and, full of anticipations, the growth of a long absence, hastened at once to his own house. The door was closed, no smoke issued from the chimney, there was no one there! After calling in vain for a long time, he ran away to her father's, endeavoring to feel certain that he would find her there. But the old man received him with a mournful shake of the head. Margaret had been gone more than a month, no one knew whither or with whom!

A report had been in circulation that Cutler was seen in the neighborhood, a few days before her disappearance; but no news having been received of his absence from the army, it had not been generally credited. But now, it was quite clear!

The old man invited Stone to enter, but he declined. Sitting down on a log, he covered his face with his hands, for a few moments, and seemed buried in grief. It did not last long, however: he rose almost immediately, and going a little aside, calmly loaded his rifle. Without noticing the old man, who stood gazing at him in wonder, he turned away, and, with his eyes fixed upon the ground, took the path toward his own house. He was seen to break the door and enter, but he remained within only a few minutes. On coming out, he threw his rifle over his shoulder, and walked away through the forest. Half an hour afterward, smoke was seen issuing from the roof of the house in several places, and on repairing thither, the neighbors found the whole place in a bright flame! It was of no use to attempt to save it or any of its contents. An hour afterward, it was a heap of smouldering ruins, and its owner had disappeared from the country!

* * * * *

Seven years passed away.

The war was over: the Indians had been driven to the north and west, and the tide of emigration had again set toward the Mississippi. The northwestern territory — especially that part of it which is now included within the limits of Illinois and Indiana — was rapidly filling up with people from the south and east. The advanced settlements had reached the site of Springfield, in the "Sangamon country,"* now the capital of Illinois, and a few farms were opened in the north of Madison county — now Morgan and Scott. The beautiful valley, most inaptly called, of the *Mauvaisterre*, was then an unbroken wilderness.

The grass was growing as high as the head of a tall man, where now well-built streets and public squares are traversed by hurrying crowds. Groves which have since become classic were then impenetrable thickets; and the only guides the emigrant found, through forest and prairie, were the points of the compass, and the courses

---

* The "Sangamon country," as the phrase was then used, included all the region watered by the river of that name, together with the counties of Cass, Morgan, and Scott, as far south as Apple creek.

of streams. But in the years eighteen hundred and seventeen, eighteen, and nineteen, the western slope of the Sangamon country began rapidly to improve. Reports had gone abroad of "the fertility of its soil, the beauty of its surface, its genial climate, and its many advantages of position"—and there is certainly no country which more richly deserves these praises.

But the first emigrant who made his appearance here, in the autumn of eighteen hundred and nineteen, was probably moved by other considerations. It was none other than Abram Cutler! And his family consisted of a wife and three young children! That wife was Margaret Roberts — or rather Margaret Stone; for, notwithstanding the representations of Cutler, her union with Stone had been perfectly legal. By what arts he had succeeded in inducing her to elope with him, we can only judge from his previous proceedings; but this is certain, that resentment toward Stone, who, she probably believed, had unfairly trapped her, was as likely to move her impulsive and unstable spirit, as any other motive. Add to this, the wound given to her vanity by the sudden departure of her young husband upon a long campaign, with the acuteness given to this feeling by the arts of Cutler, and we shall not be at a loss to explain her action.

Whether she had not bitterly repented her criminal haste, we know not; but that hardship and suffering of some sort had preyed upon her spirit, was evident in her appearance. Her beauty was much faded; she had grown pale and thin; and though she was scarcely yet in the prime of womanhood, her step was heavy and spiritless. She was not happy, of course, but her misery was not only negative: the gnawings of remorse were but too positive and real!

Cutler was changed almost as much as his victim. The lapse of seven years had added a score to his apparent age; and, if we are to credit the representations of persons who were probably looking for signs of vice, the advance of time had brought out, in well-marked lineaments, upon his countenance, the evil traits of his character. His cheeks were sunken, his features attenuated, and his figure exceedingly spare, but he still exhibited marks of great personal strength and activity. His glance, always of doubtful meaning, was now unsettled and furtive; and I have heard one of the actors in this history assert, that it had a scared, apprehensive expression, as if he were in constant expectation of meeting a dangerous enemy.

Nor is this at all improbable, for during the seven years which had elapsed since the consummation of his design upon Margaret, he had emigrated no less than three times — frightened away, at each removal, by some intimation, or suspicion, that the avenger was on his track! No wonder that his look was wary, and his face pale and haggard!

On this, his fourth migration, he had crossed the prairies from the waters of the Wabash; and having placed the wide expanse of waving plain between him and the settlements, he at length considered himself safe from pursuit. Passing by the little trading-station, where Springfield now stands, he traversed the beautiful country lying between that and the Mauvaisterre. But the alternation of stately timber and lovely prairie had no charms for him: he sought not beauty or fertility, but seclusion; for his pilgrimage had become wearisome, and his step was growing heavy. Remorse was at his heart, and fear — the appealing face of his patient victim kept his crime in continual remembrance — and he knew, that like a bloodhound, his enemy was following behind. It was a weary load! No wonder that his cheeks were thin or his eyes wild!

He passed on till he came to a quiet, secluded spot, where he thought himself not likely soon to be disturbed by emigration. It was sixteen miles west of the place where Jacksonville has since been built, upon the banks of the lower Mauvaisterre, seven miles from the Illinois river. The place was long known as Cutler's grove, but a town grew up around it, and has been christened by the sounding name of Exeter. Those who visit it now, and have heard the story of Cutler, will commend his judgment in selecting it for retirement; for, town as it is, a more secluded, dreamy little place is nowhere to be found. It would seem that the passage of a carriage through its *street*—for it has but one—would be an event in its history; and the only things which redeem it, in the fancy, from the category of visionary existences, are a blacksmith's shop and a mill!

But Cutler's trail was seen upon the prairies, and the course of many an emigrant was determined by the direction taken by his predecessor. It was not long before others came to "settle" in the neighborhood. Emigration was gradually encroaching, also, from the south; families began to take possession of the river "bottoms;" the smoke from frontier cabins ascended in almost every point of timber; and by the summer of eighteen hundred and twenty, Cutler found himself as far from the frontier as ever! But he was resolved not to move again: a dogged spirit—half weariness, half despair —had taken possession of him. "I have moved often enough," he said to Margaret, "and here I am determined to remain, come what may!"

Actuated by such feelings—goaded by a fear which he could not conquer, and yet was resolute not to indulge—the lurking devil in his nature could not long remain dormant. Nothing develops evil tendencies so rapidly as the consciousness of wrong and the fear of punishment. His life soon became reckless and abandoned, and the first sign of his degradation was his neglect of his household. For days together Margaret saw nothing of him; his only companions were the worthless and outlawed; and, when intoxicating liquors could be procured, which was, fortunately, not often, he indulged in fearful excesses.

Of evil company, there was, unhappily, but too much; for the settlement was cursed with a band of desperadoes, exiles from organized society, who had sought the frontier to obtain impunity for their misdeeds. The leaders of this band were three brothers, whom no law could control, no obligation restrain; and with these men Cutler soon formed a close and suspicious intimacy. The eyes of the citizens had been for some time directed toward the companions, by circumstances attending various depredations; and, though unknown to themselves, they were constantly watched by many of their neighbors. It is uncertain whether Cutler was acquainted with the character of the men when his association with them first commenced, for in none of the places where he had lived, had he hitherto been suspected of crime. It is most probable that he sought their company because they were "dissipated" like himself: and that, in the inception of their acquaintance, there was no other bond between them than the habit of intoxication.

Had we time and space, we would fain pause here to reflect upon the position and feelings of the false wife — deserted, in her turn, by him for whom she had given up truth and honor — alone in the wilderness with her children, whose birth she could not but regret, and harassed by thoughts which could not but be painfully self-condemning. But we must hasten on.

In the autumn of eighteen hundred and twenty, information was brought to the settlement, that a store at Springfield (as it is now called), had been entered and robbed — that the leaders of the desperadoes above alluded to, were suspected — and that the goods stolen were believed to be concealed in Cutler's grove, where they lived. Warrants were issued, and the three were arrested; but the magistrate before whom they were taken for examination, was a timid and ignorant man; and by the interference of Cutler, who assumed to be a lawyer, they were examined separately, and allowed to testify, each for the other! An officer who knew no more than to permit this, of course could do no less than discharge them. The arrest and examination, however, crude and informal as they were, confirmed the suspicions of the citizens, and directed them, more vehemently than ever, against Cutler, as well as his friends. It satisfied them, moreover, that they would never be able to reach these men through the ordinary forms of law, and strengthened the counsels of those who had already suggested the organization of a company of regulators.

While these things were fermenting in the minds of the people, the desperadoes, encouraged by their success, and rendered bold by impunity, committed their depredations more frequently and openly than ever. It was remarked, too, that Cutler, having committed himself at the examination of friends, was now more constantly and avowedly their associate; and, since he was not a man to play a second part, that they deferred to him on all occasions, never moving without him, and treating him at all times as an acknowledged leader. The people observed, moreover, that from being, like his neighbors, a small farmer of limited possessions, he rose rapidly to what, on the frontier, was considered affluence. He soon ceased to labor on his lands, and set up a very considerable "store," importing his goods from Saint Louis, and, by means of the whiskey he sold, collecting all the idle and vicious of the settlement constantly about him. His "store" was in exceedingly bad repute, and the scanty reputation which he had retained after the public part he had taken before the magistrate, was speedily lost.

Things were in this state in the spring of eighteen hundred and twenty-one, when an old gentleman of respectable appearance, who had emigrated to this country by water, having been pleased with the land in the neighborhood of the place where the town of Naples now stands, landed his family and effects, and settled upon the "bottom." It was soon rumored in the settlement, that he had brought with him a large amount of money; and it was also remarked that Cutler and his three companions were constantly with him, either at the "Grove" or on the "bottom." Whether the rumor was the cause of their attention, or their assiduity the foundation of the report, the reader must determine for himself.

One evening in May, after a visit to this man, where Cutler had been alone, he came home in great haste, and suddenly announced to Margaret his intention to "sell out," and move further westward! His unhappy victim supposed she knew but too well the meaning of this new movement: she asked no questions, but, with a sigh of weariness, assented. On the following day, he commenced hastily disposing of his "store," his stock, his cabin—everything, in fact, save a few farming utensils, his furniture, and a pair of horses. It was observed—for there were many eyes upon him—that he never ventured out after twilight, and, even in the broad sunshine, would not travel far, alone or unarmed. In such haste did he seem, that he sold many of his goods at, what his friends considered, a ruinous sacrifice. The fame of great bargains brought many people to his counter, so that, within ten days, his arrangements were complete; and, much to the satisfaction of his neighbors, he set out toward the river.

Two of his associates accompanied him on his journey — a precaution for which he would give no reason, except that he wished to converse with them on the way. He crossed the Illinois near the mouth of the Mauvaisterre, and, turning northward, in the evening reached a cabin on the banks of M'Kee's creek, not more than ten miles from his late residence. This house had been abandoned by its former occupant, on account of the forays of the Indians; but was now partially refitted, as for a temporary abode. Here, the people about "the grove" were surprised to learn, a few days after Cutler's departure, that he had halted with the apparent intention to remain, at least for some time.

Their surprise was dissipated, however, within a very few weeks. The old gentleman, spoken of above, had left home upon a visit to Saint Louis; and during his absence, his house had been entered, and robbed of a chest containing a large amount of money — while the family were intimidated by the threats of men disguised as savages.

This was the culmination of villany. The settlement was now thoroughly aroused; and, when one of these little communities was once in earnest, it might safely be predicted that *something* would be *done!*

The first step was to call "a meeting of the friends of law and order;" but no proclamation was issued, no handbills were circulated, no notices posted: not the least noise was made about the matter, lest those against whom it was to act, might hear of and prepare for it. They came together quietly but speedily — each man, as he heard of the appointment, going forthwith to his neighbor with the news. They assembled at a central point, where none need be late in coming, and immediately proceeded to business. The meeting was not altogether a formal one — for purposes prescribed by law — but it was a characteristic of those men, to do everything "decently and in order" — to give all their proceedings the sanction and solemnity of mature deliberation. They organized the assemblage regularly — calling one of the oldest and most respectable of their number " to the chair" (which, on this occasion, happened to be the root of a large oak), and appointing a younger man secretary (though they gave him no desk on which to write). There was no man there who did not fully understand what had brought them together; but one who lived in the " bottom," and had been the mover of the organization, was still called upon to " explain the object of the meeting." This he did in a few pointed sentences, concluding with these significant words: " My friends, it is time that these rascals were punished, and it is our duty to punish them."

He sat down, and a silence of some moments ensued, when another arose, and, without any preliminary remarks, moved that " a company of regulators be now organized, and that they be charged with the duty of *seeing the law administered.*" The motion was seconded by half a dozen voices — the question was put in due form by the chairman, and decided unanimously in the affirmative.

A piece of paper was produced, and the presiding officer called on the meeting for volunteers. Ten young men stepped forward, and gave their names as rapidly as the secretary could enrol them. In less than five minutes, the company was complete — the chairman and four of the meeting, as a committee, were directed to retire with the volunteers, and see that they were fully organized — and the meeting adjourned. All, except the volunteers and the committee, went directly home — satisfied that the matter needed no further attention. Those who remained entered the house and proceeded to organize in the usual manner.

A "compact" was drawn up, by the terms of which the regulators bound themselves to each other, and to their neighbors, to ferret out and punish the perpetrators of the offences, which had recently disturbed the peace of the settlement, and to rid the country of such villains as were obnoxious to the friends of law and order. This was then signed by the volunteers as principals, and by the committee, as witnesses; and was placed in the hands of the chairman of the meeting for safekeeping. It is said to be still in existence, though I have never seen it, and do not know where it is to be found.

When this arrangement was completed, the committee retired, and the company repaired to the woods, to choose a leader. They were not long in selecting a certain Major B——, who had, for some weeks, made himself conspicuous, by his loud denunciations of Cutler and his associates, and his zealous advocacy of "strong measures." They had — one or two of them, at least — some misgivings about this appointment; for the major was inclined to be a blusterer, and the courage of these men was eminently silent. But after a few minutes' discussion, the matter was decided, and the leader was chosen without opposition. They at once dispersed, to make arrangements for the performance of their duties — having first appointed an hour and a place of meeting. They were to assemble at sunset on the same day, at the point where the state road now crosses the "bluff;" and were to proceed thence, without delay, to Cutler's house on M'Kee's creek, a distance of little more than eight miles. There they were to search for the stolen property, and whether they found it or not, were resolved to notify Cutler to leave the country. But under no circumstances were they to take his life, unless it became necessary in self-defence.

The hour came, and with it, to the bluff, came all the regulators — *save one*. But that one was a very important personage — none other, indeed, than the redoubtable major, who was to head the party. The nine were there a considerable time before sunset, and waited patiently for their captain's arrival; though, already, there were whisperings from those who had been doubtful of him in the outset, that he would not keep his appointment. And these were right — for, though they waited long beyond the time, the absentee did not make his appearance. It was afterward ascertained that he excused himself upon the plea of sudden illness; but he was very well again on the following day, and his excuse was not received. The ridicule growing out of the affair, and his reduction from the rank of major to that of captain, in derision, finally drove him in disgrace from the country.

His defection left the little company without a leader; and though they were determined not to give up the enterprise, an obstacle to its prosecution arose, in the fact that no one was willing to replace the absent captain. Each was anxious to play the part of a private, and all had come prepared to discharge the duties of the expedition, to the utmost of their ability. But they were all young men, and no one felt competent to take the responsibility of command.

They were standing in a group, consulting eagerly about their course, and, as one of them afterward said, "nearly at their wits' end," when the circle was suddenly entered by another. He had come upon them so noiselessly, and they had been so much absorbed in their council, that no one saw him until he stood in their midst. Several of them, however, at once recognised him, as a hunter who had recently appeared in the southern part of the county, and had lived a singularly solitary life. No one knew his name, but, from his mode of life, he was already known among those who had heard of him, as "the wild hunter." He was but little above the medium height, and rather slender in figure; but he was well and firmly built, and immediately impressed them with the idea of great hardihood and activity. His face, though bronzed by exposure, was still handsome and expressive; but there was a certain wildness in the eye, and a compression about the mouth, which gave it the expression of fierceness, as well as resolution. He was dressed in a hunting-shirt and "leggings" of deerskin, fringed or "fingered" on the edges; and his head and feet were covered, the one by a cap of panther's hide, and the others by moccasins of dressed buckskin.

At his belt hung a long knife, and in his hand he carried a heavy "Kentucky rifle."

As he entered the circle, he dropped the breech of the latter to the ground, and, leaning calmly upon the muzzle, quietly surveyed the countenances of the group, in profound silence. The regulators were too much surprised to speak while this was going on; and the stranger seemed to be in no haste to open the conversation. When he had finished his scrutiny, however, he stepped back a pace or two, and resuming his easy attitude, addressed them:—

"You must pardon me, my friends," he commenced, "when I tell you, that I have overheard all you have said in the last half hour. I did not remain in that thicket, however, for the purpose of eaves-dropping; but having accidentally heard one of you mention a name, the sound of which touches a chord whose vibrations you can not understand, I remained, almost against my own will, to learn more. I thus became acquainted with the object of your meeting, and the dilemma in which you find yourselves placed by the absence of your leader. Now, I have but little interest in this settlement, and none in the preservation of peace, or the vindication of law, anywhere: but I have been seeking this man,

Cutler, of whom you spoke, nearly nine years. I supposed, a few days ago, that I had at last found him; but on going to his house, I learned that he had once more emigrated toward the west. You seem to know where he is to be found, and are without a leader: I wish to find him, and, if you will accept my services, will fill the place of your absent captain!"

He turned away as he finished, allowing them an opportunity for consultation among themselves. The question was soon decided: they called him back — announced their willingness to accept him as their leader — and asked his name.

"My name is *Stone*," he replied.

It was after nightfall when the little party set out from the bluff. They had, then, more than eight miles to travel, over a country entirely destitute of roads, and cut up by numberless sloughs and ponds. They had, moreover, a considerable river to cross, and, after that, several miles of their way lay through a dense and pathless forest. But they were not the men to shrink from difficulties, at any time; and now they were carried along even more resolutely, by the stern, unwavering spirit of their new leader. Having once learned the direction, Stone put himself at the head of the party, and strode forward, almost "as the bird flies," directly toward the point indicated, regardless of slough, and swamp, and thicket. He moved rapidly, too — so rapidly, indeed, as to tax the powers of some of his followers almost too severely. Notwithstanding this swiftness, however, they could not avoid a long delay at the river; and it was consequently near midnight, when, having at last accomplished a crossing, they reached the bank of M'Kee's creek, and turned up toward Cutler's house.

This stood in the centre of a "clearing," some two or three acres in extent; and upon reaching its eastern limit, the little company halted to reconnoitre. Notwithstanding the lateness of the hour, they discovered that the people of the house were still awake; and by a bright light, which streamed through the open door, they could see several men, sitting and standing about the room.

"We shall make a good haul," said one of the regulators; "the whole gang is there." And immediately the party were for rushing forward. But Stone restrained them.

"My friends," said he, "you have taken me for your leader, and must obey my directions."

He then announced his determination to go forward alone; instructing his men, however, to follow at a little distance, but in no case to show themselves until he should give the signal. They agreed, though reluctantly, to this arrangement, and then — silently, slowly, but surely — the advance commenced. The hour had at last arrived!

In the meantime, Cutler and his three friends were passing the time quite pleasantly over a bottle of backwoods nectar — commonly called whiskey. They seemed well pleased, too, with some recent exploit of theirs, and were evidently congratulating themselves upon their dexterity; for, as the "generous liquid" reeked warmly to their brains, they chuckled over it, and hinted at it, and winked knowingly at each other, as if they enjoyed both the recollection and the whiskey — as they probably did, exceedingly. There were four present, as we said — Cutler and the three worthies so often alluded to. These last sat not far from the open door; and each in his hand held a kerchief, or something of that description, of which the contents were apparently very precious; for, at intervals of a few moments, each raised his bundle between him and the light, and then were visible many circular prints, as if made by the coinage of the mint. This idea was strengthened, too, by several piles of gold and silver, which lay upon the table near the bottle, to which Cutler directed no infrequent glances.

They had all been indulging pretty freely in their devotions to the mythological liquid — rewarding themselves, like soldiers after storming a hostile city, for their hardships and daring. There were a few coals in the chimney, although it was early in the autumn; and on them were lying dark and crumpled cinders, as of paper, over which little sparks were slowly creeping, like fiery insects. Cutler turned them over with his foot, and there arose a small blue, flickering blaze, throwing a faint, uncertain light beneath the table, and into the further corners of the room, and casting shadows of the money-bundles on the open door.

If the betrayer could have known what eyes were strained upon him, as he thus carelessly thrust his foot among the cinders, how changed his bearing would have been. Stone had now approached within fifty paces of the house, and behind him, slowly creeping after, were the regulators. A broad band of light streamed out across the clearing from the door, while, on each side of this, all lay in shadow deepened by the contrast. Through the shadows, cautiously and silently came the footsteps of the avenger! There was no trepidation, no haste — the strange leader rather lingered, with a deadly slowness, as if the movement was a pleasant one, and he disliked to end it. But he never halted — not even for a moment — he came, like fate, slowly, but surely!

"Come, boys," said Cutler, and his voice penetrated the stillness quite across the clearing, "let us take another drink, and then lie down; we shall have a long journey to-morrow."

They all advanced to the table and drained the bottle. Cutler drank last, and then went back to the fire. He again stirred the smouldering cinders with his foot, and, turning about, advanced to close the door. But — he halted suddenly in the middle of the room — his face grew ashy pale — his limbs trembled with terror! Stone stepped upon the threshhold, and, without speaking, brought his rifle to his shoulder! Cutler saw that it pointed to his heart, but he had not the power to speak or move!

"Villain!" said Stone, in a low, suppressed voice, "your hour has come, at last!"

Cutler was by no means a coward; by any one else he would not have been overcome, even for an instant. As it was, he soon recovered himself and sprang forward; but it was only to fall heavily to the floor; for at the same moment Stone fired, and the ball passed directly through his heart! A groan was the only sound he uttered—his arm moved, as in the act of striking, and then fell to the ground—he was dead!

The regulators now rushed tumultuously into the house, and at once seized and pinioned the three desperadoes; while Stone walked slowly to the hearth, and resting the breech of his gun upon the floor, leaned calmly upon its muzzle. He had heard a scream from above—a voice which he knew too well. Margaret had been aroused from sleep by the report of the gun; and now, in her night-dress, with her hair streaming in masses over her shoulders, she rushed down the rude stairway. The first object that met her wild gaze was the body of Cutler, stretched upon the floor and already stiffening in death. With another loud scream, she threw herself upon him—mingling lamentations for his death, with curses upon his murderers.

Stone's features worked convulsively, and

once or twice his hand grasped the hilt of the knife which hung at his belt. At last, with a start, he drew it from the sheath. But, the next moment, he dashed it into the chimney, and leaning his gun against the wall, slowly advanced toward the unhappy woman. Grasping her arm, he lifted her like a child from the body to which she clung. Averting his head, he drew her, struggling madly, to the light; and having brought her face full before the lamp, suddenly threw off his cap, and turned his gaze directly into her eyes. A scream, louder and more fearful than any before, rang even to the woods beyond the clearing; she closed her eyes and shuddered, as if she could not bear to look upon him, whom she had so deeply wronged. He supported her on his arm, and perused her sunken and careworn features, for many minutes, in silence. Then slowly relaxing his grasp —

"You have been punished sufficiently," he said; and seating her gently upon the floor, he quietly replaced his knife in its sheath, resumed his rifle, and left the house.

He was never again seen by any of the parties, except Margaret. She, soon after this event, returned to Virginia; and here Stone paid her an annual visit. He always came without notice, and departed as suddenly, always bearing his rifle, and habited as a hunter. At such times he sought to be alone with her but a few moments, and never spoke more than three words: "Your punishment continues," he would say, after gazing at her worn and haggard face for some minutes; and, then, throwing his rifle over his shoulder, he would again disappear for twelve months more.

And truly her punishment *did* continue; for though no one accurately knew her history, she was an object of suspicion to all; and though she led a most exemplary life, her reputation was evil, and her misery was but too evident. One after the other, her children died, and she was left utterly alone! At last *her* lamp also began to flicker, and when Stone arrived in the country, upon his twelfth annual visit, it was but to see her die, and follow her to the grave! He received her last breath, but no one knew what passed between them in that awful hour. On the day after her burial he went away and returned no more.

The regulators hastily dug a grave on the bank of the creek, and in the silence of the night placed Cutler within it. Then, taking possession of the stolen money, they released their prisoners, notifying them to leave the country within ten days, and returned to the east side of the river. A few years ago, a little mound might be seen, where they had heaped the dirt upon the unhappy victim of his own passions. It was "*the first grave*" in which a white man was buried in that part of the Illinois valley.

At the expiration of the ten " days of grace," it became the duty of the regulators to see that their orders had been obeyed ; and, though the death of Cutler had been more than they had designed or foreseen, they had no disposition to neglect it. They met, accordingly, on the morning of the eleventh day, and having chosen a new leader, proceeded to Cutler's grove. They found the houses of all those to whom they had given "notice" deserted *excepting one*. This was the cabin of the youngest of the three brothers ; and declaring his intention to remain, in defiance of regulators and "Lynch law," he put himself upon his defence. Without ceremony the regulators set fire to the house in which he had barricaded himself, and ten minutes sufficed to smoke him out. They then discovered what they had not before known:

that his elder brothers were also within; and when the three rushed from the door, though taken by surprise, they were not thrown off their guard. The trio were at once seized, and, after a sharp struggle, securely pinioned. A short consultation then decided their course.

Leaving the house to burn at leisure, they posted away for the river, driving their prisoners before them, and a march of three hours brought them to the mouth of the Mauvaisterre. Here they constructed a "raft," by tying half-a-dozen drift-logs together, and warning them that death would be the penalty of a return, they placed their prisoners upon it, pushed it into the middle of the stream, and set them adrift without oar or pole! Although this seems quite severe enough, it was a light punishment compared to that sometimes administered by regulators; and in this case, had not blood been spilt when they did not intend it, it is probable that the culprits would have been first tied to a tree, and thoroughly "lynched."

The involuntary navigators were not rescued from their unpleasant position until they had nearly reached Saint Louis; and though they all swore vengeance in a loud voice, not one of them was ever again seen in the Sangamon country.

Vigorous measures, like those we have detailed, were usually effectual in restoring good order. Where there was no trial, there was no room for false witnesses; and where a punishment, not unfrequently disproportioned to the offence, so rapidly and certainly followed its commission, there was little prospect of impunity, and therefore slight inducement to violate the law. In most localities, it required but few severe lessons to teach desperadoes that prudence dictated their emigration; and, it must be acknowledged, that the regulators were prompt and able teachers.

But we should give only a partial and incomplete view of this institution (for such, in fact, it was), were we to notice its uses and say nothing of its abuse; because, like everything else partaking so largely of the mob element, it was liable to most mischievous perversions. Had the engine been suffered to rest, when it had performed its legitimate functions, all would have been well; but the great vice of the system was its obstinate vitality: it refused to die when its life was no longer useful.

As soon as the danger was past, and the call for his services had ceased, the good citizen, who alone could confine such a system to its proper limits, retired from its ranks: it was consequently left, with all its dangerous authority, in the hands of the reckless and violent. The selfish and designing soon filled up the places of the sober and honest, and from being a terror to evil-doers, and a protection to the peaceful citizen, it became a weapon in the hands of the very men against whom it should have been directed.

When this came to be the case, the institution was in danger of doing more harm in its age, than it had accomplished of good in its youth. But it must not thence be inferred that it should never have been adopted, or that it was vicious in itself. In seasons of public danger, extraordinary powers are often intrusted to individuals — powers which nothing but that danger can justify, and which would constitute the dictators intolerable despots, if they were retained after the crises are passed. The Congress of our confederacy, for example, found it necessary, at one period of our Revolutionary struggle, to invest Washington with such authority; had he exercised it beyond the pressure of immediate peril, the same outcry which has been made against others in similar circumstances, would have been justly raised against him. And most men, less soberly constituted than Washington, would have endeavored to retain it; for power is a pleasant thing, which few have the self-denial to resign without a struggle. The wrong consists not in the original delegation of the authority — for that is justified by the highest of all laws, the law of self-preservation — but in its retention and exercise, when the exigency no longer supports it.

Having parted with the authority to redress grievances, and provide for protection and defence, the citizen can not at once recover it — it remains for a time in the hands of the representative, and is always difficult to regain. But it does not therefore follow, that he should never intrust it to another, for the inconvenience sometimes resulting from its delegation, is one of the incidents to human life, teaching, not obstinacy or jealousy, but circumspection.

The following story, related by one who is well-acquainted with the early history of this country, will illustrate the manner in which the regulator system was sometimes made subservient to men's selfish purposes; and there have, unhappily, been too many instances, in which such criminal schemes were more successful than they were in this. I have entitled it "The Stratagem."

THE STRATAGEM.

Robert Elwood emigrated from Kentucky to Illinois, about the year in which the latter was erected into a state, and passing to the northwest of the regions then occupied by the French and Virginians, pitched his tent upon the very verge of the frontier. He was a man of violent passions, impatient of the restraints of law — arrogant, overbearing, and inclined to the use of "the strong-hand." His removal had been caused by a difficulty with one of his neighbors, in which he had attempted to right himself without an appeal to the legal tribunals. In this attempt, he had not only been thwarted, but also made to pay rather roundly for his temerity; and, vexed and soured, he had at once abandoned his old name, and marched off across the prairies, seeking a country in which, as he said, " a man need not meet a cursed constable every time he left his own door." His family consisted of three sons and one daughter, the latter being, at the time of his emigration, about sixteen years of age.

In journeying toward the north, he halted one day, at noon, within a "point" of timber, which extended a mile into the prairie, and was surrounded by as beautiful a piece of rolling meadow-land, as one need wish to see. He was already half-a-day's journey beyond the thicker settlements; and, indulging a reasonable hope that he would not speedily be annoyed by neighbors, he at once determined here to erect his dwelling and open a new farm. With this view, he marked off a tract of about four hundred acres, including the point of timber in which he was encamped; and before the heats of summer came on, he had a cabin ready for his reception, and a considerable amount of grain planted.

About a mile to the south, there was a similar strip of timber, surrounded, like that of which he took possession, by a rich tract of "rolling prairie;" and this he at once resolved to include in his farm. But, reflecting that it must probably be some years, before any one else would enter the neighborhood to take it up — and having only the assistance of his sons, but two of whom had reached manhood — he turned his attention, first, to the tract upon which he lived. This was large enough to engross his efforts for the present; and, for two years, he neglected to do anything toward establishing his claim to the land he coveted.

It is true, that he told several of his neighbors, who had now begun to settle around him, that he claimed that piece, and thus prevented their enclosing it; but he neither "blazed" nor marked the trees, nor "staked off" the prairie.

In the meantime emigration had come in, so much more rapidly than he had expected, that he found himself the centre of a populous neighborhood; and among other signs of advancing civilization, a company of regulators had been organized, for the protection of life and property. Of this band, Elwood, always active and forward, had been chosen leader; and the vigor and severity with which he had exercised his functions, had given a degree of quiet to the settlements, not usually enjoyed by these frontier communities. One example had, at the period of the opening of our story, but recently been made; and its extreme rigor had frightened away from the neighborhood, those who had hitherto disturbed its peace. This was all the citizens desired; and, having accomplished their ends, safety and tranquillity, those whose conservative character had prevented the regulator system from running into excesses, withdrew from its ranks — but took no measures to have it broken up. It was thus left, with recognised authority, in the hands of Elwood, and others of his violent and unscrupulous character.

Things were in this position, when, on his return from an expedition of some length, Elwood bethought him of the handsome tract of land, upon which he had so long ago set his heart. What were his surprise and rage on learning — a fact, which the absorbing nature of his regulator-duties had prevented his knowing sooner — that it was already in possession of another! And his mortification was immeasurably increased, when he was told, that the man who had thus intruded upon what he considered his own proper demesne, was none other than young Grayson, the son of his old Kentucky enemy! Coming into the neighborhood, in the absence of Elwood, the young man, finding so desirable a tract vacant, had at once taken possession; and by the return of the regulator had almost finished a neat and "roomy" cabin. He had "blazed" the trees, too, and "staked off" the prairie — taking all those steps then deemed necessary, on the frontier, to complete appropriation.

Elwood's first step was to order him peremptorily, to desist, and give up his "improvement"— threatening him, at the same time, with certain and uncertain pains and penalties, if he refused to obey. But Grayson only laughed at his threats, and went stoutly on with his work. When the young men, whom he had hired to assist him in building his house, gave him a friendly warning, that Elwood was the leader of a band of regulators, and had power to make good his menaces, he only replied that "he knew how to protect himself, and, when the time came, should not be found wanting?" Elwood retired from the contest, discomfited, but breathing vengeance; while Grayson finished his house and commenced operations on his farm. But those who knew the headlong violence of Elwood's character, predicted that these operations would soon be interrupted; and they were filled with wonder, when month after month passed away, and there were still no signs of a collision.

In the meantime, it came to be rumored in the settlement, that there was some secret connection between Grayson and Elwood's daughter, Hannah. They had been seen by several persons in close conversation, at times and places which indicated a desire for concealment; and one person even went so far as to say, that he had been observed to kiss her, on parting, late in the evening. Whatever may have been the truth in that matter, it is, at all events, certain, that Grayson was an unmarried man; and that the quarrel between the parents of the pair in Kentucky, had broken up an intimacy, which bade fair to issue in a marriage; and it is probable, that a subordinate if not a primary, motive, inducing him to take possession of the disputed land, was a desire to be near Hannah. Nor was this wish without its appropriate justification; for, though not strictly beautiful, Hannah was quite pretty, and — what is better in a frontier girl — active, fresh, and rosy. At the time of Grayson's arrival in the settlement, she was a few months past eighteen; and was as fine material for a border wife, as could be found in the new state. The former intimacy was soon renewed, and before the end of two months, it was agreed that they should be married, as soon as her father's consent could be obtained.

But this was not so easily compassed; for, all this time, Elwood had been brooding over his defeat, and devising ways and means of recovering the much-coveted land.

At length, after many consultations with a fellow named Driscol, who acted as his lieutenant in the regulator company, he acceded to a proposition, made long before by that worthy, but rejected by Elwood on account of its dishonesty. He only adopted the plan, now, because it was apparently the only escape from permanent defeat; and long chafing under what he considered a grievous wrong, had made him reckless of means, and determined on success, at whatever cost.

One morning, about a week after the taking of this resolution, it was announced that one of Elwood's horses had been stolen, on the night before; and the regulators were straightway assembled, to ferret out and punish so daring an offender. It happened (accidently, *of course*) to be a horse which had cast one of its shoes, only the day before; and this circumstance rendered it easy to discover his trail. Driscol, Elwood's invaluable lieutenant, discovered the track and set off upon it, almost as easily as if he had been present when it was made. He led the party away into the prairie toward the east; and though his companions declared that they could now see nothing of the trail, the sharp-sighted lieutenant swore that it was "as plain as the nose on his face" — truly, a somewhat exaggerated expression: for the color, if not the size, of that feature in his countenance, made it altogether too apparent to be overlooked! They followed him, however, convinced by the earnestness of his asseverations, if not by their own eyes, until, after going a mile toward the east, he began gradually to verge southward, and, having wound about at random for some time, finally took a direct course, for the point of timber on which Grayson lived!

On arriving at the point, which terminated, as usual, in a dense hazel-thicket, Driscol at once pushed his way into the covert, and lo! there stood the stolen horse! He was tied to a sapling by a halter, which was clearly recognised as the property of Grayson, and leading off toward the latter's house, was traced a man's footstep — *his*, of course! These appearances fully explained the theft, and there was not a man present, who did not express a decided conviction that Grayson was the thief.

Some one remarked that his boldness was greater than his shrewdness, else he would not have kept the horse so near. But Driscol declared, dogmatically, that this was "the smartest thing in the whole business," since, if the trail could be obliterated, no one would think of looking *there* for a horse stolen only a mile above! "The calculation" was a good one, he said, and it only failed of success because he, Driscol, happened to have a remarkably sharp sight for all tracks, both of horses and men. To this proposition, supported by ocular evidence, the regulators assented, and Driscol stock, previously somewhat depressed by sundry good causes, forthwith rose in the regulator market to a respectable premium!

Having recovered the stolen property, the next question which presented itself for their consideration, was in what way they should punish the thief. To such men as they, this was not a difficult problem: without much deliberation, it was determined that he must be at once driven from the country. The "days of grace," usually given on such occasions, were ten, and in pursuance of this custom, it was resolved that Grayson should be mercifully allowed that length of time, in which to arrange his affairs and set out for a new home: or, as the regulators expressed it, "make himself scarce." Driscol, having already, by his praiseworthy efforts in the cause of right, made himself the hero of the affair, was invested with authority to notify Grayson of this decree. The matter being thus settled, the corps adjourned to meet again ten days thereafter, in order to see that their judgment was duly carried into effect.

Meantime, Driscol, the official mouthpiece of the self-constituted court of general jurisdiction, rode away to discharge himself of his onerous duties. Halting at the low fence which enclosed the scanty door-yard he gave the customary "Halloo! the house!" and patiently awaited an answer. It was not long, however, before Grayson issued from the door and advanced to the fence, when Driscol served the process of the court *in hæc verba:* —

"Mr. Grayson, the regulators of this settlement have directed me to give you ten days' notice to leave the country. They will meet again one week from next Friday, and if you are not gone by that time, it will become their duty to punish you in the customary way."

"What for?" asked Grayson, quietly.

"For stealing this horse," the functionary replied, laying his hand on the horse's mane, "and concealing him in the timber with the intention to run him off."

"It's Elwood's horse, isn't it?"

"Yes," answered Driscol, somewhat surprised at Grayson's coolness.

"When was he stolen?" asked the notified.

"Last night," answered the official; "I suppose you know very well without being told."

"Do you, indeed?" said Grayson, smiling

absently. And then he bent his eyes upon the ground, and seemed lost in thought for some minutes.

"Well, well," said he at length, raising his eyes again. "I didn't steal the horse, Driscol, but I suppose you regulators know best who ought to be allowed to remain in the settlement, so of course I shall have to obey."

"I am glad to find you so reasonable," said Driscol, making a movement to ride away.

"Stop! stop!" said Grayson: "don't be in a hurry! I shall be gone before the ten days are up, and you and I may not meet again for a long time, so get down and come in: let us take a parting drink together. I have some excellent whiskey, just brought home."

Now, the worthy functionary, as we have intimated, or as the aforesaid nose bore witness, was "quite partial" to this description of produce: some of his acquaintances even insinuating that he took sometimes "a drop too much;" and though he felt some misgiving about remaining in Grayson's company longer than his official duties required, the temptation was too strong for him, and, silencing his fears, he sprang to the ground.

"Tie your horse to the fence, there," said Grayson, "and come in." Driscol obeyed, and it was not long before he was seated in the cabin with a tin-cup in his hand, and its generous contents finding their way rapidly down his capacious throat.

"Whiskey is a pleasant drink, after all, isn't it?" said Grayson, smiling at the gusto with which Driscol dwelt upon the draught, and at the same moment he rose to set his cup on the table behind the official.

"Very pleasant indeed," said Driscol, in reply, and to prove his sincerity, he raised his cup again to his lips. But this time he was not destined to taste its contents. It was suddenly dashed from his hand — a saddle-girth was thrown over his arms and body — and before he was aware of what was being done, he found himself securely pinioned to the chair! A rope was speedily passed round his legs, and tied, in like manner, behind, so that he could, literally, move neither hand nor foot! He made a furious effort to break away, but he would not have been more secure had he been in the old-fashioned stocks! He was fairly entrapped, and though he foamed, and swore, and threatened, it all did no manner of good. Of this he at length became sensible, and grinding his teeth in impotent rage, he relapsed into dogged silence.

Having thoroughly secured his prisoner,

Grayson, who was something of a wag, poured out a small quantity of the seductive liquor, and coming round in front of the ill-used official, smiled graciously in his face, and drank "a health" —

"Success to you, Mr. Driscol," said he, "and long may you continue an ornament to the distinguished company of which you are an honored officer!"

Driscol ground his teeth, but made no reply, and the toast was drunk, like some of those impressive sentiments given at public dinners, "in profound silence!"

Having drained the cup, Grayson deposited it upon the table and himself in a chair; and, drawing the latter up toward his companion, opened the conference thus: —

"I think I have you pretty safe, Driscol: eh!"

The lieutenant made no reply.

"I see you are not in a very sociable humor," continued Grayson; "and, to tell you the truth, I am not much that way inclined myself: but I am determined to get to the bottom of this affair before you shall leave the house. I am sure you know all about it; and if you don't, why the worse for you, that's all."

"What do you mean?" demanded Driscol, speaking for the first time.

"I mean this," Grayson answered sternly: "I did not take that horse from Elwood's — *but you did:* I saw you do it. But since my testimony will not be received, I am determined that you shall give me a certificate in writing that such is the fact. You need n't look so obstinate, for by the God that made us both! you shall not leave that chair alive, unless you do as I say!"

Grayson was a large, rather fleshy man, with a light complexion and blue eyes; and, though good-natured and hard to arouse, when once in earnest, as now, like all men of his stamp, he both looked, and was, fully capable of carrying his menaces into execution. The imprisoned functionary did not at all like the expression of his eye, he quailed before it in fear and shame. He was, however, resolved not to yield, except upon the greatest extremity.

"Come," said Grayson, producing materials for writing; "here are pen, ink, and paper: are you willing to write as I dictate?"

"No," said Driscol, doggedly.

"We'll see if I can't make you willing, then," muttered his captor; and, going to the other end of the cabin, he took down a coil of rope, which hung upon a peg, and returned to his captive. Forming a noose at one end, he placed it about Driscol's neck, and threw the other end over a beam which supported the roof.

"Are you going to murder me?" demanded the official in alarm.

"Yes," answered Grayson, drawing the loose end down, and tightening the noose about Driscol's throat.

"You'll suffer for this," said the lieutenant furiously.

"That won't help *you* much," coolly replied Grayson, tugging at the rope, until one leg of the chair gave signs of rising from the floor, and Driscol's face exhibited unmistakable symptoms of incipient strangulation.

"Stop! stop!" he exclaimed, in a voice reduced to a mere wheeze — and Grayson "eased off" to hear him.

"Won't anything else satisfy you but a written certificate?" he asked — speaking with difficulty, and making motions as if endeavoring to swallow something too large to pass the gate of his throat.

"Nothing but that," answered Grayson, decidedly; "and if you don't give it to me, when your regulator friends arrive, instead of me, they will find you, swinging from this beam by the neck!" And, seeing his victim hesitate, he again tugged at the rope, until the same signs were exhibited as before — only a little more apparently.

"Ho — hold, Grayson!" begged the frightened and strangling lieutenant; and, as his executioner again relaxed a little, he continued: "Just let me up, and I'll do anything you want."

"That is to say," laughed Grayson, "you would rather take the chances of a fight, than be hung up like a sheep-stealing dog! Let you up, indeed!" And once more he dragged the rope down more vigorously than ever.

"I — didn't — mean that — indeed!" gulped the unhappy official, this time almost strangled in earnest.

"What *did* you mean then?" sternly demanded Grayson, relaxing a little once again.

"I will write the certificate," moaned the unfortunate lieutenant, "if you will let one arm loose, and won't tell anybody until the ten days are out —"

"Why do you wish it kept secret!"

"If I give such a certificate as you demand," mournfully answered the disconsolate officer, "I shall have to leave the country — and I want time to get away."

"Oh! that's it, is it? Well — very well."

About an hour after this, Driscol issued from

the house, and, springing upon the horse, rode away at a gallop toward Elwood's. Here he left the animal, but declined to enter; telling Hannah, who happened to be in the yard, to say to her father that "it was all right," he pushed on toward home — tenderly rubbing his throat, first with the right hand and then with the left, all the way. Three days afterward, he disappeared from the settlement, and was heard of no more.

Grayson waited until near nightfall, and then took his way, as usual, to a little clump of trees, that stood near Elwood's enclosures, to meet Hannah. Here he stayed more than an hour, detailing the circumstances of the accusation against him, and laughing with her, over the ridiculous figure cut by her father's respectable lieutenant. Before they parted their plans were all arranged, and Grayson went home in excellent humor. What these plans were, will be seen in the sequel.

Eight days went by without any event important to our story — Hannah and Grayson meeting each evening, in the grove, and parting again undiscovered. On the ninth day, the former went to the house of a neighbor, where it was understood that she was to remain during the night, and return home on the following morning. Grayson remained on his farm until near sunset, when he mounted his horse and rode away. This was the last of his "days of grace;" and those who saw him passing along the road, concluded that he had yielded to the dictates of prudence, and was leaving the field.

On the following morning, the regulators assembled to see that their orders had been obeyed; and, though Elwood was a little disconcerted by the absence of Driscol, since it was understood that Grayson had left the country, the meeting was considered only a formal one, and the presence of the worthy lieutenant was not indispensable. They proceeded in high spirits to the premises, expecting to find the house deserted and waiting for an occupant. Elwood was to take immediate possession, and, all the way across the prairie, was felicitating himself upon the ease and rapidity of his triumph. What was their surprise, then, on approaching the house, to see smoke issuing from the chimney, as usual — the door thrown wide open, and Grayson standing quietly in front of it! The party halted and a council was called, but its deliberations were by no means tedious: it was forthwith determined, that Grayson stood *in defiance of the law*, and must be punished — that is, "lynched" — without delay! The object of this fierce decree, all unarmed as he was, still stood near the door, while the company slowly approached the fence. He then advanced and addressed them:—

"I think the ten days are not up yet, gentlemen," said he mildly.

"Yes, they are," answered Elwood quickly; "and we are here to know whether you intend to obey the authorities, and leave the country?"

"I think, Elwood," said the young man, not directly replying, "this matter can be settled between you me, without bloodshed, and even without trouble. If you will come in with George and John [his sons], I will introduce you to my wife, and we can talk it over, with a glass of whiskey."

Another consultation ensued, when, in order to prove their dignified moderation, they agreed that Elwood and his sons should "go in and see what he had to say."

Elwood, the elder, entered first: directly before him, holding her sides and shaking with laughter, stood his rosy daughter, Hannah!

"*My wife*, gentlemen," said Grayson, gravely introducing them. Hannah's laughter exploded.

"O, father, father, father!" she exclaimeh, leaning forward and extending her hands; "a'n't you caught, beautifully!"

The laugh was contagious; and though the elder knit his brows, and was evidently on the point of bursting with very different emotions, his sons yielded to its influence, and, joining Hannah and her husband, laughed loudly, peal after peal!

The father could bear it no longer — he seized Hannah by the arm and shook her violently, till she restrained herself sufficiently to speak; as for him, he was speechless with rage.

"It's entirely too late to make a 'fuss,' father," she said at length "for here is the marriage-certificate, and Grayson is your son!"

"I have not stolen your horse, Elwood," said the bridegroom, taking the paper which the father rejected, "though I have run away with your daughter. And," he added, significantly, "since if you had this land, you would probably give it to Hannah, I think you and I had better be friends, and I'll take it as her marriage-portion."

"If you can show that you did not take the horse, Grayson," said George, the elder of the two sons, "I'll answer for that: but——"

"That I can do very easily," interrupted the

young husband, "I have the proof in my pocket."

He caught Elwood's eye as he spoke, and reassured him with a look, for he could see that the old man began to apprehend an exposure in the presence of his sons. This forbearance did more to reconcile him to his discomfiture than aught else, save the influence of George; for, like all passionate men, he was easily swayed by his cooler children. While Hannah and her brothers examined the marriage certificate, and laughed over "the stratagem," Grayson drew Elwood aside and exhibited a paper, written in a cramped, uneven hand, as follows:—

"This is to certify, that it was not Josiah Grayson who took Robert Elwood's horse from his stable, last night—but I took him myself, by arrangement, so as to accuse Grayson of the theft, and drive him to leave his new farm.

"THOMAS DRISCOL."

Elwood blushed as he came to the words "by arrangement," but read on without speaking. Grayson then related the manner in which he had entrapped the lieutenant, and the joke soon put him in a good humor. The regulators were called in, and heard the explanation, and all laughing heartily over the capture of Driscol, they insisted that Hannah and her husband should mount, and ride with them to Elwood's. Neither of them needed much persuasion — the whole party rode away together — the "lads and lasses" of the neighborhood were summoned, and the day and night were spent in merriment and dancing.

Grayson and his wife returned on the following morning to their new home, where a life of steady and honorable industry, was rewarded with affluence and content. Their descendants still live upon the place, one of the most beautiful and extensive farms upon that fertile prairie. But on the spot where the disputed cabin stood, has since been built a handsome brick-house, and I pay only a just tribute to amiable character, when I say that a more hospitable mansion is not to be found in the western country.

This was the last attempt at "regulating" in that region, for emigration came in so rapidly, that the supremacy of the law was soon asserted and maintained. Whenever this came to be so, the regulators, of course, ceased to be types of the state of society, and were succeeded by other characters and institutions.

To these we must now proceed.

[NOTE.—The following is a copy of a compact, such as is spoken of in the story of the "The First Grave," entered into by a company of regulators in somewhat similar circumstances. I am not sure that I can vouch for its authenticity, but all who are familiar with the history of those times, will recognise, in its peculiarities, the characteristics of the people who then inhabited this country. The affectation of legal form in such a document as this, would be rather amusing, were it not quite too significant; at all events, it is entirely "in keeping" with the constitution of a race who had some regard for law and its vindication, even in their most high-handed acts. The technical phraseology, used so strangely, is easily traceable to the little "Justice's Form Book," which was then almost the only law document in the country; and though the words are rather awkwardly combined, they no doubt gave solemnity to the act in the eyes of its sturdy signers: —

" *Know all men by these presents:*
"That we [*here follow twelve names*], citizens of ——— settlement, in the state of Illinois, have this day, *jointly and severally*, bound ourselves together as a company of Rangers and Regulators, to protect this settlement against the crimes and misdemeanors of, all and singular, every person or persons whomsoever, and especially against *all horse-thieves, renegades, and robbers*. And we do by these presents, hereby bind ourselves, jointly and severally as aforesaid, unto each other, and to the fellow-citizens of this settlement, to punish, according to the code of his honor, Judge Lynch, all violations of the law, *against the peace and dignity of the said people* of ——— settlement; and to discover and bring to speedy punishment, *all illegal combinations* — to rid the country of such as are dangerous to the welfare of this settlement — to preserve the peace, and *generally to vindicate the law*, within the settlement aforesaid. All of which purposes we are to accomplish as

peaceably as possible: *but we are to accomplish them one way or another.*

"In testimony whereof, we have hereunto set our hands and affixed our seals, this twelfth day of October, *Anno Domini*, eighteen hundred and twenty.

(Signed by twelve men.)

"Acknowledged and subscribed in the presence of

"C——— T. H———n,
"J——— P. D———n,"

and five others, who seem to have been a portion of "the fellow-citizens of this settlement," referred to in the document.]

VI.

THE JUSTICE OF THE PEACE.

> "I beseech you,
> Wrest once the law to your authority:
> To do a great right, do a little wrong."—
> MERCHANT OF VENICE.

THE reign of violence, when an evil at all, is an evil which remedies itself: the severity of its proceeding hastens the accomplishment of its ends, as the hottest fire soonest consumes its fuel. A nation will endure oppression more patiently immediately after a spasmodic rebellion or a bloody revolution, than at any other time; and a community requires less law to govern it, after a violent and illegal assertion of the law's supremacy, than was necessary before the outbreak. After having thrown off the yoke of a knave—and perhaps hung the knave up by the neck, or chopped his head off with an axe—mankind not unfrequently fall under the control of a fool; frightened at their temerity in dethroning an idol of metal, they bow down before a paltry statue of wood.

Men are not easily satiated with power, but when it is irregular, a pause in its exercise must eventually come. And there is a principle of human nature, which teaches, that whatsoever partakes of the mob-spirit is, at best, but temporary, and ought to have a speedy end. This is especially true of such men as first permanently peopled the western country; for though they sometimes committed high-handed and unjustifiable acts, the moment it was discovered that they had accomplished the purposes of order, they allowed the means of vindication to fall into disuse. The regulator system, for example, was directed to the stern and thorough punishment of evil men, but no sooner was society freed from their depredations, than the well-meaning citizens withdrew from its ranks; and, though regulator companies still patroled the country, and, for a time, assumed as much authority as ever, they were not supported by the solid approbation of those who alone could give them lasting strength. They did many outrageous things for which they were never punished, and for some years, the shield which the good citizen had raised above his head for protection and defence, threatened to fall upon and crush him. But the western people are not the first who have been temporarily enslaved by their liberators, though, unlike many another race, they waited patiently for the changes of years, and time brought them a remedy.

As the government waxed stronger, and public opinion assumed a direction, the regulators, like their predecessors, the rangers, found their "occupation gone," and gradually faded out from the land. Proclamations were issued—legislatures met—laws were enacted, and officers appointed to execute them; and though forcing a legal system upon a people who had so long been "a law unto themselves," was a slow and difficult process, it was powerfully assisted by the very disorders consequent upon their attempts at self-government. They had burnt their hands by seizing the hot iron-rod of irregular authority, and were, therefore, better inclined to surrender the baton to those who could handle it. Like Frankenstein, they had created a power which they could not immediately control: the regulators, from being their servants, had come to be their masters: and they willingly admitted any authority which promised deliverance. They had risen in wrath, and chastised, with no hesitating hand, the violators of their peace; but the reaction had taken place, and they were now content to be governed by whatsoever ruler Providence might send them.

The state governments were established, then, without difficulty, and the officers of the new law pervaded every settlement. The character which I have selected as the best representative of this period, is one of these new officers — *the early justice of the peace.*

So far as history or tradition informs us, there was never yet a country in which appointments to office were invariably made with reference only to qualification, and though the west is an exception to more than one general rule, in this respect we must set it down in the common category. The lawyer-period had not yet arrived; and, probably, there was never an equal number of people in any civilized country, of whom a larger proportion were totally ignorant of legal forms. There were not three in each hundred who had ever seen the inside of a courthouse, and they were quite as few who had once looked upon a law-book! Where such was the case, some principle of appointment was of course necessary, other than that which required fitness, by training, for the office conferred; and it is probable that the rule adopted was but little different to that in force among those who have the appointing power, where no such circumstances restrict the choice.

Men were appointed conservators of the *peace*, because they had distinguished themselves in *war;* and he who had assumed the powers of the law, as a regulator, was thought the better qualified to exercise them, as a legal officer! Courage and capacity, as an Indian-fighter, gave one the prominence requisite to his appointment; and zeal for the preservation of order, exhibited as a self-constituted judge and executioner, was a guaranty for the faithful performance of new and regular duties.

Nor was the rule a bad one. A justice of the peace chosen upon this principle, possessed two qualities indispensable to an efficient officer, in the times of which we write — he was prompt in the discharge of his duties, and was not afraid of responsibility. To obviate the danger, however, which might arise from these, he had also a rigid sense of justice, which usually guided his determinations according to the rights of parties in interest. This, the lawyers will say, was a very questionable trait for a judicial officer; and perhaps it *is* better for society, that a judge should know the law, and administer it without reference to abstract justice, than that his own notions of right and wrong should be taken, however conscientiously, as the standard of judgment: for in that case, we shall, at least, have uniformity of adjudication; whereas, nothing is more uncertain, than a man's convictions of right.

But, in the times of which we are writing, society was not yet definitely shaped — its elements were not bound together by the cohesive power of any legal cement — and no better rule was, therefore, to be expected, than the spontaneous suggestions of common sense. The minds of men were, moreover, habituated to a certain course of thought and action — (such as naturally obtains in a new state of society, where the absence of organization remits them to their own exertions for safety) — and it was, therefore, impossible that any artificial system should be at once adopted. The people had been accustomed to such primitive associations, as they had entered into "for the common defence and general welfare" of their infant communities ; the rule of action had been swift, and sometimes very informal punishment, for every transgression; and this rule, having very well answered its purpose, though at the expense of occasional severity and injustice, they could not immediately understand the necessity for any other course of proceeding.

One of the characteristics of the early justice, then, was a supreme contempt for all mere form. He called it "nonsense" and could never comprehend its utility. To him, all ceremony was affectation, and the refinements of legal proceeding were, in his estimation, anti-republican innovations upon the original simplicity of mankind. Technicalities he considered merely the complicated inventions of lawyers, to exhibit their perverse ingenuity — traps to catch the well-meaning or unwary, or avenues of escape for the guilty. The rules of evidence he neither understood nor cared for; he desired "to hear all about" every cause brought before him; and the idea of excluding testimony, in obedience to any rule, he would never entertain. He acted upon the principle — though he probably never heard of the maxim — that "the law furnishes a remedy for every wrong;" and, if he knew of none in positive enactment, he would provide one, from the arsenal of his own sense of right. He never permitted anything to obstruct the punishment of one whom he had adjudged guilty; and, rather than allow a culprit to escape, he would order his judgment to be carried at once into effect, in the presence, and under the direction of the court.

He had a strong prejudice against every man accused of crime; and sometimes almost reversed the ancient presumption of the law, and held the prisoner guilty, until he proved himself innocent. He had unbounded confidence in the honesty of his neighbors and friends, and was unwilling to believe, that they would accuse a man of crime or misdemeanor, without very good cause. When it was proven that a crime *had been committed*, he considered the guilt of the prisoner already half established: it was, in his judgment, what one, better acquainted with legal terms, might have called "a *prima facia* case," devolving the *onus probandi* (or burthen of proof) upon the accused. And this may have been one cause of the frequent resort to *alibis* — a mode of defence which, as we have already remarked, is even yet in great disrepute. If a defence, of some sort, was not, then, very clearly and satisfactorily made out, the justice had no hesitation in entering judgment, and ordering immediate punishment; for the right of appeal was not generally recognised, and the justice took original and final jurisdiction, where now his duties are merely those of preliminary examination and commitment.

In civil controversies — where such causes were presented for adjudication, which, however, was not very often — the order of proceeding was quite as summary. The justice heard the statements of the parties, and sometimes, not always, would listen to witnesses, also; then, taking the general "rights, interests, claims, and demands," of both sides into consideration — and viewing himself, not as a judicial officer, but as a sort of referee or arbitrator — he would strike a balance between the disputants, and dismiss them to their homes, with a significant admonition to "keep the peace." He usually acted upon the principle — no very erronous one, either — that, when two respectable men resort to the law, as arbitrater of their controversies, they are both about equally blameable; and his judgments were accordingly based upon the corollary, that neither deserved to have all he claimed. This was the practice when any decision was made at all; but, in most cases, the justice acted as a pacificator, and, by his authority and persuasion, induced the parties to agree upon a compromise. For this purpose, he not unfrequently remitted both fees and costs — those due to the constables, as well as his own.

An instance of this pacific practice has been related to me as follows: Two neighbors had quarrelled about a small amount of debt, and, after sundry attempts to " settle," finally went to law. The justice took them aside, on the day of trial, and proposed a basis of settlement, to which they agreed, *on condition*, that all costs should be remitted, and to this the magistrate at once pledged himself. But a difficulty arose: the constable, who had not been consulted in the arrangement, had had a long ride after the defendant, and having an unquestionable right to demand his fees, was unwilling to give them up. The justice endeavored to prevail with him by persuasion, but in vain. Finally, growing impatient of his obstinacy, he gave him a *peremptory order* to consent, and, on his refusal, *fined him* the exact amount of his fees *for contempt*, entered up judgment on the basis of the compromise, and adjourned the court!

The man who thus discourages litigation at the expense of his own official emoluments, may be forgiven a few irregularities of proceeding, in consideration of the good he effects; for although under such a system it was seldom that either party obtained his full and just rights, both were always benefited by the spirit of peace infused into the community. It would, perhaps, be well for the country now, were our legal officers actuated by the same motives; unfortunately, however, such men belong only to primitive times.

But the love of peace was not accompanied, in this character, as it usually is, by merciful judgment, for, as he was very swift in determining a prisoner's guilt, he was equally rigid in imposing the penalty. The enactments of the criminal code were generally so worded as to give some scope for the exercise of a compassionate and enlightened discretion; but when the decision lay in the breast of our justice, if he adjudged any punishment at all, it was usually the severest provided for by the statute. Half-measures were not adapted to the temper of the times or the character of the people; indeed, they are suited to *no* people, and are signal failures at all times, in all circumstances. Inflicting light punishments is like firing blank cartridges at a mob, they only irritate, without subduing; and as the latter course usually ends in unnecessary bloodshed, the former invariably increases the amount of crime.

Certainty of punishment may be—unquestionably *is*—a very important element in the administration of justice, but as nothing so strongly disinclines a man to entering the water as the sight of another drowning, so nothing will so effectually deter him from the commission of crime, as the knowledge that another has been severely punished for yielding to the same temptation. The justice, however, based the rigor of his judgments upon no such argument of policy. His austerity was a part of his character, and had been rendered more severe by the circumstances in which he had lived—the audacity of law-breakers, and the necessity for harsh penalties, in order to protection.

It will be observed that I say nothing of juries, and speak of justices of the peace, as officers having authority to decide causes alone. And, it must be recollected, that in the days of which I am writing, resort was very seldom had to this cumbersome and uncertain mode of adjudication. In civil causes, juries were seldom empanelled, because they were attended by very considerable expense and delay. The chief object, in going to law, moreover, was, in most cases, to have *a decision* of the matter in dispute; and juries were as prone to "hang" then as now. Suitors generally, therefore, would rather submit to the arbitration of the justice, than take the risk of delay and uncertainty, with a jury. In criminal causes, the case was very similar: the accused would as lief be judged by one prejudiced man as by twelve; for the same rigorous spirit which actuated the justice, pervaded also the juries; and (besides the chance of timidity or favor in the justice) in the latter he must take the additional risks of personal enmity and relationship to the party injured. Thus, juries were often discarded in criminal causes also, and we think their disuse was no great sacrifice. Such a system can derive its utility, in this country, only from an enlightened public sentiment: if that sentiment be capricious and oppressive, as it too often is, juries are quite as likely to partake its vices as legal officers: if the sentiment be just and healthy, no judicial officer dare be guilty of oppression. So that our fathers lost nothing in seldom resorting to this "palladium of our liberties," and, without doubt, gained something by avoiding delay, uncertainty, and expense.

The reader will also observe, that I say nothing of higher courts. But the lines between the upper and lower tribunals were not so strictly drawn then as they now are, and the limits of jurisdiction were, consequently, very indefinite. Most of the characteristics, moreover, here ascribed to the justice of the peace, belonged, in almost an equal degree, to the judges of the circuit courts; and, though some of the latter were men of respectable legal requirements, the same off-hand mode of administering the law which distinguished the inferior magistrates, marked the proceedings of their courts also. Both occasionally assumed powers which they did not legally possess; both were guided more by their own notions of justice, than by the rules of law; and both were remarkable for their severity upon all transgressors. Neither cared much for the rules of evidence, each was equal to any emergency or responsibility, and both had very exalted ideas of their own authority.

But the functions of the justice were, in his estimation, especially important — his dignity was very considerable also, and his powers anything but circumscribed. A few well-authenticated anecdotes, however, will illustrate the character better than any elaborate portraiture. And, for fear those I am about to relate may seem exceptions, not fairly representing the class, I should state, in the outset, that I have selected them from a great number which I can recall, particularly because they are *not* exceptive, and give a very just impression of the character which I am endeavoring to portray.

'Squire A—— was a plain, honest farmer, who had distinguished himself as a pioneer and ranger, and was remarkable as a man of undoubted courage, but singularly peaceable temper. In the year eighteen hundred and twenty, he received from Governor Bond of Illinois, a commission as justice of the peace, and though he was not very clear what his duties, dignities, and responsibilities, precisely were, like a patriot and a Roman, he determined to discharge them to the letter. At the period of his appointment, he was at feud with one of his neighbors about that most fruitful of all subjects of quarrel, a division-fence; and as such differences always are, the dispute had been waxing warmer for several months. He received his docket, blanks, and "Form-Book," on Saturday evening, and though he had as yet no suits to enter and no process to issue, was thus provided with all the weapons of justice. On the following Monday morning, he repaired, as usual, to his fields, about half-a-mile from home, and though full of his new dignity, went quietly to work.

He had not been there long, before his old and only enemy made his appearance, and opened upon him a volley of abuse in relation to the division-fence, bestowing upon his honor, among other expressive titles, the euphonious epithet of "jackass." A—— bore the attack until it came to this point — which, it would seem, was as far as a man's patience ought to extend — and, it is probable, that had he not been a legal functionary, a battle would have ensued " then and there." But it was beneath the dignity thus outraged, to avenge itself by a vulgar fisticuff, and A—— bethought him of a much better and more honorable course. He threw his coat across his arm, and marched home. There he took down his new docket, and upon the first page, recorded the case of the "*People of the State of Illinois* vs. *John Braxton*" (his enemy). He then entered up the following judgment: "*The defendant in this case, this day, fined ten dollars and costs, for* CONTEMPT OF COURT, *he having called* US *a jackass !*" On the opposite page is an entry of satisfaction, by which it appears that he forthwith issued an execution upon the judgment, and collected the money!

This pretext of "contempt" was much in vogue, as a means of reaching offences not expressly provided for by statute; but the justice was never at a loss for expedients, even in cases entirely without precedent, as the following anecdote will illustrate:—

A certain justice, in the same state of Illinois, was one day trying, for an aggravated assault, a man who was too much intoxicated fully to realize the import of the proceedings or the dignity of the court. He was continually interrupting witnesses, contradicting their testimony, and swearing at the justice. It soon became evident that he must be silenced or the trial adjourned. The justice's patience at length gave way. He ordered the constable to take the obstreperous culprit to a creek, which ran near the office, "and duck him until he was sober enough to be quiet and respect the court!" This operation the constable alone could not perform, but in due time he brought the defendant back dripping from the creek and thoroughly sobered, reporting, at the same time, that he had availed himself of the assistance of two men, Messrs. B—— and L——, in the execution of his honor's commands. The trial then went quietly on, the defendant was fined for a breach of the peace, and ordered to pay *the costs:* one item of which was two dollars to Messrs. B—— and L—— "for assisting the constable in ducking the prisoner!" But, as the justice could find no form nor precedent for hydropathic services, he entered the charge as "*witness fees*," and required immediate payment! The shivering culprit, glad to escape on any terms, paid the bill and vanished!

Whatever might have been the prevailing opinion, as to the legality of such a proceeding, the ridicule attaching to it would effectually have prevented any remedy — most men being willing to forgive a little irregularity, for the sake of substantial justice and "a good joke." But the summary course, adopted by these magistrates, sometimes worked even greater injustice — as might have been expected; and of this, the following is an example:—

About the year eighteen hundred and twenty-six, there lived, in a certain part of the west, a man named Smedley, who, so far as the collection of debts was concerned, was entirely "law-proof." He seemed to have a constitutional indisposition to paying anything he owed: and, though there were sundry executions in the hands of officers against him — and though he even seemed thrifty enough in his pecuniary affairs — no property could ever be found, upon which they could be levied. There was, at the same time, a constable in the neighborhood, a man named White, who was celebrated, in those days of difficult collections, for the shrewdness and success of his official exploits; and the justice upon whom he usually attended, was equally remarkable, for the high hand with which he carried his authority. But, though two executions were placed in the hands of the former, upon judgments on the docket of the latter, months passed away, without anything being realized from the impervious defendant, Smedley.

Whenever the constable found him in possession of property, and made a levy, it was proven to belong to some one else; and the only result of his indefatigable efforts, was the additions of heavy costs to the already hopeless demand.

At length, however, White learned that Smedley had *traded horses* with a man named Wyatt, and he straightway posted off to consult the magistrate. Between them, the plan of operations was agreed upon. White levied first upon the horse then in the possession of Smedley, taking him under *one* of the two writs: he then levied *the other* execution upon the horse which Smedley had traded to Wyatt. The latter, apprehending the loss of his property, claimed the first horse — that which he had traded to Smedley. But, upon the "trial of the right of property," the justice decided that the horse was found in the possession of Smedley, and was, therefore, subject to levy and sale. He was accordingly sold, and the first judgment was satisfied. Wyatt then claimed the *second* horse — that which he had received from Smedley. But, upon a similar "trial" — after severely reprimanding Wyatt for claiming *both* horses, when, on his own showing, he never owned but *one* — the justice decided that the property in dispute had been in the possession of Smedley at the rendition of the judgment, and was therefore, like the other, subject to a lien, and equally liable to levy and sale! And accordingly, this horse, also, was sold, to satisfy the second execution, and Wyatt was dismissed by the justice, with no gentle admonition, " to be careful in future with whom he swapped horses!" A piece of advice which he probably took, and for which he ought to have been duly grateful! Fallen humanity, however, is very perverse; and it is at least supposable, that, having lost his horse, he considered himself hardly used — an opinion in which my legal readers will probably concur.

Before leaving this part of my subject, I will relate another anecdote, which, though it refers more particularly to constables, serves to illustrate the characteristics of the early officers of the law — justices, as well as others:—

The constable who figured so advantageously in the anecdote last related, had an execution against a man named Corson, who was almost as nearly "law proof" as Smedley. He had been a long time endeavoring to realize something, but without success. At length, he was informed, that Corson had sued another man, upon an account, before a justice in a distant part of the same county. This, the delinquent officer at once saw, gave him a chance to secure something; and, on the day of trial, away he posted to the justice's office. Here, he quietly seated himself, and watched the course of the proceeding. The trial went on, and, in due time, the justice decided the cause in favor of Corson. At this juncture, White arose, and, while the justice was entering up judgment, approached the table. When the docket was about to be laid aside, he interposed:—

"Stop!" said he, placing his hand upon the docket, "*I levels on this judgment!*" And, giving no attention to remonstrances, he demanded and obtained the execution. On this he collected the money, and at once applied it to that, which he had been so long carrying — thus settling two controversies, by diligence and force of will. He was certainly a valuable officer!

Thus irregular and informal were many of the proceedings of the primitive legal functionaries; but a liberal view of their characters must bring us to the conclusion, that their influence upon the progress of civilization of the country, was, on the whole, decidedly beneficial.

VII.

THE PEDDLER.

> "This is a traveller, sir; knows men and Manners."— BEAUMONT AND FLETCHER.

PREVIOUS to the organization of civil government, and "the form and pressure" given to the times by this and its attendant circumstances, the primitive tastes and habits of the western people, excluded many of those artificial wants which are gratified by commerce, and afforded no room for traders, excepting those who sold the absolute necessaries of life.

In those days, housekeeping was a very simple matter. Neither steam-engines nor patent cook-stoves were yet known, as necessary adjuncts to a kitchen; the housewife would have "turned up her nose" in contempt of a bake-oven: would have thrown a "Yankee reflector" over the fence, and branded the innovator with the old-fashioned gridiron. Tin was then supposed to be made only for cups and coffee-pots:

pie-pans had not yet even entered "the land of dreams;" and the tea-kettle, which then "sang songs of family glee," was a quaint, squat figure, resembling nothing so much as an overfed duck, and poured forth its music from a crooked, quizzical spout, with a notch in its iron nozzle. If its shut-iron lid was ornamented with a brass button, for a handle, it was thought to be manufactured in superior style? Iron spoons were good enough for the daintiest mouth; and a full set of pewter was a household treasure. China dishes and silver plate had been heard of, but belonged to the same class of marvellous things, with Aladdin's lamp and Fortunatus's purse. Cooking was not yet reduced to a science, and eating was like sleep —a necessity, not a mere amusement. The only luxuries known, were coffee and sugar; and these, with domestics and other cotton fabrics, were the chief articles for which the products of the earth were bartered.

French cloths and Parisian fashions were still less known than silver spoons and "rotary stoves." The men wore homemade jeans, cut after the *mode* of the forest: its dye a favorite "Tennessean" brownish-yellow; and the women were not ashamed to be seen in linsey-wolsey, woven in the same domestic loom. Knitting was then not only an accomplishment, but a useful art; and the size which a "yarn" stocking gave to a pretty ankle, was not suffered to overbalance the consideration of its comfort. The verge of nakedness was not then the region of modesty: the neck and its adjacent parts were covered in preference to the hands; and, in their barbarous ignorance, the women thought it more shame to appear in public half-dressed, than to wear a comfortable shoe.

They were certainly a very primitive people — unrefined, unfashionable, "coarse"— and many of their sons and daughters are even now ashamed to think what "savages" their parents were! In their mode of life, they sought comfort, not " appearances;" and many things which their more sophisticated descendants deem necessaries, they contemned as luxuries.

But, in the course of time, these things began to change, for simplicity is always " primitive," and the progress of refinement is only the multiplication of wants. As the country was reduced to cultivation, and peace settled upon its borders, new classes of emigrants began to take possession of the soil; and, for the immediate purposes of rapid advancement, and especially of social improvement, they were better classes than their predecessors: for, as the original pioneers had always lived a little beyond the influences of regular civilization, these had remained within its limits until the pressure of legal organization began to grow irksome to their partially untamed spirits. There was, indeed, an unbroken gradation of character, from the nearly savage hunter, who visited the country only because it was uninhabited, except by wild beasts, to the genuine *citizen*, who brought with him order, and industry, and legal supremacy.

The emigrants, of whom we are now writing, constituted the third step in this progression; and they imported along with them, or drew after them, the peculiarities belonging to their own degree of advancement. Their notions of comfort and modes of living, though still quite crude, indicated an appreciable stage of refinement. They were better supplied, for example, with cooking utensils — their household furniture was not so primitive — and in wearing apparel, they manifested some regard to elegance as well as comfort. Social intercourse disseminated these ideas among those to whom they were novel; where, previously, the highest motive to improvement had been a desire for convenience, the idea of gentility began to claim an influence; and some of the more moderate embellishments of life assumed the place of the mere necessaries.

The transition was not rapid nor violent, like all permanent changes, it was the work of years, marked by comparatively slow gradations. First, tin-ware, of various descriptions, became necessary to the operations of the kitchen; and that which had been confined to one or two articles, was now multiplied into many forms. A housewife could no more bake a pie without a "scalloped" pie-pan, than without a fire: a tin-bucket was much more easily handled than one of cedar or oak; and a pepper-box, of the same material, was as indispensable as a salt-cellar. A little tea was occasionally added to the ancient regimen of coffee, and thus a tin-canister became necessary for the preservation of the precious drug. With tea came queensware: and half-a-dozen cups and saucers, usually of a dingy white, with a raised blue edge, were needful for the pranking of the little cupboard.

But it was not only in the victualing department that the progress of refinement could be traced; for the thrifty housewife, who thought it proper to adorn her table, and equip her kitchen with all the late improvements, could not, of course, entirely overlook "the fashions:" the decoration of her person has been, in all ages, the just and honest pride of woman. Linsey-wolsey began to give place to calicoes and many-colored prints; calf-skin shoes were antiquated by the use of kid; and ribands fluttered gracefully upon new-fashioned bonnets. Progress of this kind never takes a step backward: once possessed of an improvement in personal comfort, convenience, or adornment, man — or woman — seldom gives it up. Thus, these things, once used, thenceforth became wants, whose gratification was not to be foregone: and it is one of the principles governing commerce, that the demand draws to it the supply.

There were few "country stores," in those days, and the settlements were so scattered as to make it sometimes very inconvenient to visit them. From ten to twenty miles was a moderate distance to the dépôt of supplies; and a whole day was usually consumed in going and returning. The visits were, therefore, not very frequent — the purchases for many weeks — perhaps months — being made on each occasion. This was a very inconvenient mode of "shopping," even for the energetic women of that day; and, since the population would not justify more numerous "stores," it was desirable that some new system should be introduced, capable of supplying the demand at the cost of less trouble, and fewer miles of travel. To answer this necessity there was but one way — the "storekeeper" must carry his wares to the doors of his customers. And thus arose the occupation of the *Peddler*, or, as he called himself, the "travelling merchant."

The population of the country was then almost exclusively agricultural — the mechanic arts belong to a more advanced period. The consequence was, that the first articles carried about from house to house, were such as are manufactured by artisans — and the chief of these was tin-ware.

The tinkers of the rural districts in older countries, were, however, not known in this — they were not adapted to the genius of the people. The men who sold the ware were, scarcely ever, the same who made it; and, though the manual dexterity of most of these ready men, might enable them to mend a broken pan, or a leaky coffeepot, their skill was seldom put in requisition. Besides, since the mending of an old article might interfere with the sale of a new one, inability to perform the office was more frequently assumed than felt.

In the course of time — as the people of the country began to acquire new ideas, and discover new wants — other articles were added to the peddler's stock. Calicoes were often carried in the same box with tin pans — cotton checks and ginghams were stowed away beneath tin-cups and iron-spoons — shining coffee-pots were crammed with spools of thread, papers of pins, cards of horn-buttons, and cakes of shaving-soap — and bolts of gaudy riband could be drawn from pepper-boxes and sausage-stuffers. Table-cloths, of cotton or brown linen, were displayed before admiring eyes, which had turned away from all the brightness of new tin plates; and knives and forks, all "warranted pure steel," appealed to tastes, which nothing else could excite. New razors touched the men "in tender places," while shining scissors clipped the purses of the women. Silk handkerchiefs and "fancy" neckcloths — things till then unknown — could occupy the former, while the latter covetously turned over and examined bright ribands and fresh cotton hose. The peddler was a master of the art of pleasing all tastes: even the children were not forgotten; for there were whips and jew's-harps for the boys, and nice check aprons for the girls. (The taste for "playing mother" was as much an instinct, with the female children of that day, as it is in times more modern; but life was yet too earnest to display it in the dressing and nursing of waxen babies.) To suit the people from whom the peddler's income was derived, he must consult at least the appearance of utility, in every article he offered; for, though no man could do more, to coax the money out of one's pocket, without leaving an equivalent, even *he* could not succeed in such an enterprise, against the matter-of-fact pioneer.

The "travelling merchants" of this country were generally what their customers called "Yankees"—that is, New-Englanders, or descendants of the puritans, whether born east of the Hudson or not. And, certainly, no class of men were ever better fitted for an occupation, than were those for "peddling." The majority of them were young men, too; for the "Yankee" who lives beyond middle age, without providing snug quarters for the decline of life, is usually not even fit for a peddler. But, though often not advanced in years, they often exhibited qualities, which one would have expected to find only in men of age and experience. They could "calculate," with the most absolute certainty, what precise stage of advancement and cultivation, was necessary to the introduction of every article of merchandise their stock comprised. Up to a certain limit, they offered, for example, linen table-cloths: beyond that, cotton was better and more saleable; in certain settlements, they could sell numbers of the finer articles, which, in others, hung on their hands like lead; and they seemed to know, the moment they breathed the air of a neighborhood, what precise character of goods was most likely to pay."

Thus — by way of illustration — it might seem, to one not experienced in reading the signs of progress, a matter of nice speculation and subtle inquiry, to determine what exact degree of cultivation was necessary, to make profitable the trade in *clocks*. But I believe there is no instance of an unsuccessful clock-peddler on record; and, though this fact may be accounted for, superficially, by asserting that time is alike important to all men, and a measure of its course, therefore, always a want, a little reflection will convince us, that this explanation is more plausible than sound.

It is, perhaps, beyond the capacity of any man, to judge unerringly, by observation, of the usual signs of progress, the exact point at which a community, or a man, has arrived in the scale of cultivation; and it may seem especially difficult, to determine commercially, what precise articles, of use or ornament, are adapted to the state indicated by those signs. But that there are such indications, which, if properly attended to, will be unfailing guides, is not to be denied. Thus, the quick observation of a clock-peddler would detect among a community of primitive habits, the growing tendency to regularity of life; for, as refinement advances, the common affairs of everyday existence, feeling the influence first, assume a degree of order and arrangement; and from the display of this improvement, the trader might draw inferences favorable to his traffic. Eating, for example, as he would perceive, is done at certain hours of the day — sleep is taken between fixed periods of the night and morning — especially, public worship — which is one of the best and surest signs of social advancement — must be held at a time generally understood.

The peddler might conclude, also, when he saw a glazed window in a house, that the owner was already possessed of a clock — which, perhaps, needed repairing — or, at least, was in great need of one, if he had not yet made the purchase. One of these shrewd "calculators" once told me, that, when he saw a man with four panes of glass in his house, and no clock, he either sold him one straightway, or "set him down crazy, or a screw."

"Have you no other 'signs of promise'?" I asked.

"O yes," he replied, "many! For instance: When I am riding past a house — (I always ride slowly) — I take a general and particular survey of the premises — or, as the military men say, I make a *reconnaissance;* and it must be a very bare place, indeed, if I can not see some 'sign,' by which to determine, whether the owner needs a clock. If I see the man, himself, I look at his extremities; and by the appearance of hat and boot, I make up my opinion as to whether he knows the value of time: if he wears anything but a cap, I can pretty fairly calculate upon selling him a clock; and if, to the hat, he has added *boots*, I halt at once, and, without ceremony, carry a good one in.

"When I see the wife, instead of the husband, I have no difficulty in making up my mind — though the signs about the women are so numerous and minute, that it would be hard to explain them. If one wears a check-apron and sports a calico dress, I know that a 'travelling merchant' has been in the neighborhood; and if he has succeeded in making a reasonable number of sales, I am certain that he has given her such a taste for buying, that I can sell her anything at all: for purchasing cheap goods, to a woman, is like sipping good liquor, to a man — she soon acquires the appetite, and thenceforward it is insatiable.

"I have some customers who have a *passion* for clocks. There is a man on this road, who has one for every room in his house; and I have another with me now — with a portrait of General Jackson in the front — which I expect to add to his stock. There is a farmer not far from here, with whom I have 'traded' clocks every year since I first entered the neighborhood — always receiving about half the value of the article I sell, in money, 'to boot.' There are clock-fanciers, as well as fanciers of dogs and birds; and I have known cases, in which a man would have two or three timepieces in his house, and not a pair of shoes in the family! But such customers are rare — as they ought to be; and the larger part of our trade is carried on, with people who begin to feel the necessity of regularity — to whom the sun has ceased to be a sufficient guide — and who have acquired some notions of elegance and comfort. And we seldom encounter the least trouble in determining, by the general appearance of the place, whether the occupant has arrived at that stage of refinement."

We perceive that the principal study of the peddler is human nature; and though he classifies the principles of his experience, more especially with reference to the profits of his trade, his rapid observation of minor traits and indications, is a talent which might be useful in many pursuits, besides clock-peddling. And, accordingly, we discover that, even after he has abandoned the occupation, and ceased to be a bird of passage, he never fails to turn his learning to a good account.

He was distinguished by energy as well as shrewdness, and an enterprising spirit was the first element of his prosperity. There was no corner—no secluded settlement—no out-of-the way place—where he was not seen. Bad roads never deterred him: he could drive his horses and wagon where a four-wheeled vehicle never went before. He understood bearings and distances as well as a topographical engineer, and would go, whistling contentedly, across a prairie or through a forest, where he had not even a "trail" to guide him. He could find fords and crossings where none were previously known to exist; and his pair of lean horses, by the skilful management of their driver, would carry him and his wares across sloughs and swamps, where a steam-engine would have been clogged by the weight of a baby-wagon. If he broke his harness or his vehicle in the wilderness, he could repair it without assistance, for his mechanical accomplishments extended from the shoeing of a horse to the repair of a watch, and embraced everything between. He was never taken by surprise—accidents never came unexpected, and strange events never disconcerted him. He would whistle "Yankee Doodle" while his horses were floundering in a quagmire, and sing "Hail Columbia" while plunging into an unknown river!

He never met a stranger, for he was intimately acquainted with a man as soon as he saw him. Introductions were useless ceremonies to him, for he cared nothing about names. He call a woman "ma'am" and a man "mister," and if he could sell either of them a few goods, he never troubled himself or them with impertinent inquiries. Sometimes he had a habit of learning each man's name from his next neighbor, and possessing an excellent memory, he never lost the information thus acquired.

When he had passed through a settlement once, he had a complete knowledge of all its circumstances, history, and inhabitants; and, the next year, if he met a child in the road, he could tell you whom it most resembled, and to what family it belonged. He recollected all who were sick on his last visit — what peculiar difficulties each was laboring under — and was always glad to hear of their convalescence. He gathered medicinal herbs along the road, and generously presented them to the housewives where he halted, and he understood perfectly the special properties of each. He possessed a great store of good advice, suited to every occasion, and distributed it with the disinterested benevolence of a philanthropist. He knew precisely what articles of merchandise were adapted to the taste of each customer; and the comprehensive "rule of three" would not have enabled him to calculate more nicely the exact amount of "talk" necessary to convince them of the same.

His address was extremely insinuating, for he always endeavored to say the most agreeable things, and no man could judge more accurately what would best please the person addressed. He might be vain enough, but his egotism was never obtruded upon others. He might secretly felicitate himself upon a successful trade, but he never boasted of it. He seemed to be far more interested in the affairs of others than in his own. He had sympathy for the afflictions of his customers, counsel for their difficulties, triumph in their success.

Before the introduction of mails, he was the universal news-carrier, and could tell all about the movements of the whole world. He could gossip over his wares with his female customers, till he beguiled them into endless purchases, for he had heard of every death, marriage, and birth within fifty miles. He recollected the precise piece of calico from which Mrs. Jones bought her last new dress, and the identical bolt of riband from which Mrs. Smith trimmed her "Sunday bonnet." He knew whose children went to "meeting" in "store-shoes," whose daughter was beginning to wear long dresses, and whose wife wore cotton hose. He could ring the changes on the "latest fashions" as glibly as the skilfulest *modiste*. He was a *connoisseur* in colors, and learned in their effects upon complexion. He could laugh the husband into half-a-dozen shirts, flatter the wife into calico and gingham, and praise the children till both parents joined in dressing them anew from top to toe.

He always sold his goods "at a ruinous sacrifice," but he seemed to have a dépôt of infinite extent and capacity, from which he annually drew new supplies. He invariably left a neighborhood the loser by his visit, and the close of each season found him inconsolable for his "losses." But the next year he was sure to come back, risen, like the Phœnix, from his own ashes, and ready to be ruined again — in the same way. He could never resist the pleading look of a pretty woman, and if she "jewed" him twenty per cent. (though his profits were only two hundred), the tenderness of his heart compelled him to yield. What wonder is it, then, if he was a prime favorite with all the women, or that his advent, to the children, made a day of jubilee?

But the peddler, like every other human "institution," only had "his day." The time soon came when he was forced to give way before the march of newfangledness. The country grew densely populated, neighborhoods became thicker, and the smoke of one man's chimney could be seen from another's front-door. People's wants began to be permanent — they were no longer content with transient or periodical supplies — they demanded something more constant and regular. From this demand arose the little neighborhood "stores," established for each settlement at a central and convenient point — usually at "cross-roads," or next door to the blacksmith's shop — and these it was which superseded the peddler's trade.

We could wish to pause here, and, after describing the little dépôt, "take an account of stock:" for no store, not even a sutler's, ever presented a more amusing or characteristic assortment. But since these modest establishments were generally the *nuclei*, around which western towns were built, we must reserve our fire until we reach that subject.

But the peddler had not acquired his experience of life for nothing, he was not to be outdone, even by the more aristocratic stationary shop-keeper. When he found his trade declining, he cast about him for a good neighborhood, still uninvaded by the Lombards, and his extensive knowledge of the country soon enabled him to find one. Here he erected his own cabin, and boldly entered the lists against his new competitors. If he could find no eligible point for such an establishment, or if he augured unfavorably of his success in the new walk, he was not cast down. If he could not "keep store," he could at least "keep tavern," an occupation for which his knowledge of the world and cosmopolitan habits, admirably fitted him. In this capacity, we shall have occasion to refer to him again; and have now only to record, that in the progress of time, he grew rich, if not fat, and eventually died, " universally regretted."

VIII.

THE SCHOOLMASTER.

> "There, in his quiet mansion, skilled to rule,
> The village *master* taught his little school.
> * * * * *
> I knew him well, and every truant knew:
> * * * * *
> Yet he was kind; or, if severe in aught,
> The love he bore to learning was in fault.
> The village all declared how much he knew:
> 'Twas certain he could write, and cipher too."—
> GOLDSMITH'S "DESERTED VILLAGE."

IN the progress of society, the physical wants are felt before the intellectual. Men appreciate the necessity for covering their backs and lining their stomachs before storing their minds, and they naturally provide a shelter from the storms of heaven, before they seek (with other learning) a knowledge of the heavenly bodies. Thus the rudest social system comprises something of the mechanic arts — government begins to advance toward the dignity of a science — commerce follows the establishment of legal

THE SCHOOLMASTER.

supremacy — and the education of the citizen comes directly after the recognition of his social and political rights. So, the justice of the peace (among other legal functionaries) indicates subjection, more or less complete, to the regulations of law; the peddler represents the beginning of commercial interests; and the schoolmaster succeeds him, in the natural order of things.

It may be possible to preserve a high respect for a *calling*, while we despise the men who exercise it: though I believe this is not one of the rules which "work both ways," and the converse is, therefore, not equally true. A man's occupation affects *him* more nearly than *he* does his occupation. A thousand contemptible men will not bring a respectable profession into so much disrepute, as a contemptible profession will a thousand respectable men. All the military talents, for example, of the commander-in-chief of our armies, would not preserve him from contempt, should he set up a barber-shop, or drive a milk-cart: but the barber, or the milkman, might make a thousand blunders at the head of an army, should extravagant democracy elevate him to that position, and yet the rank of a general would be as desirable, because as honorable, as ever.

It is certainly true, however, that the most exalted station may be degraded by filling it with a low or despicable incumbent, for the mental effort necessary to the abstraction of the employment from him who pursues it, is one which most men do not take the trouble to make : an effort, indeed, which the majority of men are *incapable* of making. A vicious priest degrades the priestly vocation — a hypocrite brings reproach upon the religious profession — a dishonest lawyer sinks the legal character — and even the bravest men care but little for promotion in an army, when cowardice and incompetency are rewarded with rank and power. But manifest incapacity, culpable neglect of duty, or even a positively vicious character, will not reduce a calling to contempt, or bring it into disrepute so soon, as any quality which excites ridicule.

An awkward figure, a badly-shaped garment, or an ungainly manner, will sometimes outweigh the acquirements of the finest scholar; and the cause of religion has suffered more, from the absence of the softer graces, in its clerical representations, than from all the logic of its adversaries. A laugh is more effectual to subvert an institution, than an argument — for it is easier to make men ashamed, than to convince them. Truth and reason are formidable weapons, but ridicule is stronger than either — or both.

Thus: All thinking men will eagerly admit, that the profession of the schoolmaster is, not only respectable, but honorable, alike to the individual, and to the community in which he pursues it: yet, rather than teach a school for a livelihood, the large majority of the same men would "split rails" or cut cord-wood! And this is not because teaching is laborious — though it *is* laborious, and thankless, too, beyond all other occupations; but because a number and variety of causes, into which we need not inquire, have combined to throw ridicule upon him, who is derisively called the pedagogue — for most men would rather be shot at, than laughed at. Cause and effect are always interreactive: and the refusal of the most competent men, to "take up the birch"—which is the effect of this derision — has filled our school-rooms with men, who are, not unfairly, its victims. Thus the profession — (for such is its inherent dignity) — itself, has fallen into discredit — even though the judgment of men universally is, that it is not only useful, but indispensable.

Nor is that judgment incorrect. For, though

home-education may sometimes succeed, it is usually too fragmentary to be beneficial — private tutors are too often the slaves of their pupils, and can not enforce "attention," the first condition of advancement, where they have not the paraphernalia of command — and, as for self-education, logically there can be no such thing : " one might as well attempt to lift himself over the fence, by the straps of his boots," as to educate himself "without a master."

The schoolmaster, then, is a useful member of society — not to be spared at any stage of its progress. But he is particularly necessary to communities which are in the transition state; for, upon the enlightenment of the rising generation depend the success and preservation of growing institutions. Nor does his usefulness consist altogether — or even in a great measure — in the number of facts, sciences, or theories, with which he may store the minds of his pupils. These are not the objects of education, any more than a knowledge of the compartments in a printer's "letter-case," is the ultimate result of the art of printing. The types are so arranged, in order to enable the compositors more conveniently to attain the ends, for which that arrangement is only a preparation: facts and sciences are taught for the improvement of the faculties, in order that they may work with more ease, force, and certainty, upon other and really important things; for education is only the marshalling of powers, preliminary to the great " battle of life."

The mind of an uneducated man, however strong in itself, is like an army of undisciplined men — a crowd of chaotic, shapeless, and often misdirected elements. To bring these into proper subjection — to enable him to bind them, with anything like their native force, to a given purpose — a prescribed "training" is necessary; and it is this which education supplies. If you can give a mind the *habit of attention*, all the power it has will be made available: and it is through this faculty, that even dull minds are so frequently able to mount the car of triumph, and ride swiftly past so many, who are immeasurably their superiors. The first element of the discipline which develops this power, is submission to control; and without such subordination, a school can not exist. Thus, the first lesson that children learn from the schoolmaster, is the most valuable acquisition they can make.

But it was no easy task to teach this princi-

ple to the sturdy children of the early Western
"settler;" in this, as in all other things, the
difficulty of the labor was in exact proportion
to its necessity. The peculiarities of the people, and the state of the country, were not
favorable to the establishment of the limited
monarchy, requisite to successful teaching. In
the first place, the parents very generally undervalued, what they called "mere book-learn-
ing." For themselves, they had found more
use for a rifle than a pen; and they naturally
thought it a much more valuable accomplishment, to be able to scalp a squirrel with a
bullet, at a hundred paces, than to read the
natural history of the animal in the "picture-
book." They were enthusiastic, also, upon the
subject of independence; and, though they
could control their children sternly enough at
home, they were apt to look, with a jealous eye,
upon any attempt to establish dominion elsewhere. The children partook largely of the
free, wild spirit of their fathers. They were
very prompt to resist anything like encroach-
ment upon their privileges or rights, and were,
of course, pretty certain to consider even salu-
tary control an attempt to assert a despotism.
I believe history contains no record, whatever
the annals of fiction may display, of a boy,

with much spirit, submitting without a murmur to the authority of the schoolmaster: if such a prodigy of enlightened humility ever existed, he certainly did not live in the west. But a more important difficulty than either of these, was the almost entire want of money in the country; and without this there was but little encouragement for the effort to overcome other obstacles. Money *may* be only a *representative* of value, but its absence operates marvellously like the want of the value itself, and the primitive people of those days, and especially that class to which the schoolmaster belonged, had a habit, however illogical, of considering it a desirable commodity, *per se.*

All these impediments, however, could, in the course of time, be conquered: the country was improving in social tone; parents must eventually take some pride even in the accomplishments they despised; and patience and gentleness, intermingled, now and then, with a little wholesome severity, will ultimately subdue the most stubborn spirit. As for the pecuniary difficulty, it was, as the political economists will tell us, only the absence of a medium at the worst: and, in its stead, the master could receive boarding, clothing, and the agricultural products of the country. So many barrels of corn, or bushels of wheat, "per quarter," might not be so conveniently handled, but were quite as easy to be counted, as an equal number of dollars; and this primitive mode of payment is even yet practised in many rural districts, perhaps, in both the east and west. To counterbalance its inconvenience of bulk, this "currency" possessed a double advantage over the more refined "medium of exchange" now in use: it was not liable to counterfeits, and the bank from which it issued was certain not to "break."

So the schoolmaster was not to be deterred from pursuing his honorable calling, even by the difficulties incident to half-organized communities. Indeed, teaching was the resort, at least temporary, of four fifths of the educated, and nearly an equal number of the uneducated young men, who came to the west: for certainly that proportion of both classes arrived in the country, without money to support, friends to encourage, or pride to deter them.

They were almost all what western people call "Yankees"—born and bred east of the Hudson: descendants of the sturdy puritans—and distinguished by the peculiarities of that strongly-marked people, in personal appearance, language, manners, and style and tone of thought. Like the peddlers, they were generally on the sunny side of thirty, full of the hopeful energy which belongs to that period of life, and only submitting to the labors and privations of the present, because through these they looked to the future for better and brighter things.

The causes which led to their emigration, were as many and as various as the adventurers whom they moved. They were, most of them, mere boys: young Whittingtons, whom the bells did *not* ring back, to become lord-mayors; who, indeed, had not even the limited possessions of that celebrated worthy; and, thus destitute, they wandered off, many hundreds of miles, "to see the world and make their fortunes," at an age when the youth of the present day are just beginning to think of college. They brought neither money, letters of introduction, nor bills of exchange: they expected to find neither acquaintance nor relatives. But they knew — for it was one of the wise maxims of their unromantic fathers — that industry and honesty must soon gather friends, and that all other desirable things would speedily follow. They had great and just confidence in their own abilities to "get along;" and if they did not actually think that the whole world belonged to them, they were well-assured, that in an incredibly short space of time, they would be able to possess a respectable portion of it.

A genuine specimen of the class to which most of the early schoolmasters belonged, never felt any misgivings about his own success, and never hesitated to assume any position in life. Neither pride nor modesty was ever suffered to interfere with his action. He would take charge of a numerous school, when he could do little more than write his own name, just as he would have undertaken to run a steamboat, or command an army, when he had never studied engineering or heard of strategy. Nor would he have failed in either capacity: a week's application would make him master of a steam-engine, or a proficient (after the *present manner* of proficiency) in tactics; and as for his school, he could himself learn at night what he was to teach others on the following day! Nor was this mere "conceit" — though, in some other respects, that word, in its limited sense, was not inapplicable — neither was it altogether ignorant presumption; for one of these men was seldom known to fail in anything he undertook: or, if he did fail, he was never found to be cast down by defeat, and the resiliency of his nature justified his confidence.

The pursuit of a certain avocation, for a long period, is apt to warp one's nature to its inequalities; and as the character gradually assumes the peculiar shape, the personal appearance changes in a corresponding direction and degree. Thus, the blacksmith becomes brawny, square, and sturdy, and the characteristic swing of his arm gives tone to his whole bearing: the silversmith acquires a peering, cunning look, as if he were always examining delicate machinery: the physician becomes solemn, stately, pompous, and mysterious, and speaks like "Sir Oracle," as if he were eternally administering a bread-pill, or enjoining a regimen of drugs and starvation: the lawyer assumes a keen, alert, suspicious manner, as if he were constantly in pursuit of a latent perjury, or feared that his adversary might discover a flaw in his "case:" and so on, throughout the catalogue of human avocations. But, among all these, that which marks its votaries most clearly, is school-teaching.

There seems to be a sort of antagonism between this employment and all manner of neatness, and the circle of the schoolmaster's female acquaintance never included the Graces. Attention to personal decoration is usually, though not universally, in an inverse ratio to mental garniture; and an artistically-tied cravat seems inconsistent with the supposition of a well-stored head above it. A mind which is directed toward the evolution of its own powers, has but little time to waste in adorning the body; and a fashionable costume would appear to cramp the intellect, as did the iron-vessel the genius of the Arabian tale. Although, therefore, there are numerous exceptions — persons whose externals are as elegant as their pursuits are intellectual — men of assiduously-cultivated minds are apt to be careless of appearances, and the principle applies, with especial force, to those whose business it is to develop the minds of others.

Nor was the schoolmaster of early days in the west, an exception to the rule. He might not be as learned, nor as purely intellectual, as some of our modern college-professors, but he was as ungraceful, and as awkwardly clad, as the most slovenly of them all. Indeed, he came of a stock which has never been noted for any of the lighter accomplishments, or "carnal graces;" for at no period of its eventful history, has the puritan type been a remarkable elegant one. The men so named have been better known for bravery than taste, for zeal than polish; and since there is always a correspondence between habits of thought and feeling and the external appearance, the *physique* of the race is more remarkable for rigor of muscle and angularity of outline, than for accuracy of proportion or smoothness of finish. Neither Apollo nor Adonis was in any way related to the family; and if either had been, the probability is that his kindred would have disowned him.

Properly to represent his lineage, therefore, the schoolmaster could be neither dandy nor dancing-master; and, as if to hold him to his integrity, nature had omitted to give him any temptation, in his own person, to assume either of these respectable characters. The tailor that could shape a coat to fit *his* shoulders, never yet handled shears; and he would have been as ill at ease, in a pair of fashionable pantaloons, as if they had been lined with chestnut-burrs. He was generally above the medium height, with a very decided stoop, as if in the habit of carrying burthens; and a long, high nose, with light blue eyes, and coarse, uneven hair, of a faded weather-stain color, gave his face the expression answering to this lathy outline.

Though never very slender, he was always thin: as if he had been flattened out in a rolling-mill; and rotundity of corporation was a mode of development not at all characteristic. His complexion was seldom florid, and not often decidedly pale; a sort of sallow discoloration was its prevailing hue, like that which marks the countenance of a consumer of " coarse" whiskey and strong tobacco. But these failings were not the cause of his cadaverous look — for a faithful representative of the class held them both in commendable abhorrence — *they were not the vices of his nature.*

There was a subdivision of the class, a secondary type, not so often observed, but common enough to entitle it to a brief notice. *He* was, generally, short, square, and thick — the latitude bearing a better proportion to the longitude than in his lank brother — but never approaching anything like roundness. With this attractive figure, he had a complexion of decidedly bilious darkness, and what is commonly called a "dish-face." His nose was depressed between the eyes, an arrangement which dragged the point upward in the most cruel manner, but gave it an expression equally ludicrous and impertinent. A pair of small, round, black eyes, encompassed

THE SCHOOLMASTER. 303

—like two little feudal fortresses, each by its moat—with a circle of yellowish white, peered out from under brows like battlements. Coarse, black hair, always cut short, and standing erect, so as to present something the appearance of a *chevaux de frise*, protected a hard, round head—a shape most appropriate to his lineage —while, with equal propriety, ears of corresponding magnitude stood boldly forth to assert their claim to notice.

Both these types were distinguished for large feet, which no boot could enclose, and hands broad beyond the compass of any glove. Neither was ever known to get drunk, to grow fat, to engage in a game of chance, or to lose his appetite: it became the teacher of "ingenuous youth" to preserve an exemplary bearing before those whom he was endeavoring to benefit; while respectable "appearances," and proper appreciation of the good things of life, were the *alpha* and *omega* of his system of morality.

But the schoolmaster—and we now include both subdivisions of the class—was not deficient as an example in many other things, to all who wished to learn the true principles of living. Among other things, he was distinguished for a rigid, iron-bound economy: a characteristic which it might have been well to impart to many of his pupils. But that which the discreet master denominated *prudence*, the extravagant and wrong-headed scholar was inclined to term *meanness:* and historical truth compels us to admit, that the rigor of grim economy sometimes wore an aspect of questionable austerity. Notwithstanding this, however, when we reflect upon the scanty compensation afforded the benefactor of the rising generation, we can not severely blame his penurious tenacity any more than we can censure an empty wine-cask for not giving forth the nectar which we have never poured into it. If, accordingly, he was out at the elbows, we are bound to conclude that it was because he had not the money to buy a new coat; and if he never indulged himself in any of the luxuries of life, it was, probably, because the purchase of its necessaries had already brought him too near the bottom of his purse.

He was always, moreover, "a close calculator," and, with a wisdom worthy of all imitation, never mortgaged the future for the convenience of the present. Indeed, this power of "calculation" was not only a talent but a passion: you would have thought that his progenitors had been arithmeticians since the time of Noah! He could "figure up" any proposition whatsoever: but he was especially great upon the question, how much he could save from his scanty salary, and yet live to the end of the year.

In fact, it was only *living* that he cared for. The useful, with him, was always superior to the ornamental; and whatever was not absolutely necessary, he considered wasteful and extravagant. Even the profusion of western hospitality was, in his eyes, a crime against the law of prudence, and he would as soon have forgiven a breach of good morals as a violation of this, his favorite rule.

As might have been expected, he carried this principle with him into the schoolroom, and was very averse to teaching anything beyond what would certainly "pay." He rigidly eschewed embellishment, and adorned his pupils with no graceful accomplishments. It might be that he never taught anything above the useful branches of education, because he had never learned more himself; but it is certain that he would not have imparted merely polite learning, had his own training enabled him to do so: for he had, constitutionally, a high contempt for all "flimsy" things, and, moreover, he was not employed or paid to teach rhetoric or *belles-lettres*, and, "on principle," he never gave more in return than the value of the money he received.

With this reservation, his duties were always thoroughly performed, for neither by nature, education, nor lineage, was he likely to slight any recognised obligation. He devoted his time and talents to his school, as completely as if he had derived from it the income of a bishop; and the iron constitution, of both body and mind, peculiar to his race, enabled him to endure a greater amount of continuous application than any other man. Indeed, his powers of endurance were quite surprising, and the fibre of his mind was as tough as that of his body. Even upon a quality so valuable as this, however, he never prided himself; for, excepting the boast of race, which was historical and not unjustifiable, he *had* no pride. He might be a little vain; and, in what he said and did, more especially in its manner, there might occasionally be a shade of self-conceit: for he certainly entertained no mean opinion of himself. This might be a little obtrusive, too, at times; for he had but slight veneration for men, or their feelings, or opinions; and he would sometimes pronounce a judgment in a tone of superiority justly offensive. But he possessed the uncommon virtue of sincerity: he thoroughly believed in the infallibility of his own conclusions; and for this the loftiness of his tone might be forgiven.

The most important of the opinions thus expressed, were upon religious subjects, for Jews, puritans, and Spaniards, have always been very decided controversialists. His theology was grim, solemn, and angular, and he was as combative as one of Cromwell's disputatious troopers. In his capacious pocket, he always carried a copy of the New Testament — as, of old, the carnal controvertists bore a sword buckled to the side. Thus armed, he was a genuine polemical "swash-buckler," and would whip out his Testament, as the bravo did his weapon, to cut you in two without ceremony. He could carve you into numerous pieces, and season you with scriptural salt and pepper; and he would do it with a gusto so serious, that it would have been no unreasonable apprehension that he intended to eat you afterward. And the value of his triumph was enhanced, too, by the consideration that it was won by no meretricious graces or rhetorical flourishes; for the ease of his gesticulation was such as you see in the arms of a windmill, and his enunciation was as nasal and monotonous as that of the Reverend Eleazer Poundtext, under whose ministrations he had been brought up in all godliness.

But he possessed other accomplishments beside those of the polemic. He was not, it is true, overloaded with the learning of "the schools"—was, in fact, quite ignorant of some of the branches of knowledge which he imparted to his pupils: yet this was never allowed to become apparent, for as we have intimated, he would frequently himself acquire, at night, the lessons which he was to teach on the morrow. But time was seldom wasted among the people from whom he sprang, and this want of preparation denoted that his leisure hours had been occupied in possessing himself of other acquirements. Among these, the most elegant, if not the most useful, was music, and his favorite instrument was the flute.

In "David Copperfield," Dickens describes a certain flute-playing tutor, by the name of Mell, concerning whom, and the rest of mankind, he expresses the rash opinion, "after many years of reflection," that "nobody ever could have played worse." But Dickens never saw Strongfaith Lippincott, the schoolmaster, nor heard his lugubrious flute, and he therefore knows nothing of the superlative degree of detestable playing.

There *are* instruments upon which even an unskilful performer may make tolerable music, but the flute is not one of them — the man who murders *that*, is a malefactor entitled to no " benefit of clergy :" and our schoolmaster *did* murder it in the most inhuman manner! But, let it be said in mitigation of his offence, he had never received the benefit of any scientific teaching — he had not been " under the tuition of the celebrated Signor Wheeziana," nor had he profited by "the invaluable instructions of the unrivalled Bellowsblauer"— and it is very doubtful whether he would have gained much advantage from them, had he met the opportunity.

He knew that, in order to make a noise on the flute, or, indeed, anywhere else, it was necessary to *blow*, and blow he did, like Boreas! He always carried the instrument in his pocket, and on being asked to play — a piece of politeness for which he always looked — he drew it out with the solemnity of visage with which a tender-hearted sheriff produces a death-warrant, and while he screwed the joints together, sighed blasts like a furnace. He usually deposited himself upon the door-sill — a favorite seat for him — and collecting the younger members of the family about him, thence poured forth his strains of concentrated mournfulness.

He invariably selected the most melancholy

tunes, playing, with a more profound solemnity, the gloomiest psalms and lamentations. When he ventured upon secular music, he never performed anything more lively than "The Misletoe Bough," or "Barbara Allen," and into each he threw a spirit so much more dismal than the original, as almost to induce his hearers to imitate the example of the disconsolate "Barbara," and "turn their faces to the wall" in despair of being ever again able to muster a smile!

He was not a scientific musician, then — fortunately for his usefulness — because thorough musicians are generally "good-for-nothing" else. But music was not a science among the pioneers, though the undertone of melancholy feeling, to which all sweet sounds appeal, was as easily reached in them as in any other people. Their wants in this, as in other things, were very easily satisfied — they were susceptible of pleasure from anything which was in the least commendable: and not feeling obliged, by any captious canon, to condemn nine true notes, because of the tenth false one, they allowed themselves to enjoy the best music they could get, without thinking of the damage done their musical and critical reputation.

But his flute was not the only means of

pleasing within the schoolmaster's reach: for he could flatter as well as if the souls of ten courtiers had transmigrated into his single body. He might not do it quite so gracefully as one of these, nor with phrases so well-chosen, or so correctly pronounced, but what he said was always cunningly adapted to the character of the person whom he desired to move. He had "a deal of candied courtesy," especially for the women; and though his sturdy manhood and the excellent opinion of himself — both of which came to him from his ancestry — usually preserved him from the charge of servility, he was sometimes a "cozener" whose conscience annoyed him with very few scruples. Occasionally he might be seen fawning upon the rich; but it was not with him — as it usually is with the parasites of wealthy men — because he thought Dives more respectable, but more *useful*, on account of his money: the opulent possessed what the indigent wanted, and the shortest road to the goal of Cupidity, lay through the region of Vanity. There was none of that servility which Mr. Carlyle has attempted to dignify with the name of "hero-worship," for the rich man was rather a bird to be plucked, than a "hero" to be worshipped. And though it may seem that I do the schoolmaster little honor by the distinction, I can not but think cupidity a more manly trait than servility: the beast of prey a more respectable animal than the hound.

But the schoolmaster's obsequiousness was more in manner than in inclination, and found its excuse in the dependence of his circumstances. It has been immemorially the custom of the world, practically to undervalue his services, and in all time teaching and poverty have been inseparable companions. Nobody ever cared how poorly he was clad, how laborious his life, or how few his comforts; and if he failed to attend to his own interests by all the arts in his power, no one, certainly, would perform the office for him. He was expected to make himself generally useful without being particular about his compensation: he was willing to do the one, but was, very naturally, rather averse to the other: that which justice would not give him, he managed to procure by stratagem.

His manners thus acquired the characteristics we have enumerated, with also others. He was, for example, very officious; a peculiarity which might, perhaps, be derived from his parentage, but which was never repressed by his occupation. The desire to make himself agreeable, and his high opinion of his ability to do so, rendered his tone and bearing very familiar; but this was, also, a trait which he shared with his race, and one which has contributed, as much as any other, to bring the people called "Yankees" into contempt in the west. The men of that section are not themselves reserved, and hate nothing more than ceremonious politeness: but they like to be the first to make advances, and their demonstrations are all hearty, blunt, and open. They therefore disliked anything which has an insinuating tone, and the man who attempts to ingratiate himself with them, whether it be by elaborate arts or sidelong familiarity, at once arms them against them.

The schoolmaster was inquisitive, also, and to that western men most decidedly object. They have little curiosity themselves, and seldom ask impertinent questions. When they do so, it is almost always for the purpose of insulting the man to whom they are put, and *never* to make themselves agreeable. The habit of asking numerous questions was, therefore, apt to prejudice them against men whose characteristics might be, in other respects, very estimable; and it must be acknowledged, that vulgar and obtrusive impertinence is an unfortunate accompaniment to an introduction. But the schoolmaster never meant to be impertinent, for he was far from being quarrelsome (except with his scholars), and the idea that any one could be otherwise than pleased with his notice, however given, never entered his mind. Though his questions were, for the most part, asked to gratify a constitutional curiosity, he was actuated in some degree, also, by the notion that his condescension would be acceptably interpreted by those whom he thus favored. But, like many other benevolent men, who put force upon their inclinations for the benefit of their neighbors, he was mistaken in his "calculation;" and where he considered himself a benefactor, he was by others pronounced a "bore." The fact is, he had some versatility, and, like most men of various powers, he was prone to think himself a much greater man than he really was.

He was not peculiarly fitted to shine as a gallant "in hall or bower," but had he been the climax of knightly qualities, the very impersonation of beauty, grace, and accomplishment, he could not have been better adapted than, in his own estimation, he already was, to please the fancy of a lady. He was blissfully unconscious of every imperfection; and displayed himself before what he thought the admiring gaze of all *dames* and *demoiselles*, as proudly as if he had been the all-accomplished victor in some passage of arms. Yet he carried himself, in outward appearance, as meekly as the humblest Christian, and took credit to himself accordingly. He seldom pressed his advantages to the utter subjugation of the sighing dames, but deported himself with commendable forbearance toward the weak and defenceless whom his perfections had disarmed. He was as merciful as he was irresistible : as considerate as he was beautiful.

"What a saint of a knight is the knight of Saint John!"

The personal advantages which he believed made him so dangerous to the peace of woman, were counteracted, thus, by his saintly piety. For — as it became him to be, both in the character of a man, and in that of a descendant of the puritans — he was always habited in "the livery of heaven." Some ill-natured and suspicious people, it is true, were inclined to call his exemplary "walk" hypocritical, and to stigmatise his pious "conversation" as *cant*. But the ungodly world has always persecuted the righteous, and the schoolmaster was correct in attributing their sneers to the rebuke which his example gave to their wickedness, and to make "capital" out of the "persecution." And who shall blame him — when in the weary intervals of a laborious and thankless profession, fatigue repressed enthusiasm — if he sometimes eked out the want of inspiration by a godly snuffle? True piety reduces even the weapons of the scorner to the service of religion, and the citadel of the Gloomy Kingdom is bombarded with the artillery of Satan! Thus, the nose, which is so serviceable in the production of the devilish and unchristian sneer, is elevated by a saintlike zeal, to the expression of a devout whine: and this I believe to be the only satisfactory explanation which has ever been given, of the connection, in so many good men, between the *nasal* and the *religious!*

But the schoolmaster usually possessed genuine religious feeling, as well as a pious manner; and, excepting an occasional display of hereditary, and almost unconscious, cunning, he lived "a righteous and upright life."

The process of becoming a respectable and respected citizen was a very short and simple one — and whether the schoolmaster designed to remain only a lord of the ferrule, or casting the insignia of his office behind him, to seek higher things, he was never slow in adopting it. Among his scholars, there were generally half-a-dozen or more young women — marriageable daughters of substantial men; and from this number he selected, courted, and espoused, some healthy, buxom girl, the heiress of a considerable plantation or a quantity of "wild land." He always sought these two requisites combined — for he was equally fond of a fine person and handsome estate. Upon the land, he generally managed to find an eligible town-site; and, being a perfect master of the art of building cities on paper, and puffing them into celebrity, his sales of town-lots usually brought him a competent fortune. As years rolled on, his substance increased with the improvement of the country — the rougher points of his character were gradually rubbed down — age and gray hairs thickened upon his brow — honors, troops of friends, and numerous children, gathered round him — and the close of his career found him respected in life and lamented in death. His memory is a monument of what honesty and industry, even without worldly advantages, may always accomplish.

[NOTE.—A friend expresses a doubt whether I have not made the foregoing portrait too hard-featured for historical accuracy; and, by way of fortifying his opinion, points to illustrious examples of men who have taught schools in their youth — senators and statesmen — some of whom now hold prominent positions before the people, even for the highest offices in their gift. But these men never belonged to the class which I have attempted to portray. Arriving in this country in youth, without the means of subsistence — in many cases, long before they had acquired the professions which afterward made them famous — they resorted to school-teaching as a mere expedient for present support, without any intention to make it the occupation of their lives, or the means of their advancement. They were moved by an ambition which looked beyond it, and they invariably abandoned it so soon as they had prepared themselves for another pursuit.

But the genuine *character* took it up as a permanent employment — he looked to it not only as a means of temporary subsistence, but as a source, by some of the direct or indirect channels which we have indicated, of lasting income — and he never threw it up until he had already secured that to which the other class, when *they* abandoned the occupation, were still looking forward. In the warfare against Ignorance, therefore, these, whom we have described, were the regular army, while the exceptions were but volunteers for a limited period, and, in the muster-roll of permanent strength, they are, therefore, not included.

THE SCHOOLMISTRESS.

IX.

THE SCHOOLMISTRESS.

> "And yet I love thee not — thy brow
> Is but the sculptor's mould:
> It wants a shade, it wants a glow—
> It is less fair than cold."   L. E. L.

But the family of the pioneer consisted of girls as well as boys; and though the former were never so carefully educated as the latter, they were seldom allowed to go wholly untaught.

The more modern system, which separates the sexes while infants, and never suffers them to come together again until they are "marriageable," was not then introduced; and we think it would have been no great misfortune to the country had it remained in Spain, whence it would seem to have been imported. Children of both sexes were intended to grow up together — to be educated in company — at least until they have reached the points where their paths naturally diverge, for thus only can they be most useful to each other, in the duties, trials, and struggles, of after life. The artificial refinement which teaches a little girl that a boy is something to be dreaded — a sort of beast of prey — before she recognises any difference, save in dress, can never benefit her at best; for by-and-by she will discover the falsehood: the very instincts of her nature would unveil it, did she learn it in no other way: and as action and reaction are equal, the rebound may cause her to entertain opinions altogether too favorable to those whom she has so foolishly been taught to fear.

Nor is the effect of such a system likely to be any better upon the other sex: for it is association with females (as early as possible, too, all the better), which softens, humanizes, graces, and adorns the masculine character. The boy who has been denied such association — the incidents to whose education have made him shy, as so many are, even of little girls — is apt to grow up morose and selfish, ill-tempered, and worse mannered. When the impulses of his developing nature finally force him into female society, he goes unprepared, and comes away without profit: his ease degenerates into familiarity, his conversation is, at best, but washy sentimentalism, and the association, until the accumulated rust of youth is worn away, is of very doubtful benefit to both parties. Indeed, parents who thus govern and educate their children, can find no justification for the practice, until they can first so alter the course of Nature, as to establish the law, that each family shall be composed altogether of girls, or shall consist exclusively of boys!

But these modern refinements had not obtained currency, at the period of which we are writing; nor was any such nonsense the motive to the introduction of female teachers. But one of the lessons learned by observation of the domestic circle, and particularly of the influence of the mother over her children, was the principle, that a woman can teach males of a certain age quite as well as a man, and *females much better;* and that, since the school-teacher stands, for the time in the place of the parent, a *mistress* was far more desirable, especially for the girls, than a *master.* Hence, the latter had exercised his vocation in the west, but a few years, before he was followed by the former.

New England was the great nursery of this class, as it was of so many others, transplanted beyond the Alleganies. Emigration, and the enticements and casualties of a seafaring life — drawing the men into their appropriate channels of enterprise and adventure, had there reduced their number below that of the women — thus remitting many of the latter, to other than the usual and natural occupations of "the sex." Matrimony became a remote possibility to large numbers — attention to household matters gave place to various kinds of light labor — and, since they were not likely to have progeny of their own to rear, many resorted to the teaching of children belonging to others. Idleness was a rare vice; and New England girls — to their honor be it spoken — have seldom resembled "the lilies of the field," in aught, save the fairness of their complexions! They have never displayed much squeamishness — about work: and if they could not benefit the rising generation in a maternal, were willing to make themselves useful in a tutorial capacity. The people of that enlightened section, have always possessed the learning necessary to appreciate, and the philanthropy implied in the wish to dispel, the benighted ignorance of all other quarters of the world; and thus a competent number of them have ever been found willing to give up the comforts of home, for the benefit of the "barbarous west."

The schoolmistress, then, generally came from the "cradle" of intelligence, as well as "of liberty," beyond the Hudson; and, in the true spirit of benevolence, she carried her blessings (herself the greatest) across the mountain barrier, to bestow them, *gratis*, upon the spiritually and materially needy, in the valley of the Mississippi. Her vocation, or, as it would now be called, her "mission" was to teach an impulse not only given by her education, but belonging to her nature. She had a constitutional tendency toward it—indeed, a genius for it; like that which impels one to painting, another to sculpture—this to a learned profession, that to a mechanical trade. And so perfectly was she adapted to it, that "the ignorant people of the west" not recognising her "divine appointment," were often at a loss to conjecture, who, or whether anybody, could have taught *her!*

For that same "ignorant," and too often, ungrateful people, she was full of tender pity—the yearning of the single-hearted missionary, for the welfare of his flock. *They* were steeped in darkness, but *she* carried the light—nay, she *was* the light! and with a benignity, often evinced by self-sacrifice—she poured it graciously over the land—

> "Heaven doth with us, as we with torches do:
> Not light them for themselves; for if our virtues
> Did not go forth of us, 't were all alike
> As if we had them not."

For the good of the race, or of any (male) individual, she would immolate herself, even upon the altar of Hymen; and, since the number, who were to be benefited by such self-devotement, was small in New England, but large in the west, she did well to seek a field for her benign dedication, beyond the Alleganies! Honor to the all-daring self-denial, which brought to the forlorn bachelor of the west, a companion in his labors, a solace in his afflictions, and a mother to his children!

Her name was invariably Grace, Charity, or Prudence; and, if names had been always descriptive of the personal qualities of those who bore them, she would have been entitled to all three.

In the early ages of the world, names were, or, at least, were supposed to be, fair exponents of the personal characters of those, upon whom they were bestowed. But, *then*, the qualities must be manifested, before the name could be earned, so that all who had never distinguished themselves, in some way, were said to be "nameless." In more modern times, however, an improvement upon this system was introduced: the character was anticipated, and parents called their children what they *wished* them to be, in the hope that they would grow to the standard thus imposed. And it is no doubt, true, that names thus bestowed had much influence in the development of character—on the same principle, upon which the boards, to which Indian women lash their infants soon after birth, have much to do with the erect carriage of the mature savage. Such an appellation is a perpetual memento of parental counsels—a substitute for barren precept—an endless exhortation to Grace, Charity, or Prudence.

I do not mean, that calling a boy Cicero will certainly make him an orator, or that all Jeremiahs are necessarily prophets; nor is it improbable, that the same peculiarities in the parents, which dictate these expressive names, may direct the characters of the children, by controlling their education; but it is unquestionable, that the characteristics, and even the fortunes of the man, are frequently daguerreotyped by a name given in infancy. There is not a little wisdom in the advice of Sterne to godfathers—not "to Nicodemus a man into nothing."—" Harsh names," says D'Israeli, the elder, " will have, in spite of all our philosophy, a painful and ludicrous effect on our ears and our associations; it is vexatious, that the softness of delicious vowels, or the ruggedness of inexorable consonants, should at all be connected with a man's happiness, or even have an influence on his fortune."

"That which we call a rose,
By any other name would smell as sweet;"

but this does not touch the question, whether, if it had not smelt as sweet we would not have given it some other name. The celebrated demagogue, Wilkes, is reported to have said, that, "without knowing the comparative merits of the two poets, we would have no hesitation in preferring John Dryden to Elkanah Settle, *from the names only*." And the reason of this truth is to be found in the fact, that our impressions of both men and things depend upon associations, often beyond our penetration to detect — associations with which *sound*, depending on hidden laws, has quite as much to do, as *sense*.

Among those who have carried the custom of picturesque or expressive naming, to an extent bordering on the ridiculous, were the hard-headed champions of the true church-militant, the English puritans — as Hume, the bigoted old tory, rather ill-naturedly testifies! And the puritans of *New* England—whatever advancing intelligence may have made them in the present—were, for a long time, faithful representatives of the oddities, as well as of the virtues, of their fathers.

And, accordingly, we find the schoolmistress —being a descendent of the Jason's-crew, who landed from the Argo-Mayflower, usually bearing a name thus significant, and manifesting, even at her age, traits of character justifying the compellation. What that age precisely *was*, could not always be known; indeed, a lady's age is generally among indeterminate things; and it has, very properly, come to be considered ungallant, if not impertinent, to be curious upon so delicate a subject. A man has no more right to know how many years a woman has, than how many skirts she wears; and, if he have any anxiety about the matter, in either case, his eyes must be the only questioners. The principle upon which the women themselves proceed, in growing old, seems to be parallel to the law of gravitation: when a storm, for example, is thrown into the air the higher it goes the slower it travels; and the momentum toward Heaven, given to a woman at her birth, appears to decrease in about the same ratio.

We will not be so ungallant, then, as to inquire too curiously into the age of the schoolmistress; but, without disparagement to her youthfulness, we may be allowed to conjecture that, in order to fit her so well for the duties of her responsible station (and incline her to undertake such labors), a goodly number of years must needs have been required. Yet she bore time well; for, unless married in the meanwhile, at thirty, she was as youthful in manners, as at eighteen.

But this is not surprising: for, even as early as her twelfth year, she had much the appearance of a mature woman—something like that noticed in young quakers, by Clarkson*—and her figure belonged to that rugged type, which is adapted to bear, unscathed, more than the ravages of time. She was never above the medium height, for the rigid rule of economy seemed to apply to flesh and blood, as to all other things pertaining to her race; at all events, material had not been wasted in giving her extra longitude—at the ends. Between the extremities, it might be different—for she was generally very long-waisted. But this might be accounted for in the process of *flattening*

---

* Author of the Life of William Penn, whose accuracy has lately been questioned.

out: for like her compeer, the schoolmaster, she had much more breadth than thickness. She was somewhat angular, of course, and rather bony; but this was only the natural correspondence, between the external development, and the mental and moral organization. Her eyes were usually blue, and, to speak with accuracy, a little cold and grayish, in their expression—like the sky on a bleak morning in Autumn. Her forehead was very high and prominent, having, indeed, an *exposed* look, like a shelterless knoll in an open prairie: but, not content with this, though the hair above it was often thin, she usually dragged the latter forcibly back, as if to increase the altitude of the former, by extending the skin. Her mouth was of that class called "primped," but was filled with teeth of respectable dimensions.

Her arms were long, and, indeed, a little skinny, and she swung them very freely when she walked; while hands, of no insignificant size, dangled at the extremities, as if the joints of her wrists were insecure. She had large feet, too, and in walking her toes were assiduously turned out. She had, however, almost always one very great attraction—a fine, clear, healthy complexion—and the only blemishes upon this, that I have ever observed, were a little *red* on the tip of her nose and on the points of her cheek-bones, and a good deal of *down* on her upper lip.

In manners and bearing, she was brisk, prim, and sometimes a little "fidgety," as if she was conscious of sitting on a dusty chair; and she had a way of searching nervously for her pocket, as if to find a handkerchief with which to brush it off. She was a very fast walker, and an equally rapid talker — taking usually very short steps, as if afraid of splitting economical skirts, but using very long words, as if entertaining no such apprehension about her throat. Her gait was too rapid to be graceful, and her voice too sharp to be musical; but she was quite unconscious of these imperfections, especially of the latter: for at church — I beg pardon of her enlightened ancestors! I should say at "*meeting*" — her notes of praise were heard high over all the tumult of primitive singing; and, with her chin thrown out, and her shoulders drawn back, she looked, as well as sounded, the impersonation of *melody*, as contra-distinguished from *harmony!*

But postponing, for the present, our consideration of her qualifications as a teacher, we find that her characteristics were still more respectable and valuable as a private member of society. And in this relation, her most prominent trait, like that of her brother teacher, was her stainless piety. In this respect, if in no other, women are always more sincere and single-hearted than men — perhaps because the distribution of social duties gives her less temptation to hypocrisy — and even the worldly, strong-minded, and self-reliant daughter of the church-hating Puritan-Zion, displayed a tendency toward genuine religious feeling.*

But in our subject, this was not a mere bias, but a constant, unflagging sentiment, an every-day manifestation. She was as warm in the cause of religion on one day as upon another, in small things as in great — as zealous in the repression of all unbecoming and ungodly levity, as in the eradication of positive vice. Life was too solemn a thing with her to admit of thoughtless amusements — it was entirely a state of probation, not to be enjoyed in itself, or for itself, but purgatorial, remedial, and prepara-

---

* By this form of expression, which may seem awkward, I mean to convey this idea: That consistency of character would seem to preclude any heartfelt reverence in the descendant of those whose piety was manifested more in the *hatred of earthly*, than in *the love of heavenly*, things.

tory. She hated all devices of pleasure as her ancestors did the abominations of popery. A fiddle she could tolerate only in the shape of a bass-viol; and dancing, if practised at all, must be called "calisthenics." The drama was to her an invention of the Enemy of Souls — and if she ever saw a play, it must be at a *museum*, and not within the walls of that temple of Baal, the theatre. None but "serious" conversation was allowable, and a hearty laugh was the expression of a spirit ripe for the destination of unforgiven sinners.

Errors in religion were too tremendous to be tolerated for a moment, and the form (or rather anti-form) of worship handed down by her fathers, had cost too much blood and crime to be oppugned. She thought Barebones's the only godly parliament that ever sat, and did not hate Hume half so much for his infidelity, as for his ridicule of the roundheads. Her list of martyrs was made up of the intruders ousted by Charles's "Act of Conformity," and her catalogue of saints was headed by the witch-boilers of Massachusetts bay. She abhorred the memory of all *popish* persecutions, and knew no difference between catholic and cannibal. Her running calendar of living saints were born "to inherit the earth," and heaven, too: they possessed a monopoly of all truth, an unlimited "indulgence" to enforce conformity, and, in their zeal, an infallible safeguard against the commission of error. She had no patience with those who could not "see the truth;" and he who reviled the puritan mode of worship, was "worse than the infidel." The only argument she ever used with such, was the *argumentum ad hominem*, which saves the trouble of conviction by "giving over to hardness of heart." New England was, to her, the land of Goshen — whither God's people had been led by God's hand — "the land of the patriarchs, where it rains righteousness"* — and all the adjacent country was a land of Egyptian darkness.

She was commendably prudent in her personal deportment: being thoroughly pure and circumspect herself, she could forgive no thoughtless imprudence in her sister-woman: but she well-understood metaphysical distinctions, and was tolerant, if not liberal, to marriageable men. These she could hope to reform at some future time: and she had, moreover, a just idea of the weakness of man's nature. But being a woman, and a staid and sober-minded woman, she could

* The language of a precious pamphlet, even now in circulation in the west.

never understand the power of temptation upon her own sex, or the commonest impulses of high spirits. Perhaps she was a little deficient in charity : but, as we have seen, it was chiefly toward her female friends, and since none can bear severe judgment more safely than woman, her austerity did little harm.

But she sincerely regretted what she could never palliate ; she hated not the guilty, though she could not forgive the sin ; and no one was more easily melted to tears by the faults, and particularly by the *follies*, of the world. Wickedness is a very melancholy thing, but it is to be punished as well as lamented : and like the unfortunate governor who was forced to condemn his own son, she wept while she pronounced judgment. But earthly sorrow, by her, was given only to earthly faults : violations of simple good morals, crimes against heavenly creeds and forms (or rather *the* form) of worship, claimed no tear. Her blood rose to fever-heat at the mention of an unbeliever, and she would as soon have wept for the errors of the fallen angels, as for those of anti-Robinsonians.

But though thus rigid and austere, I never heard that she was at all disinclined to being courted : especially if it gave her any prospect

THE SCHOOLMISTRESS. 335

of being able to make herself useful as a wife, either to herself, her husband, or her country. She understood the art of rearing and managing children, in her capacity as a teacher: she was thus peculiarly well-fitted for matrimonial duties, and was unwilling that the world should lose the benefit of her talents. But the man who courted her must do so in the most sober, staid, and regulated spirit, for it was seldom any unmixed romance about "love and nonsense," which moved *her* to the sacrifice : if she entertained notions of that sort, they were such only as could find a place in her well-balanced mind, and, above all, were the subject of no raptures or transports of delight. If she indulged any enthusiasm, in view of the approaching change, it was in the prospect of endless shirt-making, and in calculations about how cheaply (not how happily) she could enable her husband to live. She had no squeamish delicacy about allowing the world to know the scope and meaning of her arrangements, and all her friends participated in her visions of comfort and economy. False modesty was no part of her nature — and her sentiment could be reduced to an algebraic formula — excluding the "unknown quantities" usually represented by the letters b, c, and $d:$ meaning "bliss," "cottages," and "devotion."

Yet, though she cared little for poetry, and seldom understood the images of fancy, she was not averse to a modicum of scandal in moments of relaxation : for the faults of others were the illustrations of her prudent maxims, and the thoughtlessness of a sister was the best possible text for a moral homily. The tense rigidity of her character, too, sometimes required a little unbending, and she had, therefore, no special aversion to an occasional surreptitious novel. But this she would indulge only in private; for in her mind, the worst quality of transgression was its bad example ; and she never failed, in public, to condemn all such things with becoming and virtuous severity. Nor must this apparent inconsistency be construed to her disadvantage; for her strong mind and well-fortified morals, could withstand safely what would have corrupted a large majority of those around her ; and it was meet, that one whose "mission" it was to reform, should thoroughly understand the enemy against which she battled. And these things never unfavorably affected her life and manners, for she was as prudent in her deportment (ill-natured people say *prudish*) as if some ancestress of hers had been deceived, and left in the family a tradition of man's perfidy and woman's frailty.

She was careful, then, of three things — her clothes, her money, and her reputation: and, to do her justice, the last was as spotless as the first, and as much prized as the second, and that is saying a good deal, both for its purity and estimation. Neat, economical, and prudent, were, indeed, the three capital adjectives of her vocabulary, and to deserve them was her eleventh commandment.

With one exception, these were the texts of all her homilies, and the exception was, unluckily, one which admitted of much more argument.

It was the history of the puritans. But upon this subject, she was as dexterous a special pleader as Neale, and as skilful, in giving a false coloring to facts, as D'Aubigné. But she had the advantage of these worthies in that her declamation was quite honest: she had been taught sincerely and heartily to believe all she asserted. She was of the opinion that but two respectable ships had been set afloat since the world began: one of which was Noah's ark, and the other the Mayflower. She believed that no people had ever endured such persecutions as the puritans, and was especially eloquent upon the subject of "New England's Blarney-stone," the Rock of Plymouth.

Indeed, according to the creed of her people, historical and religious, this is the only piece of granite in the whole world "worth speaking of;" and geologists have sadly wasted their time in travelling over the world in search of the records of creation, when a full epitome of everything deserving to be known, existed in so small a space! All the other rocks of the earth sink into insignificance, and "hide their diminished heads," when compared to this mighty stone! The Rock of Leucas, from which the amorous Lesbian maid cast herself disconsolate into the sea, is a mere pile of dirt: the Tarpeian, whence the Law went forth to the whole world for so many centuries, is not fit to be mentioned in the same day: the Rock of Cashel, itself, is but the subject of profane Milesian oaths; and the Ledge of Plymouth is the real "Rock of Ages!" It is well that every people should have something to adore, especially if that "something" belongs exclusively to themselves. It elevates their self-respect: and, for this object, even historical fictions may be forgiven.

But, as we have intimated, in the course of time the schoolmistress became a married woman; and as she gathered experience, she gradually learned that New England is not the whole "moral vineyard," and that one might be more profitably employed than in disputing about questionable points of history. New duties devolved upon her, and new responsibilities rained fast. Instead of teaching the children of other people, she now raised children for other people to teach. New sources of pride were found in these, and in her husband and his prosperity. She discovered that she could be religious without bigotry, modest without prudery, and economical without meanness: and, profiting by the lessons thus learned, she subsided into a true, faithful, and respectable matron, thus, at last, fulfilling her genuine "mission."

X.

THE POLITICIAN.

> "All would be deemed, e'en from the cradle, fit
> To rule in politics as well as wit:
> The grave, the gay, the fopling, and the dunce,
> Start up (God bless us !) statesmen all at once !"
> CHURCHILL.

In a country where the popular breath sways men to its purposes or caprices, as the wind bends the weeds in a meadow, statesmanship may become a *system*, but can never rise to the dignity of a *science;* and politics, instead of being an *art*, is a series of *arts*.

A system is order without principle: a science is order, based upon principle. Statesmanship has to do with generalities — with the relations of states, the exposition and preservation of constitutional provisions, and with fundamental organizations. Politics relates to measures, and the details of legislation. The *art* of governing is the accomplishment of the true politician:

the *arts* of governing are the trickeries of the demagogue. *Right* is the key-note of one: *popularity* of the other.

The large majority of men are sufficiently candid to acknowledge — at least to themselves — that they are unfit for the station of lawgiver; but the vanity and jealousy begotten by participation in political power, lead many of them, if not actually to believe, at all events to *act* upon the faith, that men, no more able than themselves, are the best material for rulers. It is a kind of compromise between their modesty and self-love: not burthening them with the trials and responsibilities of positions for which they feel incompetent, but soothing their vanity by the contemplation of office-holders not at all their superiors. Below a certain (or uncertain) grade, therefore, political stations are usually filled by men of very moderate abilities: and their elevation is favored — indeed, often effected — by the very causes which should prevent it. Such men are prone to thrust themselves upon public notice, and thus secure, by persistence and impudence, what might not be awarded them on the score of merit.

It is a trite remark, that people are inclined to accept a man's estimate of himself, and to put him in possession of that place, in their consideration, which he has the hardihood to claim. And the observation is just, to this extent: if the individual does not respect himself, probably no one else will take that trouble. But in a country where universal suffrage reigns, it may be doubted whether the elevation of an ordinary man indicates any recognition of the justice of his claims. On the contrary, they may be endorsed precisely because they are false: that is, because he really possesses no other title to the support of common men, than that which is founded upon fellow-feeling or sympathy of character. Many a man, therefore, who receives his election as a compliment from the voters, if he understood the motives of their action, would throw up his office in disgust; for in a large majority of cases, the popular choice, so far from being an assertion of the candidate's peculiar fitness to be singled out from among his brethren, is only a declaration that neither talent nor character entitles him to the distinction. The cry that a man is "one of the people," will bring him great strength at the ballot-box: but this is a phrase which means very different things, according as it is used by the candidate or the voter; and, in many cases, if they could thoroughly understand each other, the latter would not give his support, and the former would not ask it.

These remarks are applicable to all stages of society's progress; for, if the world were so enlightened, that, in the scale of intellect, such a man as Daniel Webster could only be classed as an idiot, there would still be the "ignorant vulgar," the "uneducated classes." Society is one entire web — albeit woven with threads of wool and silk, of silver and gold: turn it as you will, it must all turn together; and if a whirlwind of enlightenment should waft it to the skies, although each thread would be immeasurably above its present condition, the relation of one to another would still be the same. If the baser wool should be transmuted into gold, the very same process would refine and sublimate the precious metal, in a corresponding ratio; and the equilibrium of God's appointed relations would remain undisturbed.

But it is more especially in the primitive periods, before the great political truths become household words, and while the reign of law and municipal organization is a vague and distant thing, that most citizens shrink from official duties. Diffidence, in this matter is, fortunately, a disease which time will alleviate — a youthful weakness, which communities "outgrow," as children do physical defects; and, I believe, of late years, few offices have "gone begging," either east or west of the great barrier of the Allegany.

In the earlier periods of its history, we have seen that the western country was peculiarly situated. The settlements were weak and the population small; with the exception of a few narrow fields, in the vicinity of each frontier fort, or stockade, the land was a wilderness, held in undisturbed possession by the savages and wild beasts. The great struggle, which we call the Revolution, but which was, in fact, only a justifiable and successful rebellion, had exhausted the force and drained the coffers of the feeble federal government; had plunged the infant states into enormous debts; and the only means of paying these were the boundless but unclaimed lands of the west, which the same causes rendered them unable to protect. The scattered settlements on the Mississippi side of the Alleganies, were thus left to their own scanty resources; and the distance was so great, that, had the older states been able to afford assistance, the delays and losses attendant upon its transmission across so wide a tract of wilderness, would have made it almost nugatory.

In those times, therefore, though a few were looking forward to separate political organization and the erection of new states, the larger number of the western people were too constantly occupied with their defence, to give much attention to internal politics. Such organization as they had was military, or patriarchal: the early pioneer, who had distinguished himself in the first explorations of the country, or by successfully leading and establishing a new settlement, as he became the commander of the local fort, was also the lawgiver of the community. The pressure of external danger was too close to allow a very liberal democracy in government; and, as must be the case in all primitive assemblages of men, the counsels and commands of him whom they knew to be the *most able*, were always observed. He who had proven himself competent to lead was, therefore, the leader *ipso facto* and *de jure ;* and the evidence required was the performance of such exploits, and the display of such courage and sagacity, as were necessary to the defence, well-being, and protection of the community.

It is obvious that no mere pretender could

exhibit these proofs; and that, where they were taken as the sole measure of a man's worth, dexterity with a rifle must be of more value than the accomplishments of a talker — Indian-fighting a more respectable occupation than speech-making. Small politicians were, therefore, very small men, and saying that one had " a turn for politics," would have been equivalent to calling him a vagabond. The people had neither time nor patience to listen to declamation — the man who rose in a public assembly, and called upon his neighbors to follow him in avenging a wrong, made the only speech they cared to hear. "Preambles and resolutions" were unmeaning formalities — their "resolutions" were taken in their own minds, and, to use their own expressive words, they executed them "without preamble." An ounce of lead was worth more than a pound of advice; and, in the vindication of justice, a " charge" of gunpowder was more effectual than the most tedious judicial harangue. It is, even now, a proud, but well-founded boast, of western men, that these traits have been transmitted to them from their fathers — that they are more remarkable for *fighting* than for *wrangling*, for *acting* than for *talking*.

In such a state of society, civil offices existed

scarcely in name, and were never very eagerly sought. That which makes official station desirable is obedience to its authority, and if the title of "captain" gave the idea of more absolute power than that of "sheriff," one would rather command a company of militia than the "*posse comitatus*." Besides, the men of the frontier were simple-hearted and unambitious, desiring nothing so much as to be "left alone," and willing to make a compact of forbearance with the whole world—excepting only the Indians. They had never been accustomed to the restraints of municipal regulations, they were innocent of the unhealthy pleasures of office-holding, or the degrading impulses of office-seeking. Their lives had given them little or no knowledge of these things; experience had never suggested their importance, for their acquaintance with life was, almost exclusively, such as could be acquired in the woods and forest pathways.

But as time rolled away, and the population of the country became more dense—as the pressure of external danger was withdrawn, and the necessities of defence grew less urgent—the rigor of military organization came gradually to be somewhat irksome. The seeds of civil institutions began to germinate among the people, while the extending interests of communities required corresponding enactments and regulations. The instincts of social beings, love of home and family, attachment to property, the desire of tranquillity, and, perhaps, a leaven of ambition for good estimation among neighbors, all combined to open men's eyes to the importance of peaceful institutions. The day of the rifle and scalping-knife passed away, and justice without form — the rule of the elementary strong-hand — gave place to order and legal ceremony.

Then first began to appear the class of politicians, though, as yet, office-seeking had not become a trade, nor office-holding a regular means of livelihood. Politics had not acquired a place among the arts, nor had its professors become the teachers of the land. There were few, indeed, who sought to fill civil stations; and, although men's qualifications for office were, probably, not any more rigidly examined then than now, those who possessed the due degree of prominence, either deemed themselves, or were believed by their fellow-citizens, peculiarly capable of discharging such functions. They were generally men who had made themselves conspicuous or useful in other capacities

— who had become well or favorably known to their neighbors through their zeal, courage, sagacity, or public spirit. A leader of regulators, for example, whose administration of his dangerous powers had been marked by promptitude and severity, was expected to be equally efficient when clothed with more regular authority. A captain of rangers, whose enterprises had been remarkable for certainty and *finish*, would, it was believed, do quite as good service, in the capacity of a civil officer. A daring pioneer, whose courage or presence of mind had saved himself and others from the dangers of the wilderness, was supposed to be an equally sure guide in the pathless ways of politics. Lawyers were yet few, and not of much repute, for they were, for the most part, youthful adventurers, who had come into the field long before the ripening of the harvest.

There was another class, whose members held prominent positions, though they had never been distinguished for the possession of any of the qualifications above enumerated. These might be designated as the *noisy* sort — loud-talking, wise-looking men, self-constituted oracles and advice-givers, with a better opinion of their own wisdom than any one else was willing to endorse. Such men became "file-leaders," or "pivot-men," because the taciturn people of the west, though inclined to undervalue a mere talker, were simple-minded enough to accept a man's valuation of his own powers: or easy-tempered enough to spare themselves the trouble of investigating so small a matter. It was of little consequence to them, whether the candidate was as wise as he desired to be thought; and since, in political affairs, they knew of no interest which they could have in disputing it, for *his* gratification they were willing to admit it. These were halcyon days for mere pretenders — though for no very flattering reason: since their claims were allowed chiefly because they were not deemed worth controverting. Those days, thanks to the " progress of intelligence!" are now gone by: the people are better acquainted with the natural history of such animals, and — witness, ye halls of Congress! — none may now hold office except capable, patriotic, and disinterested men!

Nor must we be understood to assert that the primitive politician was the reverse of all this, save in the matter of capability. And, even in that particular, no conception of his deficiency ever glimmered in his consciousness. His own assumption, and the complaisance of his fellow-

THE POLITICIAN. 351

citizens, were inter-reactive, mutually cause and effect. *They* were willing to confirm his valuation of his own talents: *he* was inclined to exalt himself in their good opinion. Parallel to this, also, was the oracular tone of his speech: the louder he talked, the more respectfully silent were his auditors; and the more attentive *they* became, the noisier *he* grew. Submission always encourages oppression, and admiration adds fuel to the fire of vanity. Not that the politician was precisely a despot, even over men's opinions: the application of that name to him would have been as sore a wound to his self-respect as the imputation of horse-stealing. He was but an oracle of opinion, and though allowed to dictate in matters of thought as absolutely as if backed by brigades of soldiers, he was a sovereign whose power existed only through the consent of his subjects.

In personal appearance, he was well-calculated to retain the authority intrusted to him by such men. He was, in fact, an epitome of all the physical qualities which distinguished the rugged people of the west: and between these and the moral and intellectual, there is an invariable correspondence — as if the spirit within had moulded its material encasement to the planes and angles of its own "form and pressure."

National form and feature are the external marks of national character, stamped more or less distinctly in different individuals, but, in the aggregate, perfectly correspondent and commensurate. The man, therefore, who possesses the national traits of character in their best development, will be, also, the most faithful representative of his race in physical characteristics. At some periods, there are whole classes of these types ; and if there be any *one* who embodies the character more perfectly than all others, the tranquillity of the age is not calculated to draw him forth. But in all times of trouble — of revolution or national ferment — the perfect Man-emblem is seen to rise, and (which is more to the purpose) is sure to stand at the head of his fellows : for he who best represents the character of his followers, becomes, by God's appointment, their leader. To this extent, the *vox populi* is the *vox Dei ;* and the unfailing success of every such man, throughout his appointed term, is the best possible justification of the choice.

What was Washington, for example, but an epitome of the steady and noble qualities combined of cavalier and puritan, which were then coalescing in the American character? And what more perfect correspondence could be conceived between the moral and intellectual and the physical outlines? What was Cromwell but *the Englishman*, not only of his own time, but of all times? And the testimony of all who saw him, what is it, but that a child, who looked upon him, could not fail to see, in his very lineaments, the great and terrible man he was? And Napoleon, was he aught but an abridgment of the French nation, the sublimate and "proof" essence of French character? Not one, of all the great men of history, has possessed, so far as we know, a physical constitution more perfectly representing, even in its advancing grossness, both the strength and weakness of the people he led.

In tranquil times, these things are not observed in one individual more than in others of his class, and we are, therefore, not prepared to decide whether, at such periods, *the one man* exists. The great Leviathan, the king of all the creatures of the ocean, rises to the surface only in the tumult of the storm; his huge, portentous form, lies on the face of the troubled waters only when the currents are changed and the fountains of the deep are broken up.

Nature does no superfluous work, and it may require the same causes which produce the storm to organize its Ruler. If a great rebellion is boiling among men, the mingling of the elements is projecting, also, the Great Rebel: if a national cause is to be asserted, the principles upon which it rests will first create its appropriate Exponent. But when no such agitation is on the point of breaking out—when the crisis is not near, and the necessity for such greatness distant—national character probably retains its level; and though there be no *one* whom the people will recognise as the arch-man, the representatives, losing in intensity what they gain in numbers, become a class. They fill the civil stations of the country, and are known as men of mark—their opinions are received, their advice accepted, their leading followed. No one of them is known instinctively, or trusted implicitly, as the leader of Nature's appointment: yet they are, in fact, the exponents of their time and race, and in exact proportion to the degree in which they possess the character, will they exhibit, also, the physical peculiarities.

Thus it was at the time of which we are writing, with the class to which belonged the politician, and a description of his personal appearance, like that of any other man, will convey no indistinct impression of his internal character.

Such a description probably combined more characteristic adjectives than that of any other personage of his time — adjectives, some of which were applicable to many of his neighbors, respectively, but *all* of which might be bestowed upon him *only*. He was tall, gaunt, angular, swarthy, active, and athletic. His hair was, invariably, black as the wing of the raven; even in that small portion which the cap of raccoon-skin left exposed to the action of sun and rain, the gray was but thinly scattered; imparting to the monotonous darkness only a more iron character. As late as the present day, though we have changed in many things, light-haired men seldom attain eminence among the western people: many of our legislators are *young* enough, but none of them are *beardless*. They have a bilious look, as if, in case of illness, their only hope would lie in calomel and jalap. One might understand, at the first glance, that they are men of *talent*, not of *genius;* and that physical energy, the enduring vitality of the body, has no inconsiderable share in the power of the mind.

Corresponding to the sable of the hair, the politician's eye was usually small, and intensely black — not the dead, inexpressive jet, which gives the idea of a hole through white paper, or of a cavernous socket in a death's-head; but the keen, midnight darkness, in whose depths you can see a twinkle of starlight — where you feel that there is meaning as well as color. There might be an expression of cunning along with that of penetration — but, in a much higher degree, the blaze of irascibility. There could be no doubt, from its glance, that its possessor was an excellent hater; you might be assured that he would never forget an injury or betray a friend.

A stoop in the shoulders indicated that, in times past, he had been in the habit of carrying a heavy rifle, and of closely examining the ground over which he walked; but what the chest thus lost in depth it gained in breadth. His lungs had ample space in which to play — there was nothing pulmonary even in the drooping shoulders. Few of his class have ever lived to a very advanced age, but it was not for want of iron-constitutions, that they went early to the grave. The same services to his country, which gave the politician his prominence, also shortened his life.

From shoulders thus bowed, hung long, muscular arms — sometimes, perhaps, dangling a little ungracefully, but always under the command of their owner, and ready for any effort, however violent. These were terminated by broad, bony hands, which looked like grapnels — their grasp, indeed, bore no faint resemblance to the hold of those symmetrical instruments. Large feet, whose toes were usually turned in, like those of the Indian, were wielded by limbs whose vigor and activity were in keeping with the figure they supported. Imagine, with these peculiarities, a free, bold, rather swaggering gait, a swarthy complexion, and conformable features and tones of voice : and — excepting his costume — you have before your fancy a complete picture of the early western politician.

But the item of costume is too important to be passed over with a mere allusion. As well might we paint a mountain without its verdant clothing, its waving plumes of pine and cedar, as the western man without his picturesque and characteristic habiliments. The first, and indispensable article of dress, was the national hunting-shirt : a garment whose easy fit was well-adapted, both to the character of his figure and the freedom of his movements. Its nature did not admit much change in fashion : the only variations of which it was capable, were those of ornament and color. It might be fringed around the cape and skirt, or made plain; it might be blue, or copper-colored—perhaps tinged with a little madder. And the variety of material was quite as limited, since it must be of either jeans or deer-skin.

Corresponding to this, in material, style, and texture, he wore, also, a pair of wide pantaloons —not always of precisely the proper length for the limbs of the wearer, but having invariably a broad waistband, coming up close under the arms, and answering the purpose of the modern vest. People were not so dainty about "set" and "fit," in those days, as they have since become; and these primitive integuments were equally well-adapted to the figure of any one to whose lot they might fall. In their production, no one had been concerned save the family of the wearer. The sheep which bore the wool, belonged to his own flock, and all the operations, subsequent to the shearing, necessary to the ultimate result of shaping into a garment, had been performed by his wife or daughter. Many politicians have continued this affectation of plainness, even when the necessity has ceased, on account of its effect upon the masses; for people are apt to entertain the notion, that de-cent clothing is incompatible with mental ability, and that he who is most manifestly behind the improvements of the time, is best qualified for official stations.

A neck-cloth, or cravat, was never seen about the politician's throat; and for the same reason of expediency: for these were refinements of affectation which had not then been introduced; and a man who thus compassed his neck, could no more have been elected to an office, than if he had worn the cap and bells of a Saxon jester. The shirt-bosoms of modern days were in the same category; and *starch* was an article contraband to the law of public sentiment — insomuch that no epithet expressed more thorough contempt for a man, than the graphic word " starched." A raccoon-skin cap — or, as a piece of extravagant finery, a white-wool hat — with a pair of heavy shoes, not unfrequently without the luxury of hose — or, if with them, made of blue-woollen yarn, from the back of a sheep of the aforesaid flock — completed the element of costume.

He was not very extravagantly dressed, as the reader sees; but we can say of him — what could not be as truly spoken of many men, or, indeed, of many women, of this day — that his clothing bore distinct reference to his character, and was well-adapted to his "style of beauty." In fact, everything about him, form, face, manners, dress, was in "in keeping" with his characteristics.

In occupation, he was usually a farmer; for the materials of which popular tribunes are made in later times — such as lawyers, gentlemen of leisure, and pugnacious preachers — were not then to be found. The population of the country was thoroughly agricultural; and though (as I believe I have elsewhere observed) the rural people of the west were neither a cheerful nor a polished race, as a class, they possess, even yet, qualities, which, culminating in an individual, eminently fit him for the *rôle* of a noisy popular leader.

But a man who is merely fitted to such a position, is a very different animal to one qualified to give laws for the government of the citizen. After all our vain boasting, that public sentiment is the law of our land, there is really a very broad distinction between forming men's opinions and controlling their action. If the government had been so organized, that the pressure of popular feeling might make itself felt, directly, in the halls of legislation, our history, instead of being that of a great and advancing nation, would have been only a chronicle of factious and unstable violence. It does not follow, that one who is qualified to lead voters at the polls, or, as they say here, "on the stump," will be able to embody, in enlightened enactments, the sentiment which he contributes to form, any more than that the tanner will be able to shape a well-fitting boot from the leather he prepares. "*Suum cuique proprium dat Natura donum.*"* A blacksmith, therefore, is not the best manufacturer of silver spoons, a lawyer the ablest writer of sermons, nor either of them necessarily the safest law-maker.

But those things to which his qualifications were appropriate, the politician did thoroughly and well. For example, he was a skilful farmer — at least in the leading branches of that calling, though he gave little or no attention to the merely ornamental. For the latter, he had neither time nor inclination. Even in the essentials, it was only by working, as he expressed it, "to the best advantage,"—that is, contriving to produce the largest amount of results with the least expenditure of labor and patience— that he got sufficient leisure to attend to his public duties; and as for "inclination," no

* Translate "*donum,*" talent.

quaker ever felt a more supreme contempt for mere embellishment.

He was seldom very happy in his domestic relations; for, excepting at those seasons when the exigencies of his calling required his constant attention, he spent but little of his time at his own fireside. He absented himself *until* his home became strange and uncomfortable to him: and he then did the same, *because* it had become so. Every man who may try the experiment will discover that these circumstances mutually aggravate each other — are, interchangeably, cause and effect. His children were, however, always numerous, scarcely ever falling below half-a-dozen, and not unfrequently doubling that allowance. They generally appeared upon the stage in rapid succession — one had scarcely time to get out of the way, before another was pushing him from his place. The peevishness thus begotten in the mother — by the constant habit of nursing cross cherubs — though it diminished the amount of family peace, contributed, in another way, to the general welfare: it induced the father to look abroad for enjoyment, and thus gave the country the benefit of his wisdom as a political counsellor. Public spirit, and the consciousness of ability, have "brought out" many politicians: but uncomfortable homes have produced many more.

He was an oracle on the subject of hunting, and an unerring judge of whiskey — to both which means of enjoyment he was strongly attached. He was careful, however, neither to hunt nor drink in solitude, for even his amusements were subservient to his political interests. To hunt alone was a waste of time, while drinking alone was a loss of good-fellowship, upon which much of his influence was founded. He was particularly attached to parties of half-a-dozen, or more; for in such companions, his talents were always conspicuous. Around a burgou* pot, or along the trenches of an impromptu barbecue, he shone in meridian splendor; and the approving smack of his lips, over a bottle of "backwoods' nectar," was the seal of the judgment which gave character to the liquor.

"Militia musters" were days in his calendar, "marked with a white-stone;" for it was upon

---

* A kind of soup, made by boiling all sorts of game with corn, onions, tomatoes, and a variety of other vegetables. When skilfully concocted and properly seasoned, not at all unsavory. So called from a soup made by seamen.

these occasions that he appeared in his utmost magnificence. His grade was never lower than that of colonel, and it not unfrequently extended to, or even beyond, the rank of brigadier-general. It was worth "a sabbath-day's journey" on foot, to witness one of these parades; for I believe that all the annals of the burlesque do not furnish a more amusing caricature of the "pomp and circumstance" of war. Compared to one of those militia regiments, Falstaff's famous corps, whose appearance was so unmilitary as to prevent even that liberal-minded gentleman from marching through Coventry in their company, was a model of elegance and discipline. Sedeno's cavalry in the South American wars, though their uniform consisted only of "leggings," a pair of spurs, and a Spanish blanket, had more the aspect of a regular *corps d'armée* than these! A mob of rustics was never armed with a more extensive variety of weapons; and no night's "haul" of a recruiting sergeant's net, ever made a more disorderly appearance, when mustered in the morning for inspection.

The "citizen-soldier" knew no more about "dressing the line," than about dressing himself, and the front of his company presented as many inequalities as a "worm-fence." Tall men and short men — beaver hats and raccoon-skin caps — rusty firelocks and long corn-stalks — stiff brogans and naked feet — composed the grand display. There were as many officers as men, and each was continually commanding and instructing his neighbor, but never thinking of himself. At the command "Right dress!" (when the officer *par excellence* knew enough to deliver it) some looked right, others left — some thrust their heads out before — some leaned back to get a glimpse behind — and the whole line waved like a streamer in the wind. "Silence in line!" produced a greater clamor than ever, for each repeated the command to every other, sending the order along the ranks like a rolling fire, and not unfrequently enforcing it with the push of a corn-stalk, or a vigorous elbow-hint. When a movement was directed, the order reached the men successively, by the same process of repetition — so that while some files were walking slowly, and looking back to beckon on their lagging fellow-soldiers, others were forced to a quick run to regain their places, and the scramble often continued many minutes after the word "halt!" The longer the parade lasted, the worse was the drill; and after a tedious day's "muster," each man knew less, if possible, of military tactics, than he did in the morning.

But the most ludicrous part of the display, was the earnest solemnity with which the politician-colonel endeavored "to lick the mass into shape." If you had judged only by the expression of his face, you would have supposed that an invading army was already within our borders, and that this democratic army was the only hope of patriotism to repel the foreign foe. And, indeed, it might not be too much to say, that some such idea actually occupied his mind: for he was so fond of "supposing cases," that bare possibilities sometimes grew in his mind to actual realities; and it was a part of his creed, as well as his policy to preach, that "a nation's best defence" is to be found in "the undisciplined valor of its citizens." His military maxims were not based upon the history of such countries as Poland and Spain — and Hungary had not then added her example to the list. He never understood the relation between discipline and efficiency; and the doctrine of the "largest liberty" was so popular, that, on his theory, it must be universally right. Tempered thus, and modified by some of the tendencies of the demagogue, his love of military parade amounted to a propensity, a trait which he shared with most of the people among whom he lived.

The inference from this characteristic, that he possessed what phrenologists used to call "combativeness," is not unavoidable, though such was the fact. He was, indeed, quite pugnacious, ready, at all times, to fight for himself or for his friends, and never with any very special or discriminating reference to the cause of quarrel. He was, however, seldom at feud with any one whose enmity could materially injure him: extensive connections he always conciliated, and every popular man was his friend. Nor was he compelled, in order to compass these ends, to descend to any very low arts; for "the people," were not so fastidious in those days, as they seem since to have become; and a straightforward sincerity was then the first element of popularity. The politician was not forced to affect an exemplary "walk and conversation;" nor was an open declaration of principle or opinion dangerous to his success.

This liberality in public sentiment had its evils: since, for example, the politician was not generally the less esteemed for being rather a hard *swearer*. In the majority of the class, indeed, this amounted only to an energetic or emphatic mode of expression; and such the people did not less respect, than if, in the same person, they had had reason to believe the opposite tone hypocritical. The western people — to their honor be it written! — were, and are, mortal enemies to everything like *cant:* though they might regret, that one's morals were no *better* than they appeared, they were still more grieved, if they found evidence, that they were *worse* than they claimed to be.

But, though the politician was really very open and candid in all the affairs of life, in his own estimation he was a very dexterous and dangerous intriguer: he often deceived himself into the belief, that the success, which was in fact the result of his manly candor, was attributable only to his cunning management. He was always forming, and attempting to execute, schemes for circumventing his political opponents; but, if he bore down all opposition, it was *in spite of* his chicanery, and not by its assistance. Left-handed courses are never advantageous " in the long run;" and, perhaps, it would be well if this lesson were better understood by politicians, even in our own enlightened day.

For the arts of rhetoric he had small respect; in his opinion, the man who was capable of making a long, florid speech, was fit for little else. His own oratorical efforts were usually brief, pithy, and to the point. For example, here follows a specimen, which the writer heard delivered in Illinois, by a candidate for the legislature:—

"Fellow-citizens: I am no speech-maker, but what I say, *I'll do*. I've lived among you twenty years, and if I've shown myself a clever fellow, you know it, *without* a speech: if I'm *not* a clever fellow, you know that, too, and wouldn't forget it *with* a speech. I'm a candidate for the legislature: if you think I'm 'the clear grit,' *vote* for me: if you think Major R—— of a better 'stripe' than I am, vote for *him*. The fact is, that either of us will make a devilish good representative!"

For the satisfaction of the reader, we should record that the orator was triumphantly elected, and, though "no speech-maker," was an excellent member for several years.

The saddest, yet cheerfullest—the quaintest, yet most unaffected of moralists, has written "A Complaint upon the Decay of Beggars," which will not cease to be read, so long as pure English and pure feeling are understood and appreciated. They were a part of the recollections of his childhood—images painted upon his heart, impressions made in his soft and pitying nature; and the "besom of societarian reformation," legislating busybodies, and tinkers of the general welfare, were sweeping them away, with all their humanizing influences, their deep lessons of dire adversity and gentle charity.

There are some memories of the childhood of western men — unlike, and yet similar in their generous persuasions on all pure young hearts — upon whose "Decay" might, also, be written a "Complaint," which should come as truly, and yet as sadly, from the heart of him, who remembers his boyhood, as did that from the heart of Elia. Gatherings of the militia, burgou-hunts, barbecues, and anniversaries — phases of a primitive, yet true and hearty time! — are fast giving way, before the march of a barbarous "progress" (erroneously christened) "of intelligence." The hard spirit of money-getting, the harder spirit of education-getting, and the hardest of *all* spirits, that of pharasaical morality, have divorced our youth, *a vinculo*, from every species of amusement; and life has come to be a probationary struggle, too fierce to allow a moment's relaxation. The bodies of children are drugged and worried into health, their intellects are stuffed and forced into premature development, or early decay — but their *hearts* are utterly forgotten! Enjoyment is a forbidden thing, and only the miserable cant of "intellectual pleasure" is allowed. *Ideas*—of philosophy, religious observance, and mathematics —are supplied *ad nauseam ;* but the encouragement of a generous *impulse,* or a magnanimous *feeling,* is too frivolous a thing to have a place in our vile system. Children are " brought up," and " brought out," as if they were composed exclusively of intellect and body: And, since the manifestations of any other element are pronounced pernicious—even if the existence of the element itself be recognised—the means of fostering it, innocent amusements, which make the sunshine brighter, the spirits more cheerful, and the heart purer and lighter, are sternly prohibited. Alas! for the generation which shall grow up, and be "educated" (God save the mark!) as if it had no heart! And wo to the blasphemy which dares to offer, as service to Heaven, an arrogant contempt of Heaven's gifts, and claims a reward, like the self-tormentors of the middle ages, for its vain mortifications.

But, in the time of the politician, of whom we write, these things were far different. We have already seen him at a "militia muster," and fain would we pause here, to display him at a barbecue. What memories, sweet, though sad, we might evoke of "the glorious fourth" in the olden time! How savory are even the dim recollections of the dripping viands, which hung, and fried, and crisped, and crackled, over the great fires, in the long deep trenches! Our nostrils grow young again with the thought— and the flavor of the feast floats on the breezes of memory, even "across the waste of years" which lie between! And the cool, luxuriant foliage of the grove, the verdant thickets, and among them pleasant vistas, little patches of green sward, covered with gay and laughing parties—even the rosy-cheeked girls, in their rustling gingham dresses, cast now and then a longing glance, toward the yet forbidden tables! how fresh and clear these images return upon the fancy!

And then the waving banners, roaring cannon, and the slow procession, moving all too solemnly for our impatient wishes! And finally, the dropping of the ropes, the simultaneous rush upon the open feast, and the rapid, perhaps ravenous consumption of the smoking viands, the jest, the laugh, all pleasant merriment, the exhilaration of the crowd, the music, and the occasion! What glories we heard from the orator, of victories achieved by our fathers!

How we longed — O! brief, but glorious dream! to be one day spoken of like Washington! How wildly our hearts leaped in our boyish bosoms, as we listened to the accents of the solemn pledge and " declaration" — " our lives, our fortunes, and our sacred honor!" The whole year went lighter for that one day, and at each return, we went home happier, and better!

How measureless we thought the politician's greatness then! This was his proper element — here he was at home; and, as he ordered and directed everything about him, flourishing his marshal's baton, clearing the way for the march of the procession — settling the " order of exercises," and reading the programme, in a stentorian voice — there was, probably in his own estimation. and certainly in ours, no more important or honored individual in all that multitude!

In such scenes as these, he was, indeed, without a rival; but there were others, also, in which he was quite as useful, if not so conspicuous. On election days, for instance, when a free people assembled to exercise their " inestimable privilege," to choose their own rulers — he was as busy as a witch in a tempest. His talents shone forth with especial and peculiar lustre — for, with him, this was "the day for which all other days were made." He marshalled his retainers, and led them to "the polls" — not as an inexperienced tactician would have done, with much waste of time, in seeking every private voter, but after the manner of feudal times — by calling upon his immediate dependants, captains over tens and twenties, through whom he managed the more numerous masses. These were the "file-leaders," the "fugle-men," and "heads of messes;" and it was by a judicious management of these, that he was able to acquire and retain an extensive influence.

The first article of his electioneering creed was, that every voter was controlled by somebody; and that the only way to sway the privates was, to govern the officers: and, whether true or not, it must be admitted that his theory worked well in practice. He affected to entertain a high respect for those whom he described as "the boys from the heads of the hollows"— men who were never seen beyond the precincts of their own little "clearings," except upon the Fourth of July and election day, from one end of the year to the other. With these he drank bad whiskey, made stale jokes, and affected a flattering condescension. With others, more important or less easily imposed upon, he "whittled" sociably in the fence-corners, talked solemnly in conspicuous places, and always looked confidential and mysterious.

But, however earnestly engaged, he never forgot the warfare in which he was chief combatant. Like a general upon a field of battle, with his staff about him, he had sundry of his friends always near, to undertake any commission, or convey any order, which he desired to have executed; and not a voter could come upon the ground, whom there was the remotest chance to influence, that his vigilance did not at once discover and seize upon, through some one of these lieutenants. He resorted to every conceivable art, to induce the freemen to vote *properly;* and, when he could not succeed in this, his next study was to prevent their voting *at all.* The consequence usually was, that he secured his own election, or that of his chosen candidate; for, in him, vigilance and shrewdness were happily combined.

But, perhaps fortunately for the country, his ambition was generally limited to such small offices, as he was quite capable of filling. The highest point at which he aimed, was a seat in the state legislature; and on reaching that goal, he signalized his term, chiefly, if at all, in advocating laws about division fences, and trespassers upon timber—measures which he deemed desirable for his own immediate constituency, with very little care for the question of their general utility. Indeed, he never went to the capital, without having his pockets full of "private bills," for the gratification of his personal friends, or near neighbors; and if, after a reasonable term of service, he had succeeded in getting all these passed into laws, he came home, contented to "subside," and live the remainder of his days, upon the recollection of his legislative honors.

In the course of time, like all other earthly things, his class began to decay. The tide of immigration, or the increasing intelligence of the people, raised up men of larger views; and he speedily found himself outstripped in the race, and forgotten by his ancient retainers. Then—like his predecessor, the original frontierman—disgusted with civilization and its refinements—he migrated to more congenial regions, and, in the scenes of his former triumphs, was heard of no more.

EPILOGUE.

Here we must pause.

On the hither side of the period, represented by the early politician, and between that and the present, the space of time is much too narrow, to contain any distinct development: those who superseded the primitive oracles, are yet in possession of the temple. We could not, therefore, pursue our plan further, without hazarding the charge of drawing from the life.

It is remarkable, that anything like a fair or candid estimate of—for example—a public man's character, while he is yet favored with the people's suffrages, is very certain to be pronounced a caricature; and it is not less singular, that, while the complaints of popular critics, in effect, affirm that there is fidelity enough in the picture to enable even obtuse minds to fit the copy to the original, they at the same time vehemently assert that the whole portrait is a libel. A just admeasurement of a demagogue's ability is thus always abated by the imputation of partisan falsehood or prejudice; and whosoever declines to join in the adulation of a temporary idol, may consider himself fortunate, if he escape with only the reproach of envy.

Sketches of contemporaneous character—if they seek recognition among the masses, must, therefore, not reduce the altitude which blind admiration has assigned, nor cut away the foreign lace, nor tear the ornaments, with which excited parties have bedaubed their images of clay. And, yet, so prone are men to overrate their leaders, that no estimate of a prominent man can be just, without impugning popular opinion.

There is probably no other ground quite so perilous as politics, unless it be literature: and, as yet, the west is comparatively barren of those "sensitive plants," literary men. But any attempt to delineate society, by portraiture of living characters, even though the pictures were purely ideal, would, upon the present plan, involve the suspicion (and perhaps the temptation to deserve it), indicated above. Before venturing upon such uncertain paths, therefore, we must display a little generalship, and call a halt, if not a council of war. Whether we are to march forward, will be determined by the "General *Orders.*"

THE END.

MID-AMERICAN FRONTIER

An Arno Press Collection

Andreas, A[lfred] T[heodore]. **History of Chicago.** 3 volumes. 1884-1886

Andrews, C[hristopher] C[olumbus]. **Minnesota and Dacotah.** 1857

Atwater, Caleb. **Remarks Made on a Tour to Prairie du Chien: Thence to Washington City, in 1829.** 1831

Beck, Lewis C[aleb]. **A Gazetteer of the States of Illinois and Missouri.** 1823

Beckwith, Hiram W[illiams]. **The Illinois and Indiana Indians.** 1884

Blois, John T. **Gazetteer of the State of Michigan, in Three Parts.** 1838

Brown, Jesse and A. M. Willard. **The Black Hills Trails.** 1924

Brunson, Alfred. **A Western Pioneer: Or, Incidents of the Life and Times of Rev. Alfred Brunson.** 2 volumes in one. 1872

Burnet, Jacob. **Notes on the Early Settlement of the North-Western Territory.** 1847

Cass, Lewis. **Considerations on the Present State of the Indians, and their Removal to the West of the Mississippi.** 1828

Coggeshall, William T[urner]. **The Poets and Poetry of the West.** 1860

Darby, John F[letcher]. **Personal Recollections of Many Prominent People Whom I Have Known.** 1880

Eastman, Mary. **Dahcotah: Or, Life and Legends of the Sioux Around Fort Snelling.** 1849

Ebbutt, Percy G. **Emigrant Life in Kansas.** 1886

Edwards, Ninian W[irt]. **History of Illinois, From 1778 to 1833: And Life and Times of Ninian Edwards.** 1870

Ellsworth, Henry William. **Valley of the Upper Wabash, Indiana.** 1838

Esarey, Logan, ed. **Messages and Letters of William Henry Harrison.** 2 volumes. 1922

Flower, George. **The Errors of Emigrants.** [1841]

Hall, Baynard Rush (Robert Carlton, pseud.). **The New Purchase: Or Seven and a Half Years in the Far West.** 2 volumes in one. 1843

Haynes, Fred[erick] Emory. **James Baird Weaver.** 1919

Heilbron, Bertha L., ed. **With Pen and Pencil on the Frontier in 1851: The Diary and Sketches of Frank Blackwell Mayer.** 1932

Hinsdale, B[urke] A[aron]. **The Old Northwest: The Beginnings of Our Colonial System.** [1899]

Johnson, Harrison. **Johnson's History of Nebraska.** 1880

Lapham, I[ncrease] A[llen]. **Wisconsin: Its Geography and Topography, History, Geology, and Mineralogy.** 1846

Mansfield, Edward D. **Memoirs of the Life and Services of Daniel Drake.** 1855

Marshall, Thomas Maitland, ed. **The Life and Papers of Frederick Bates.** 2 volumes in one. 1926

McConnel, J[ohn] L[udlum.] **Western Characters: Or, Types of Border Life in the Western States.** 1853

Miller, Benjamin S. **Ranch Life in Southern Kansas and the Indian Territory.** 1896

Neill, Edward Duffield. **The History of Minnesota.** 1858

Parker, Nathan H[owe]. **The Minnesota Handbook, For 1856-7.** 1857

Peck, J[ohn] M[ason]. **A Guide for Emigrants.** 1831

Pelzer, Louis. **Marches of the Dragoons in the Mississippi Valley.** 1917

Perkins, William Rufus and Barthinius L. Wick. **History of the Amana Society.** 1891

Rister, Carl Coke. **Land Hunger:** David L. Payne and the Oklahoma Boomers. 1942

Schoolcraft, Henry R[owe]. **Personal Memoirs of a Residence of Thirty Years With the Indian Tribes on the American Frontiers.** 1851

Smalley, Eugene V. **History of the Northern Pacific Railroad.** 1883

[Smith, William Rudolph]. **Observations on the Wisconsin Territory.** 1838

Steele, [Eliza R.] **A Summer Journey in the West.** 1841

Streeter, Floyd Benjamin. **The Kaw:** The Heart of a Nation. 1941

[Switzler, William F.] **Switzler's Illustrated History of Missouri, From 1541 to 1877.** 1879

Tallent, Annie D. **The Black Hills.** 1899

Thwaites, Reuben Gold. **On the Storied Ohio.** 1903

Todd, Charles S[tewart] and Benjamin Drake. **Sketches of the Civil and Military Services of William Henry Harrison.** 1840

Wetmore, Alphonso, compiler. **Gazetteer of the State of Missouri.** 1837

Wilder, D[aniel] W[ebster]. **The Annals of Kansas.** 1886

Woollen, William Wesley. **Biographical and Historical Sketches of Early Indiana.** 1883

Wright, Robert M[arr]. **Dodge City.** 1913